Knoxville
Green by Nature

a history of serendipitous progress
by **Jack Neely**

J Robert Towery — Publisher
James Tomlinson — Executive Publisher
J Robert Towery — Editor & Art Director
Ardith Bradshaw — Editor
Nikki Sepsis — Profile Editor

Published by

Urban Renaissance Books
A division of the Publishing Resources Group, Inc.
Jacques Verhaak, President & CFO
www.pubresgroup.com

Photo by Sheena Patrick

Library of Congress Control Number: 2013916504

Neely, Jack 1954-   **KNOXVILLE: Green by Nature—a history of serendipitous progress** is the story of Knoxville's revitalization of its downtown and the mobilizing effect it has had on the community; also includes a photo-journal celebrating its rebirth.

Neely describes how vision, imagination and plenty elbow grease made it all happen—oftentimes with too little funding and almost always with a frightening lack of what many would consider a serious plan.

PUBLISHED BY
URBANRenaissanceBOOKS
A DIVISION OF THE PUBLISHING RESOURCES GROUP, INC.
w w w . p u b r e s g r o u p . c o m
ISBN # 978-0-9847145-5-1   Printed in South Korea

Contents

Front Cover Photo by Jacques Gautreau—The cream-colored building in the foreground is a recent renovation of what is thought to be a Victorian-era commercial building. Part of the recent boom, it now houses both commercial and professional occupants. The 1919 Farragut Hotel Building with its speckled brick facade has been predominantly an office building since the 1970s. Its ground floor, however, is home to a very popular and successful bistro. It is located at Gay and Clinch.

Back Cover Photo by Jacques Gautreau—Not renovated, but well preserved, the Fidelity Building (shown here from the back/side) is an office building on the Union side, near Gay.

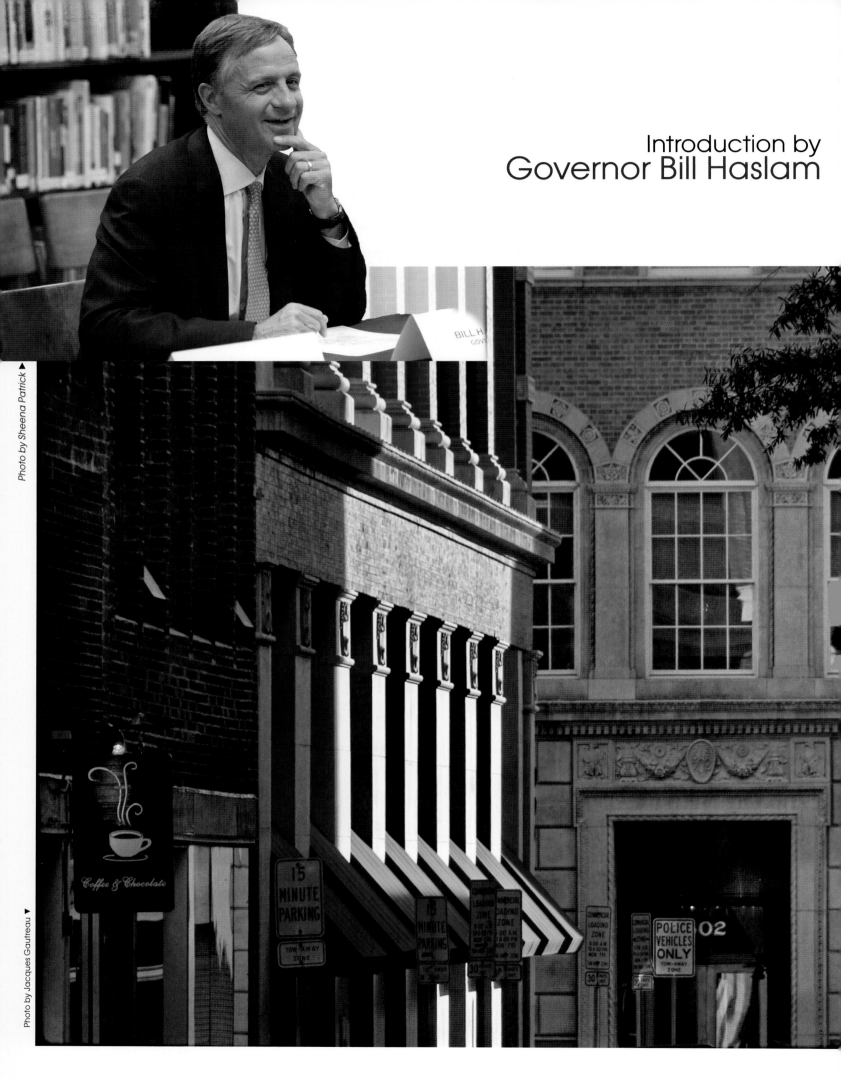

Photo by Sheena Patrick ▶

Photo by Jacques Gautreau ▶

15
MINUTE
PARKING

TOW-AWAY
ZONE

15
MINUTE
PARKING

COMMERCIAL
LOADING
ZONE

COMMERCIAL
LOADING
ZONE

COMMERCIAL
LOADING
ZONE

POLICE
VEHICLES
ONLY

TOW-AWAY
ZONE

02

Coffee & Chocolate

noxville is my home. I was born there, grew up there, and spent some years in business before I felt called to try public service. As it happened, after a particularly tough race, I became mayor of the city at what I thought was a pivotal moment.

Ten years ago, Knoxville didn't feel like one coherent city. It felt like a grouping of different communities and interests pulling in different directions, north, south, east west, each pulling their own way. Everybody was used to talking about Knoxville in terms of the piece they lived in, without looking at the city as a whole.

I thought downtown had the potential to change that. Throughout my life (I was born early in the "urban renewal" period) we'd witnessed big plans for downtown, some of which improved the place a little here and there, some of which didn't, but none of which worked as well as advertised.

When I was inaugurated in 2003, downtown was showing some signs of a different sort of renewal, as a handful of private developers were converting old buildings to new uses. A couple hundred brave people had begun moving back into downtown.

The century-old Gay Street Bridge, the oldest bridge over the Tennessee River, was undergoing a federally funded rebuild. The city had just commenced major improvements to its 150-year-old Market Square, an unusual public space that had attracted city plans and private redevelopment projects for decades, but nothing lately had worked exactly right.

Some people were talking about a new movie theater in the center of town, but when I came in, others said the idea was

Photo by David Luttrell

I knew that if we didn't move decisively forward, we'd slip, once again, into a scattered bunch of neighborhoods that resented and distrusted each other.

But I also knew Knoxville was a fiscally conservative community, and the amount that could be done with taxpayer dollars, or strong-arm government tactics like eminent domain, was likely to be very limited. Knoxville had shown a resistance to top-down urban planning, too.

So we developed a policy based on communicating, sometimes

impossible or foolish. It had been 25 years since anyone watched a new movie downtown, and skeptics said if people wanted to watch movies downtown, they wouldn't have let the old theaters close.

In 2003, Knoxville had buses but no bus station. People waited for the city bus on the sidewalk. Both of downtown's historic theaters were in need of major work. Retail had almost abandoned downtown. People who lived in the suburbs--and 10 years ago, that was an overwhelming majority of middle-class Knoxvillians--complained it was hard to park downtown, expensive and risky. Many buildings, including some very large ones, were vacant. And from my window, I could see the south side of the river, its underused riverbanks covered with kudzu. Over there, groundhogs were sometimes easier to spot than people.

It had been years since Knoxvillians were in the habit of coming downtown just for fun, and seeing other, old friends and like-minded strangers alike, out for a Sunday afternoon stroll, or a Friday-night date.

Photo by Jacques Gautreau

Knoxville

intensively, with developers and property owners who had potential to help, even when they had shown little interest in that sort of thing before.

Eventually, property owners who'd been reluctant to fix up their buildings either did so, or sold them. It became pretty obvious that there was an untapped market for urban residences. Retail was a tougher nut to crack. It had been years since Knoxvillians came downtown to shop. And though a few hundred new residences downtown makes a great news story and saved a few buildings, it wasn't nearly enough to support a whole retail district.

Most would have agreed that the era of the downtown department store was long past, but we found a surprising anchor just over the mountains. Previously concentrated in Western North Carolina, Mast General Store was a small and unusual chain of old-fashioned stores carrying a combination of outdoor gear, kitchenware, and candy--that, by company policy, favored to move into large, empty old buildings. We still had plenty of those, but luring Mast to open their first store west of the Appalachians took a lot of meetings, and a lot of convincing that we were earnest in turning downtown around. Part of that convincing came by way of our investment in a movie-theater project.

Some theater chains had already expressed an interest in our downtown, but I thought it was important that when we did open the first new downtown cinema in 75 years, it should be the one that was already headquartered

Photo by Gary Pope ▲

Photo by David Luttrell ▶

Green by Nature

in Knoxville. Regal, the biggest cinema chain in the world, was right here, but had not had positive experiences with downtown cineplexes elsewhere. With some more intensive discussions, between the city, property owners, historic-preservation experts, and Regal, the Regal Riviera opened in 2007, and became one of Regal's most popular cinemas in the region.

It seemed a turning point, because it was when you started to see lots of people on the sidewalks after 6 on, say, a Tuesday night—and when you started to hear people talk excitedly, not sarcastically or ironically, about Knoxville, Tennessee.

But by that point so many good things were happening downtown it's hard to credit any one of them. The gorgeous old Tennessee Theatre had gotten a multi-million-dollar makeover, mostly funded by private contributions, that actually added to its capacity for big live shows. When the even-older Bijou got fixed up, too, Knoxville gained an unusual dual asset, two historic theaters with a steady stream of live performances, booked by AC Entertainment, a nationally known company already based in downtown Knoxville. The old farmer's market tradition was reviving, twice a week, on Market Square, more vigorously than anyone could remember.

A whole lot of it was privately driven, both by for-profit businesses and nonprofit volunteer groups, but at the city we found we could offer a significant assist to all the new life, addressing the parking issue with a pretty simple solution. We made the city-owned parking garages free after banking hours and on weekends. New restaurants were opening, along with a few more little shops, and every year brought new residents, as energetic and imaginative developers transformed buildings that had been eyesores.

Knoxville has been an unusual case, among American cities, private developers and non-profits, doing the right thing, usually independent of instruction or government guidance, inspired by each other's successes, and leading the way with occasional assists from city government.

One such assist came when we made some structural improvements to the 100 block of Gay Street. In the 1990s, that block was dominated by dirty, empty buildings, some of them very large ones. People were afraid of its homeless shelter. But by the time we installed broader sidewalks, with benches and plantings, it was becoming, credibly, the most popular residential block in the entire city.

With festivals and outdoor plays and musical shows, as well as just coming out to Market Square for lunch, Knoxvillians really do more together today--a whole lot more than they ever did before. Moreover, we don't seem to have the personal, political battles we did in a previous generation. When I was mayor, I didn't have the feeling there was a huge number of people against me. It was more a spirit of "We want you to do a good job."

Even my opponent in my first mayoral race, Madeline Rogero worked with my administration on priorities we found we could agree on. I don't know how often that

Photo by David Luttrell

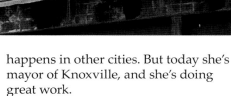

happens in other cities. But today she's mayor of Knoxville, and she's doing great work.

We still have challenges; I knew redeveloping the south side wouldn't be easy, or even something we could do in one mayoral administration, and it has taken longer than I'd like, partly due to a little recession we had to deal with. But it's still making progress.

Today, Knoxville's an obviously busy, urban place, with a diversity of attractions in a historic downtown so small the activity is concentrated and obvious. That's been happening in several other cities, but to me, Knoxville seems unlike others. In Knoxville, there's a remarkable civic spirit. You don't have that same sense of, "what's in it for me." There's more of a sense of, "What can I do to help?" Everything feels more personal.

Today, that spirit seems more important and more precious, to the future of a city, than any building or street.

Chapter 1

It may not be the most gracefully named city, combining a blocky Scottish-surname prefix with the once-fashionable French suffix. When the bluff-top town was founded in 1791, its odd name didn't trip off the tongue. And, what IS Knoxville anyway? Maybe most Americans could take a stab at an answer, but the more you know, perhaps, the less easy this particular question is to answer. No city's a simple proposition, but Knoxville, the valley city located near the spot where the Holston and French Broad Rivers flow together to form the Tennessee, may be more complicated than most.

For much of the 20th century, Knoxville suffered an unenviable reputation for ugliness, illiteracy, filth, crime, and general backwardness, some of it reasonably accurate. At times Knoxville could seem the clogged drainpipe for all of Southern Appalachia's problems. At the same time, somehow, it was becoming an intellectual and educational center; a center for arts, offering huge opera festivals and the South's oldest symphony orchestra; eventually a city with a reputation as a media powerhouse and an innovator in radiological sciences and energy technology.

Its downtown was the rotten core most ridiculed in national magazines and best-selling travel books. But in the 21st century, Knoxville has changed in ways that almost everyone notices.

Inaugurated in 2011 after decades in local public service, Mayor Madeline Rogero, a trained urban planner who had lived in several other cities in her youth, from Florida to the Midwest to the West Coast, was once critical of Knoxville. "There's a real sense of community, a real optimism" about Knoxville today, she says, describing the reborn downtown in particular. "Walk around. There are locally owned stores, restaurants, offices, theaters, music studios. It's all right

Green by Nature

Photo by David Luttrell

A block of massive and vacant old wholesale buildings and closed department stores, the 400 block of Gay Street was once considered one of the city's most daunting problems. But several imaginative developers working independently, sometimes with city encouragement, have resulted in so many attractions, including a brewpub, a coffee house, an art gallery, a music store, a wine store, and an unusual print shop—plus dozens of new upscale residences--that its sidewalks are often crowded.

there, and you can do it." She cites a busy local human-resources director who has traditionally had trouble luring newcomers to Knoxville. "But once they come here, and get here, he can't transfer them out."

Music-promoter Ashley Capps, the regional performing-arts guru who organized the mega-festival Bonnaroo and books the edgiest nightclubs of Knoxville, Asheville, and Chattanooga, thinks

his home town may be literally unique. "I've seen a lot of great downtowns," says Capps, who's been in the music business for more than 30 years, and travels widely. "I don't know that any developed in quite the same way, and with quite the same depth of character, as we've seen in downtown Knoxville."

Newcomers, like educational-media entrepreneur John Tolsma, originally from Houston, describe the city's distinctive "creative energy"

as an asset to his company, and the lively downtown that draws his employees. "This is the best place in the world to start and grow a business," claims Mike Carroll, chief of MK Technologies, a mechanical-engineering corporation with a wide variety of products. He speaks of the city's "collected prowess" of talented professionals who are attracted to Knoxville's "vibrant downtown."

That neighborhood, in particular, inspires head-shaking awe from almost everybody who knows it, especially those who knew it 25 years ago, when such statements would have sounded bizarre.

What's happened? There hasn't been any comprehensive city or state-sponsored initiative. Downtown has been the recipient of no multi-million dollar philanthropic project. No major corporate headquarters has arrived. Knoxville's still not a common tourist destination; when travelers visit the Smokies, they find tens of thousands of hotel rooms closer than Knoxville.

When asked to describe what makes Knoxville's recent growth different, Capps and several other community leaders tend to fall back on the vague, almost mystical word "organic." It's grown almost like a wildflower garden.

Photo by David Luttrell

Photo by David Luttrell

How it happened, and how it's still happening, is an interesting puzzle.

— • —

Mention Knoxville to someone a few states away, and the word may ring only a few bells. The 1982 World's Fair attracted 11 million, and left the city with an oblong park and the peculiar attraction known as the Sunsphere. It's the headquarters of New Deal survivor the Tennessee Valley Authority, today still the largest utility in America, even though it now lacks the civilization-changing idealism that fired its early decades and attracted world leaders to visit. Knoxville is home to the University of Tennessee, a large and respected institution, albeit one most popularly known for athletics. Thanks to UT, Knoxville possesses the third (or is it fourth?) largest football stadium in America, not to mention the world's only Women's Basketball Hall of Fame.

Even locals fall back on the easy simplification that it's a "college town." But as large as UT Knoxville is, it accounts for hardly 20 percent of the city's population and economy, which is diverse. Once a factory town, Knoxville maintains its industrial tradition making products for the nation ranging from automobile

Photo by Stephanie Norwood

Coffee culture has taken hold all over downtown. Coffee and Chocolate, near Market Square, offers outdoor seating. Java, Knoxville's first modern coffee house, arrived as a locally owned business in the Old City years before the city's first Starbucks.

parts to medical equipment to coffee. Bush Beans, which controls 50 percent of its national market, is headquartered in Knoxville.

Knoxville's service sector is stronger, and accounts for most of the region's fastest-growing occupations. It's a medical center for some two million people, and is East Tennessee's main concentration of banks and courts. Pilot,

the corporation that operates service-station "travel centers" across America's eastern half—and reportedly America's sixth-largest family-owned business—is home in Knoxville.

In recent years, Knoxville has emerged as an unlikely media center, home of both the largest cinema chain

Photo by David Luttrell ▼▲

in the world—Regal—and Scripps Networks Interactive, the cable-TV studio behind HGTV, DIY, the Food Network, and other specialty channels. Several smaller studios add to the city's demand for show-biz professionals. Boosters claim Knoxville is the fourth—or third, depending on whom you talk to—cable-television-production center in America.

More quietly, Knoxville has been developing technological businesses and research laboratories, some connected to UT, which is known for its engineering college, and to Oak Ridge National Laboratory; World War II's "secret city," charged with helping develop the atomic bomb, remains a national center for technological research, especially energy innovation. Since before the 1982 World's Fair—the "Energy Expo"—Knoxville has cherished its potential to be, in particular, a national leader in green technologies, though the practical, industrial realization of that dream has proven elusive.

"We've talked about the intellectual piece for years, with Oak Ridge, UT, for years," says Rogero, of somehow harnessing the Knoxville area's expertise in energy research. "The challenge is to make it happen."

The lively commercial activity in and around Knoxville is what observers remark about today. But large parts of Knoxville still lie fallow—especially old factory neighborhoods that began shriveling more than half a century ago. Lush and green in the summer, parts of Knoxville, even in the central part of the city, look like they were never developed at all. You might have to be an archaeologist, and pull back the honeysuckle and kudzu, to know any different.

— • —

Knoxville, whatever it is, carries a bit of a demographic mystery. Almost everyone with some acquaintance with the city, upon visiting today, remarks on how much bigger Knoxville is than when last encountered, perhaps 20 or 30 years ago. That's among the most common of many too-quick conclusions about the place. But today it does seem to have more, and more varied, restaurants; many more entertainment options, especially in terms of live music; more, bigger, and better public festivals; and perhaps the most elusive quality in any city, that let-me-show-you-around pride that hasn't been a regular thing here in living memory.

For much of the 20th century, Knoxville's aesthetic presence made it a butt of jokes, and magnet for several high-profile insults. In 1947, best-selling travel writer John Gunther called Knoxville "the ugliest city I ever saw in America.... Its main street is

The University of Tennessee accounts for a minority of Knoxville's economy and culture, and people argue about whether Knoxville is properly a "college town," but there's no question the university has a big effect on the city's life. The university's landmark building, collegiate-gothic Ayres Hall, completed atop UT's famous Hill in 1921, has been recently renovated.

Photo by Gary Heatherly

Downtown, as seen across the Tennessee River, from newly opened River Bluff Park.
Photo by Gary Heatherly

called Gay Street; this seems to me to be a misnomer."

In 2012, the American Planning Association walked on that same strip of pavement. In a list of 10, alongside New York's world-famous Broadway and Charleston's picturesque Broad Street, the APA selected Gay Street one of America's "Great Places."

Meanwhile, the Brookings Institution hailed Knoxville's metro area number one in the nation for green-job growth per capita. Other surveys give Knoxville superlatives for outdoor recreation, pet-friendliness, or its vigorously popular farmers' market.

How things have started looking up in Knoxville is not that simple to explain.

Despite perceptions of dramatic growth, Knoxville's municipal population has remained, for half a century, almost eerily constant. "About 180, 000," its boosters say. They may not mention they've been using that figure every year since the Kennedy administration. And in fact, no actual census has ever counted quite that many Knoxvillians. As of 2010, it's still just shy of 179,000. That number suggests a modest-sized city, not even one of America's 100 largest. Those city-limits figures have hardly changed, either in number or basic ethnic

makeup, since John Glenn first orbited the Earth.

Knoxville's metropolitan area broadens and complicates the picture, and is a big part of the answer. The burgeoning and fairly peculiar nine-county region known as the Knoxville Metropolitan Statistical Area includes both high-tech Oak Ridge on one side and, on the other, the broad appeal of tourist-oriented attractions of the Great Smoky Mountains, the nation's most popular national park. Knox County alone, reputedly an "urban county," includes Knoxville itself and its lively, urban downtown—but also the clean, orderly, and very suburban incorporated

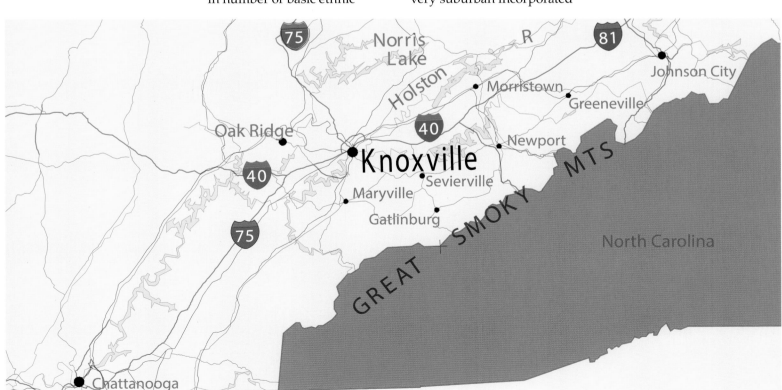

community of Farragut—and the very different corner called Gap Creek, a farming community so rural that a city, like maybe the 21st century, can seem like a remote and untrustworthy concept.

As defined, Knoxville's official metropolitan area has grown in size to about 840,000. Despite that sizeable figure, even "Metropolitan Knoxville" can seem artificially limited, because that definition does not include thousands of residents who live hardly 15 miles away from downtown Knoxville, in adjacent Sevier County. That fast-growing county, home of Gatlinburg, Pigeon Forge, and Dollywood, is driven by a tourism-based economy considered distinct from Knoxville's. But Sevier is included in an even wider census net, the Knoxville-Sevierville-LaFollette Combined Statistical Area, which is officially home to well over one million people. Despite its long-nurtured rural image, East Tennessee is a heavily populated region compared to the rest of the South, even to the rest of America.

For whatever it's worth, in this region not famous for cities, Knoxville is the largest. More than a million live within a half-hour drive of downtown Knoxville, and they're a factor in the city's successes, and its failures.

While Knoxville's metropolitan growth has been fairly steady over the decades—as the city itself remains demographically static—a sharper, recent change has been evident since about 2000, and may be a larger part of what's surprising returnees. It's a more focused and particular change in how people live in Knoxville, mostly in directing their attentions and activities toward its historic downtown.

— • —

A sizeable metropolitan area, a major university, a diverse economy, and a region known for natural beauty might make urban success seem inevitable. In fact, Knoxville has struggled, with its image, its economy, its politics, its identity. From 1930 to 1980, the most conspicuous descriptions of Knoxville in the national press emphasized its soot, its crime, its cheap architecture, its corrupt politics, its reckless growth—and its bizarre morality, which by the 1950s and '60s blandly tolerated open pornography and prostitution, while still banning wine served by the glass.

For 50 years, almost all of Knoxville's objective press was negative, culminating in a Wall Street Journal reporter's 1980 dismissal of Knoxville—a quote instantly famous among its citizens—as "a scruffy little city on the Tennessee

River" that probably lacked the wherewithal to mount a world's fair. Lacking a more clear-cut identity, 21st-century Knoxvillians have embraced that one, with the brazen motto "Keep Knoxville Scruffy."

Knoxville does struggle with some chronic challenges.

Downtown's situation, on top of a river bluff, was advantageous in the days when spring floods and hostile natives were major threats to frontier settlements. Today, it's an interesting impediment; downtown is joined to the rest of the city by a network of viaducts. Especially sharp is the grade between downtown Knoxville and its riverfront. What made for good defense in the 1790s is a liability in an era when cities are defining

themselves by reconnecting with their waterfronts with restaurants and greenways and festivals. And that grade still challenges enthusiasm for some of the elements of America's 21st-century urban revival, like bicycling. Steep topography also makes some construction more expensive than it would be elsewhere, especially considering that historic Knoxville's built on a Swiss cheese of limestone caves and sinkhole-prone karst.

In a broader view, the hilly, lush geography throughout the larger community conceals the city from itself. Knoxville can sometimes seem less a city than a loose confederation of hollers. Downtown presents an interesting skyline, from select angles—but it's easy to live in Knoxville, especially on the most populous west side, without ever catching a glimpse of it. For most suburbanites, it's easy to forget downtown Knoxville exists—and perhaps even that there's an actual city in the vicinity.

Knoxville's demographics

combine the collegiate class with a much-larger body of working-class and non-working people who lack college degrees, and in many cases even high-school degrees. Descended from independent country people, many locals are fiercely proud and fiercely resistant to notions of obligation or expected cooperation. UT is one of the larger universities east of the Mississippi, and in its home county, about 34 percent of adults are college graduates, a respectable figure compared to the nation at large. But in some rural counties it's much lower. In one county adjacent to Knox, only six percent of adults have college degrees. And over a five-county region (constituting Knoxville's old metro area), 58 percent of jobs are classified as low-skill, and low-pay.

Then there's the issue of monetary capital. "Old money" is not a phrase heard much in Knoxville, and though the city has its successful entrepreneurs, it's home to few real tycoons. The scions of its once-prosperous old families have mostly moved away. Knoxville's income is based more on present wages and salaries than profits. Its ranks of major financiers and

wealthy philanthropists are thin. Private endowments to civic improvements are often generous, but hardly ever extravagant. Knoxville lacks the lavish museums and performing-arts centers endowed by private individuals, as seen in most larger and some smaller cities.

What Knoxville lacks in public-amenity philanthropy is rarely compensated by the elected government and the taxpayer. The city and state's fiscal conservatism, along with low combined income and property-tax rates, is often cited as a factor that draws business to town, but it also means that the community has limited resources for planned public improvements, especially the sorts that are likely to impress visitors.

Some of those limitations have informed Knoxville's personality, made it noticeably different from most other cities. Eventually, perhaps, they've become a peculiar sort of asset. With a public economy based more on sales taxes than income taxes, it's possible, perhaps even likely, that a scruffy downtown hipster who dwells in the city daily will have a bigger effect on the local economy than a wealthy suburbanite who may spend much of his year out of town.

Knoxville's 21st-century revival came as the result of initiatives by a motley and particularly unlikely cadre of nonconformists, most of them acting almost independently. Among Knoxville's most influential leaders have been a career hairdresser; a public-radio disk jockey; an Iranian-immigrant chef; an aerospace engineer; an English handbag exporter; a couple of marijuana-smuggling conspirators; a modest freight-railroad executive; a former federal prosecutor—and several others who did not commence their careers with any intention of reviving a city, but were happy to help when the opportunity presented itself.

Knoxville's renaissance was a bit of complex serendipity that is not likely to replicate itself, but which may offer some interesting clues for other cities, and perhaps a reason to hope.

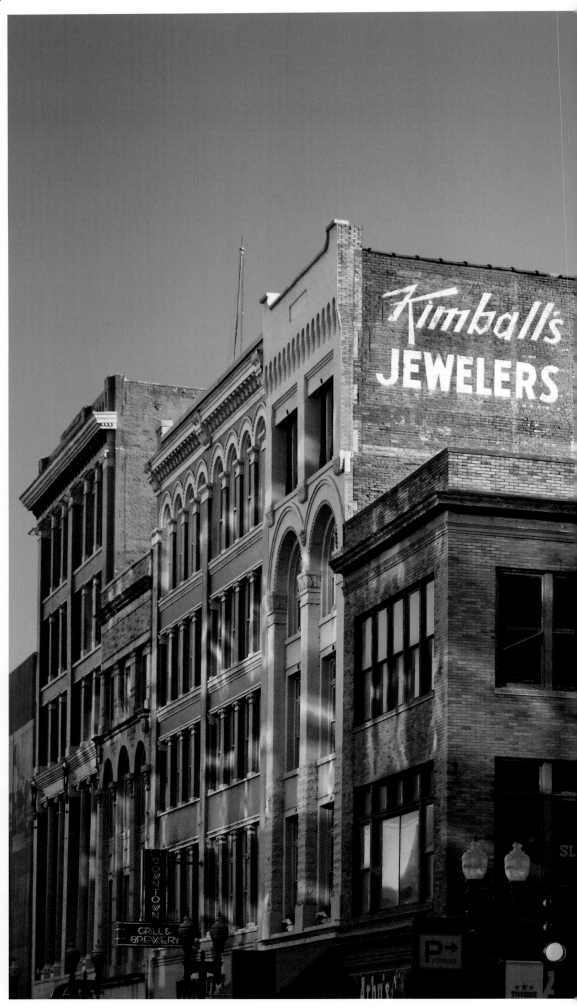

STOP
HERE ON
RED
↙

TURNING
VEHICLES
YIELD TO
PEDESTRIANS

Photo by Jacques Gautreau

Knoxville today is perhaps not as famous as it was two centuries ago when it was capital of the dynamic and sometimes startling sixteenth state. The city's narrative is a kaleidoscopic presentation composed of almost every aspect of American history.

Originally a territorial capital established during the administration of President George Washington, the bluff-top village was named for his rotund secretary of war, General Henry Knox. The French suffix ville was popular among cities founded just after the Revolutionary War, when Americans hailed France as the home of liberty, equality, and fraternity. This notable frontier settlement was in its earliest days a must-see site on the itinerary of nobles fleeing the French Revolution, before 1796, when it hosted the constitutional convention that founded Tennessee. Though it thrived as a frontier capital, home to governors and senators and frequently visited by major national figures like Andrew Jackson and Sam Houston, Knoxville slipped behind during the steam era. Thanks to its surrounding geography of mountains, valleys, and shoal-hobbled rivers, railroads and steamboats, the steam-driven wonders of the first half of the 19th century, had difficulty reaching Knoxville. The town lost state-capital status to Middle Tennessee locations in 1819. With little industry to compensate for the loss of its original political purpose, Knoxville stagnated.

Knoxville seemed a quaint historical footnote fated to lapse into modern-era insignificance—until 1855, when after three decades of trying, a railroad finally burst into town, bringing fresh perspectives and enabling industry. Attracting population from other parts of the country and from Europe, especially Ireland, Wales, Germany, and Switzerland, Knoxville grew rapidly, fueled by its abundant natural resources, coal, marble, lumber, even iron. Old Knoxville seemed on the brink of a new industrial rebirth in 1861, when war divided the city. Arriving first as violence in the

▼ *Original Blount Mansion, said to be the first frame house built west of the Appalachians, was home to Governor William Blount, who in 1791 made Knoxville the capital of the federal Southwestern Territory. It's the lone survivor of Knoxville's first quarter-century, but still was almost demolished, in the 1920s, for a parking lot.*

streets, as both the Union and Confederate armies recruited, sometimes within sight of each other, the Civil War spawned mob violence, assassinations, arson, and hangings. The civilian horrors of war insured that in Knoxville neither side would view their cause quite as idealistically as

the best-defended city in America. The Confederates learned the extent of the city's formidable ring of defenses only in November, 1863, when their three-week siege of the city culminated in a mad charge on Knoxville's biggest earthworks, Fort Sanders, a bloody 20-min-

especially those who brought money and talent. Postwar Republican politics elevated the city's regional college, known then as East Tennessee University, to the status of state university. During the city's period of astonishing growth in the 50 years after the war, when Knoxville

Photo by Gary Pope

some other parts of the country did.

Though Knoxville was home to the biggest pro-Union newspaper in the South, a Confederate occupation force ruled the city for two years, defending it from a significant cavalry raid in June, 1863. But then the Confederates evacuated Knoxville to help with the Chattanooga campaign. Thereupon the Union army occupied Knoxville without a shot, and began work to make it a citadel—as General William Tecumseh Sherman described it,

ute Confederate debacle remembered as the Battle of Knoxville. The city earned a weird distinction: Knoxville turned away assaults by both the Union and Confederate armies in a single year.

The city remained securely in Union hands for the remainder of the war— and, some would say, for the remainder of the century. Partly due to its Republican politics, extremely unusual in the South, and partly due to its openness to industry, Knoxville developed a reputation as a Southern city welcoming to Yankees,

multiplied its population by a factor of about 12, adding new factories every year, the drivers of the growth were newcomers, especially from Northern cities, but also from the deeper South, and from Europe. Knoxville made train cars, furniture, underwear, gauges, sausage, statuary, beer, mantels, and fine flour— much of it for a national and even international market.

By 1900, the burly, progressive business-minded town boasted dozens of factories and large wholesaling houses, a large opera house, two train stations, an

Photo, previous pages: Reconstructed using the timbers of the first Knoxvillian's 1786 cabin, James White's Fort contrasts with modernist Plaza Tower, in the background. The modern fort actually stands a few blocks away from its original location, but has become a Knoxville landmark in its own right, an attraction for tourists, school groups, and sometimes even Native-American events.

admirable electric-streetcar system, two and sometimes three daily newspapers, popular baseball teams, the state university, dozens of saloons, a red-light district, and a busy market square that attracted farmers and shoppers from more than 100 miles away. Knoxville became a center for

and marble. Knoxville's long period of pride in its relatively respectful race relations ended abruptly in the bizarre lynch-mob riots of 1919 and 1921.

Some regional coal and marble interests declined, co-inciding with an agricultural recession. The 1920s saw a re-

part to these new Knoxvillians who saw no point in raising taxes to solve long-term problems. A 1920s surge of progressive city politics with an emphasis on planning—seemingly a culmination of a half-century of aspirations—ended with a popular defeat of a tax increase and the departure

▲▼ Photos courtesy of Great Smoky Mountains Photographs –Thompson Brothers, McClung Historical Collection

conservationism, especially as it concerned the forests of the nearby mountains. The proud "Queen City of the Appalachians" hosted three major expositions, the largest of which, the 1913 National Conservation Exposition, drew national interest. One million visitors viewed its exhibits about the modern husbandry of natural resources.

It was a high-water point. Knoxville seemed to trip over World War I. The years to come would bring corruption, dissipation, and decline of some of the city's old-line industries like iron

gional in-migration to the city, mostly rural families looking for work in Knoxville's booming textile mills and other factories. For generations, many rural Appalachians had lived almost independently on their own land, unaccustomed to cooperative projects, and fiercely resistant to taxation. They moved to the city in numbers large enough not to be intimidated, and many continued living as they and their forefathers had in the country. Unimpressed by city values, they never felt obliged to conform. Historian Bruce Wheeler ascribes the end of Knoxville's proud progressive era in large

of Louis Brownlow, a nationally renowned urban planner hired to be Knoxville's first city manager, who resigned after suffering a reported nervous breakdown.

The country infusion also made positive marks on local and national culture. Mainly via Knoxville's far-reaching radio stations, numerous popular musicians, among them popular fiddler Roy Acuff and innovative guitarist Chet Atkins, launched careers that would establish the sound of country music.

The Smokies, once dreaded as a dangerous barrier to travel and trade, the Great Smoky Mountains became an attraction only in the 20th century, but since the 1920s they've become the nation's most popular national park. For some years Knoxville attempted, with some success, to market itself as the Gateway to the Smokies; today, there are many tourist communities closer to the mountains. At right is Alum Cave Bluffs, a popular hiking destination.

As the city suffered failure at the core, its region got serendipitous boosts from outside, from several major national projects, several of them unanticipated.

> *Franklin Roosevelt's Tennessee Valley Authority employed 3,000 in downtown Knoxville...*

The Great Smoky Mountains National Park, established in the 1920s and '30s, first as a result of Knoxville progressive initiatives, and with major contributions from local citizens and businesses, eventually resulted in the nation's most popular park. Located just 30 miles from Knoxville, it spawned a new tourist industry in the city itself. Then, designed to improve the region, President Franklin Roosevelt's Tennessee Valley Authority employed 3,000 in downtown Knoxville, many of them educated

professionals, engineers, geographers, lawyers, and even urban planners who brought a new intellectual energy to the city even as their efforts were directed mostly at projects in the countryside. Just a few years later, the wartime Manhattan Project evolved into Oak Ridge National Laboratory, which brought thousands of affluent new residents, a great many with advanced professional credentials and academic degrees, to the Knoxville area.

The University of Tennessee, which before 1900 never attracted more than 700 students, exploded in size. Its sports teams, which before the late 1920s had been of little interest to anyone but students, became a major draw, attracting thousands to games.

Contrary to assumptions, these huge economic powerhouses, some led by idealistic

urban professionals who moved to Knoxville either temporarily or permanently, did not herald a golden age for Knoxville. Beginning in 1935, one journalist after another visited Knoxville and described third-world conditions: poor sewerage, poor electrical service, general collapse. Gunther's 1947 assessment of Knoxville as "the ugliest city I've ever seen in America" was the most famous, but hardly the most severe. The assessments provoked fierce municipal ire, but the mainstream reaction was telling. It wasn't fair to appraise Knoxville by its downtown, some protested: journalists should always drive around and behold our beautiful suburbs. A few realists acknowledged that the authors had a point.

Somehow, all those new reasons to live in Knoxville were never reflected in city population growth. For about

Expanded in the 1990s, Neyland Stadium was, briefly, the largest football stadium in America; it's still in the top four, and even a mediocre season can bring in capacity crowds to see the Tennessee Vols take on another challenger. Its location right by the Tennessee River offers unusual vistas, and potential for travel to games via boat.

Inset: another aerial view UT's campus, showing the same football field, in the late 1920s.

Photo courtesy of Thompson Photograph Collection, McClung Historical Collection

Photo courtesy of University of Tennessee

30 years after the opening of the Smoky Mountains and the launching of TVA, Knoxville was demographically stagnant. In the 1950s, as the Smokies became more popular than ever, as TVA lakes hummed with new houseboats, as Oak Ridge National Lab became ever more important to Cold War defense, as UT's Vols won a national football championship, Knoxville suffered a population decline of more than 10 percent, the steepest decline of any American city

that decade. And the city continued to get terrible press. Fortune magazine jeered at its dysfunctional downtown, and Look magazine named Knoxville as one of America's "most sinful" cities, citing the proliferation of prostitution in hotels.

Part of that population decline came with continued industrial disintegration, as several textile mills closed. Part of that urban population decline came with suburbanization.

Knoxville's apparent federal-level windfalls and its urban decline may not have been purely coincidental. TVA and the Smokies park project created unprecedented popular attractions in Knoxville's region—but not in Knoxville itself. The region, more appealing to locals and visitors than ever before, boomed without bringing the city along with it. The Smokies, difficult to get to before 1930, had once been known only to a hardy few. Suddenly they became a way for a middle-class family to spend a weekend. Between 1935 and 1945, TVA created five new lakes within an hour's drive of Knoxville. All of them sprouted lake houses, marinas, public parks, many of them populated by Knoxvillians fleeing the dirty city for an afternoon or a weekend.

Many Knoxvillians left town for the newly accessible mountains and lakes, either temporarily, forsaking old urban amenities like movie theaters and baseball games and downtown festivals— or permanently, with new homes with beautiful views and lower property taxes. Many of those left behind to entertain themselves in the old-fashioned city were those who lacked dependable transportation. Knoxville's once-admirable streetcar system shut down forever in 1946.

Norris Dam, on the Clinch River about 20 miles north of Knoxville, was completed in 1936, the first of several major dams built by the Tennessee Valley Authority. The proximity of Norris was one reason Knoxville was chosen as TVA's headquarters. The planned town of Norris, established to house dam workers, is now considered a Knoxville suburb. The hydroelectric dam was considered a wonder in its time, and was visited by an astonishing array of international visitors, including Prime Minister Jawaharlal Nehru of India, philosopher Jean-Paul Sartre, and the Swiss architect Le Corbusier, who was reportedly awed by it. Today, Norris Lake is a popular weekend attraction.

Downtown residential development declined, suburban shopping bloomed, and in the mid-20th century, many affluent Knoxvillians stopped coming downtown very much except to go to work. Those

...thanks to the beautiful and suddenly accessible mountains and lakes around its outskirts, Knoxville's particular experience with suburbanization was almost nuclear.

who noticed conditions in the city had little personal reason to care about decrepit old buildings and peeling billboards.

Suburbanization was a national phenomenon, of course, as the suddenly mobile American middle class embraced a new lifestyle enabled by automobiles. Perhaps

thanks to the beautiful and suddenly accessible mountains and lakes around its outskirts, Knoxville's particular experience with suburbanization was almost nuclear.

The city became outward-directed to an extent that few cities ever are. Newspaper columnists devoted most of their attention to the countryside. Even Knoxville Chamber of Commerce literature stopped saying much about the city itself, preferring to emphasize attractions outside city limits, mountains and lakes. Tacitly they all acknowledged that Knoxville's amenities were country amenities, not city amenities.

In the 1950s, coast-to-coast Interstate 40 plowed right through downtown Knoxville—necessitating the wholesale demolition of several downtown blocks and parts of traditional Victorian-era urban subdivisions. Close on its heels was intersecting Interstate 75, connecting Michigan to Florida, again through the old town of Knoxville. A post-war generation was generally cooperative, and some downtown merchants—the ones on surviving blocks, at least—welcomed it as a likely boon to downtown. New commercial and residential development spilled alongside the freeway's route, especially to the west.

Highway construction co-incided with Urban Renewal, a term many of those affected feel should always come

smelly, even dangerous, few Knoxvillians regretted the loss.

A few years after I-40's completion, a new highway connected Neyland Drive to the interstate. James White Parkway, named for the 1786 settler who built his mill on the creek now buried in a

years: open in 1962, the Civic Coliseum addressed a long-neglected lack, that of a performing-arts center. It was downtown, but set apart from downtown, suburban style, surrounded by lawn, and with its own dedicated parking. Now one could visit downtown without walking on a downtown sidewalk. At the time, that option seemed like a good thing.

The suburban motif invaded downtown's core, as century-old Market Square became concrete-modernist Market Square Mall, and a shopping block of Gay Street got the back-door Promenade, which promised to make stores as easy to access as they were in the suburbs.

For a few years, it looked like a success. But by the time Knoxville built West Town, its first covered suburban shopping mall, about six miles west of downtown—a little belatedly, compared to the rest of the country, in 1972—it was all too obvious that downtown retail was dying.

In the 1950s and '60s, slum clearance on the east side of downtown, criticized for being too comprehensive, resulted in hundreds of acres of land for highways and the 1962 Civic Coliseum, still used for hockey games, circuses, and concerts; as well as, much later, the Women's Basketball Hall of Fame, at right.

Photo by Gary Pope

with ironic quotation marks. Reflecting national patterns, Knoxville embarked on a 15-year plan that included wholesale slum removal and construction of housing projects. As in most cities, the community removed was predominantly black. Many black businesses, traditions, and social networks did not survive the move.

A new university-oriented highway, Neyland Drive, named for the Vols' football coach, used most of the city's undervalued urban riverfront. A fast automobile connection between downtown, the university (especially burgeoning Neyland Stadium) and points west, Neyland Drive also separated the downtown pedestrian from the riverfront. At a time when the river was still seen as a liability, dirty,

culvert for the highway project, was anticipated to extend southward, across the river, toward the mountains.

A probably uncontemplated result of the construction of highways in central Knoxville was that the city's traditional downtown shrank in size, to barely half the urban neighborhood known as downtown Knoxville in 1920—retreating, roughly, to the borders of the 1870s. Though a few square blocks of northern downtown survived as an urban-looking place across the interstate, it was almost forgotten, no longer considered part of the central business district.

Urban-renewal demolition made way for downtown's first major new construction in more than 30

Other seemingly positive developments for the city and its culture and leisure habits had a deleterious effect on downtown.

During the city's pre-1925 boom years, Knoxvillians rarely had reason to set foot on UT's campus. But by 1950, college football had surpassed traditional city baseball in attendance, as Neyland Stadium, growing to be one of the nation's largest football stadiums, often filled for Vols games.

At mid century, the university began to dominate Knoxville's cultural life, both through its ever-bigger athletic programs and public amenities, some of which competed with traditional downtown attractions. Built in 1954, the University Center offered public bowling alleys, a large bookstore, restaurants, and multiple auditoriums which hosted occasional movies, famous lecturers, musical performances, and comedians; most shows were open to the public at large. McClung Museum, open in 1963, addressed Knoxville's long-bemoaned lack of a general-purpose history and arts museum. Clarence Brown Theatre. Endowed by the Hollywood Golden Age director and completed in 1970, that state-of-the-art modernist facility immediately became Knoxville's favored venue for live drama, open to the non-collegiate public but clearly run by the university, primarily for the benefit of theater students. Most of UT's public attractions were discreetly separated, and attendees might not expect to encounter any Knoxvillian who wasn't attending the same event.

Later, UT's on-campus Thompson-Boling Arena, completed in 1987 mainly

> *UT claimed more and more of Knoxville's leisure time, and perhaps also the city's sense of itself.*

for intercollegiate basketball, began hosting major-draw country, rock, and other mainstream performances for the general public—eventually many of those that had previously appeared at the Civic Coliseum and other downtown venues.

In the latter 20th century, UT claimed more and more of Knoxville's leisure time, and perhaps also the city's sense of itself. The university's attractions and facilities were

well-designed, well-kept, well-booked, often superior to those previously known in the city—but in bringing Knoxville to the clean, suburban-style, alcohol-free campus—without dinner restaurants, bars, or retail attractions in sight—it rendered a cultural Night in Knoxville, whether for a UT play, a

concert, an exhibit, or a basketball game, more a single-destination experience, and a distinctly non-urban one.

The collegiate-gothic detail of Ayres Hall established an architectural standard for the university as it grew in the middle part of the 20th century.
Photo by Gary Pope

Deliberate attempts to improve downtown, revive downtown, save downtown, date back to the 19th century. An 1890s attempt to improve Knoxville along the lines of the new City Beautiful movement sputtered. Extravagant plans for major steel mills, world-class hotels, cliff-top parks, and planned communities crashed with the devastating national recession of 1893. In the middle 1920s, an extremely ambitious progressive plan to redesign the city along modern principles that seem enlightened even today—emphasizing the riverfront, parks, and urban beauty—influenced the Henley Street Bridge project before colliding with the Great Depression and collapsing altogether.

Photo by Sheena Patrick ◀

Photo by Gary Pope ▶

In 1955, a native tree inspired Knoxville's annual Dogwood Arts Festival; at right, [something about renovation and public art].

Years of execrably bad press prodded improvements in the postwar era. Beginning in 1955, pastel-marked Dogwood Trails aimed at first to get travelers toward its suburban garden spots—and, presumably, away from the unfixed downtown. After the first modernizations of urban renewal, and the opening of the Civic Coliseum, the city, which had not sponsored public festivals in decades, launched a colorfully sober Dogwood Arts Festival which in the early '60s earned some positive national press.

It all coincided with de-segregation, which after res-taurant sit-ins in 1960, and the desegregation of UT the same year—followed by movie-theater demonstrations in 1963— came to Knoxville a little earlier and more peace-fully than in many Southern cities. However, it was hard not to notice that urban

renewal, though favored by many progressive desegrega-tionists, disproportionately affected the black community, erasing dozens of blocks of the eastern side of downtown that had supported thou-sands of residents and scores of businesses—and ultimate-ly pushed a large part of the predominantly black commu-nity about half a mile away from the business district.

Meanwhile, ambitions for downtown were habitu-ally directed at improving shopping. Though hundreds still lived downtown, most-ly in inexpensive and aging apartment buildings, residen-tial development in postwar Knoxville was almost entirely directed toward the sub-urbs. Middle class or affluent residences downtown were considered outmoded. New movie theaters, restaurants, and motels favored suburban

locations, especially those near interstate exits.

Deliberate downtown-improvement efforts pushed retail, often imitating subur-ban patterns. After some de-molitions to make way for it, a downtown "East-West Mall" was stillborn.

In the 1970s, a modern new Hyatt Regency opened near the Civic Coliseum, ac-cessed only by suburban-style parking, at a discreet distance from the tradition-al downtown; soon, both of Gay Street's traditional old grand hotels, the Andrew Johnson and the Farragut, closed. So did both of the grand old movie theaters, the Riviera and the Tennessee. Entertainment seemed to have moved decisively to suburban cinemas and to the university, which was host-ing more and more live music and drama, the sorts of shows that were once the province of downtown.

However, at the same time, downtown office development got a huge boost through a pocket financial boom. Originally from rural Union County, banker Jake Butcher, the 1978 Democratic gubernatorial nominee, and his brother, C.H., seemed poised to make Knoxville a regional banking capital. In downtown Knoxville, Jake Butcher built the tallest building ever built in East Tennessee, the 24-story modernist glass skyscraper known as Plaza Tower.

Maybe more interesting, and more relevant to downtown's long-term viability, was what was happening to one old porno theater directly across the street. Knoxville had little reputation for preservation until a few eccentrics noted that the gritty

Photo by David Luttrell ▼   Photo by Jacques Gautreau ▲

Above, left: Plaza Tower, built by charismatic banker Jake Butcher in the 1970s, was Knoxville's first modern skyscraper, and remains the tallest building in East Tennessee. Right across the street from it is a very different and much older place, the Bistro, in an 1816 brick and masonry building adjacent to the 1909 Bijou Theatre.

Adjacent to downtown is Fort Sanders, made famous by author James Agee in his essay, "Knoxville: Summer 1915" and his subsequent autobiographical novel, A Death In the Family. East Tennessee's most densely populated neighborhood, it's best known for its population of university students.

Photo by Jacques Gautreau

Photo by Florence Homolka

Bijou Theater was actually an interesting old vaudeville house—attached to an antebellum hotel. With a narrative that included Andrew Jackson, John Phillip Sousa, Rutherford B. Hayes, and the Marx Brothers, it was a building with more history than some good-sized towns.

The Bijou captured the imagination of a city that had rarely thought of itself as historic, and a grassroots organization succeeded in renovating it, offering the central part of downtown its first legitimate live-performance space in many years. The effort also spawned a permanent organization called Knoxville Heritage. The nonprofit later known as Knox Heritage would be one of the most influential factors in the city's transformation in decades to come, not just downtown, but in bringing back the city's historic neighborhoods, the "trolleyburbs" close to downtown, one old house at a time.

Adjacent to downtown and to the university is what remains of a late-Victorian, early 20th-century neighborhood known as Fort Sanders. Its history includes the region's bloodiest Civil War battle as well as the beloved home of author James Agee, whose Pulitzer winning novel, *A Death in the Family*, is set there. Its family-oriented nature declined with suburbanization, as the university grew rapidly, and it became, inevitably, UT's "student ghetto," interesting and lively but rapidly decaying, even as it was credibly claimed to include the two most densely populated census districts in East Tennessee.

Development pressures from the university and from an expanding hospital have eroded whole swaths of the neighborhood, but piecemeal renovations have saved pockets of it. Despite its reputation as one of Knoxville's noisier neighborhoods, it's home to a few affluent professionals. Knox Heritage has attempted to work with UT to consider renovated homes in Fort Sanders as residences for faculty.

Meanwhile, some other inner-city neighborhoods have flourished. Perhaps the biggest success story is Fourth and Gill, a modest Victorian neighborhood on downtown's northeastern corner. Largely abandoned by the families it was built to serve, and badly cut up by interstate development, in the 1970s, it was overwhelmingly occupied by the elderly interspersed with vacancies and some occupants who tended to get into trouble. Its organic, house-by-house redevelopment was barely underway in 1980, but by the dawn of the new century, it was once again a family neighborhood, and one of the most interesting and envied neighborhoods in the city, with many old houses valued in the hundreds of thousands.

Redevelopment has helped lift other historic neighborhoods—the inner-city "trolleyburbs" including Old North, Parkridge, Mechanicsville, and Island Home, to varying degrees of success.

— • —

It wasn't until a few years after the Bijou's renovation, in 1980, that young public-radio disk jockey Ashley Capps hosted a performance by jazz drummer Jack DeJohnette, and noticed something unexpected about the old theater's acoustics. They were very nearly perfect. "I thought, 'This is something special,'" Capps recalls. It was an unexpected bonus from the preservation effort some had criticized as foolish.

In spite of its college crowd, Knoxville then had a terrible reputation among performers. Knoxville audiences were slow to spend money on tickets for evenings watching live music, and when they did, they were stoic, hard to excite. And they'd grown fond of saying "there's nothing going on here."

"There are a couple of ways to respond to that," says Ashley Capps. "Do nothing and complain, or move somewhere else—or try to make

some stuff happen. I don't know why I chose the latter. For me, Knoxville was like a palate of opportunity. It was never the most receptive place to do what I do. It just made me want to try harder. In a way, Knoxville's reticence at embracing shows helped me be a better concert promoter."

Part of Knoxville's lack of focus was likely its major spillage to the west, in step with America's suburbanization, but exaggerated in West Knoxville by the adjacency of the newly appealing river/lake, the chain-dominant businesses clustered around the I-40/75 exits, and burgeoning Oak Ridge. The national laboratory became part of a long-cherished dream of related economic development, in accord with UT and even TVA. A 1970s project to develop the highway connector Pellissippi Parkway as a "technology corridor" comparable to North Carolina's Research Triangle attracted a great deal of interest and investment, and drew a few big firms. It was ultimately

A night at the Bistro: Today, more than half of all downtown restaurants host live music regularly.
Photo by Stephanie Norwood

Knoxville *Green by Nature*

The Third Creek Bike Trail, which here passes under an old masonry railroad trestle, was the beginning of the city's passion for greenways.
Photo by David Luttrell

disappointing—and it was all a dozen miles west of central Knoxville.

A different, almost opposite initiative started with much less fanfare, but it was the humble beginning of something that would become one of 21st-century Knoxville's chief assets.

In the early 1970s, a group of unconventional bicycling enthusiasts, with the approval of a bemused city government and a few property owners, gained right of way to about two miles of thick woods on the suburban west side of the university, and organized a paved bike trail, the city's first. Connecting the back corner of a bleak student-apartment parking lot with a little-known dead-end street, the Third Creek Bike Trail skirted the banks of an almost-forgotten brook. The relative few who experienced it in its first 20 years always remarked

that "the bike trail"—it was Knoxville's only one—was lush, pristine, almost like a favorite trail in the Smokies. In the full leaf of summer, in several portions there was no visible sign of man except for the trail itself.

The fact that Knoxville's combination of topography and lush greenery could create this illusion of wilderness between a decadent industrial area and high-traffic Kingston Pike was a cause of wonder. The bike trail remained just that peculiar two-mile stretch for a couple of decades. In years to come, that phenomenon would connect to the university, downtown, and beyond, connecting to a network of 10 miles of trails, arguably the nucleus of what became one of 21st-century Knoxville's defining principles: the Urban Wilderness.

— • —

In the 1970s, none of that destiny was clear. The key to urban success seemed to be to follow the lead of Atlanta, Charlotte, and Nashville, embracing modernity—and height. C.H. Butcher commenced his own skyscraper— the second-tallest building ever built in East Tennessee— Riverview Tower, a block away from his brother Jake's Plaza Tower. Both brothers were invested heavily in an extraordinary event that promised to transform downtown, the 1982 World's Fair.

First proposed by Mayor Kyle Testerman, encouraged by the recent success of a big fair in a similar-sized city, Spokane, and driven by international news—the mid-1970s energy crisis—the six-month International Energy Exposition would highlight the future of energy generation, and make Knoxville the smallest American city ever to attempt an event of that prominence.

Expo '82, as it was called during its planning years, was better known as the 1982 World's Fair the day it opened with a visit from President Ronald Reagan. The exposition's urban venue, unusual for such an event—it occupied an old rail yard that had been a Victorian-era industrial site—prompted the construction of three new downtown hotels, attracted 23 nations including, to the astonishment of the nation, the Peoples' Republic of China, marking the first time since 1904 that mainland China had participated in a world's fair. It drew 11 million visitors, and earned mostly positive press, hushing some cynics—and reportedly earning a slight profit.

The Butcher brothers so intimately associated with the Fair weren't so lucky. Not four months after the Fair closed,

federal agents descended on their twin skyscrapers, seizing assets and jailing the Butcher brothers for bank fraud.

Worse for Knoxville, maybe, the World's Fair didn't deliver the promised residual effect, at least not right away. The fair site languished for years to come, as city officials argued about what to do with it. One prospective developer after another withdrew their proposals for parks and residential areas. Pessimistic observers wondered aloud how long downtown would be able to sustain the three new hotels built in anticipation of the fair.

Madeline Rogero, a former union and community activist who'd lived all over the country arrived in Knoxville in the early '80s, and despite the World's Fair, found a moribund city mostly content with its "Dogpatch image," controlled by graying white men, "promoting us as a low-wage

town"—essentially, she says, "selling us on our weaknesses." At the time, she did not expect to stay in Knoxville long.

A few things were stirring. Attempting to keep some of the momentum of the fair going, the city hosted downtown festivals outside of the aegis of April's tame, matronly Dogwood Arts Festival. Saturday Night on the Town, an annual music-oriented festival launched just before the fair by a civic arts organization, swelled after the fair, ranging over much of the downtown area, with multiple stages spaced blocks away from the others. Its popularity seemed a revelation, but then

Planned in the wake of the Energy Crisis of the 1970s, the 1982 World's Fair ostensibly showed its 11 million visitors ways to conserve energy, and produce it more cheaply and cleanly. President Ronald Reagan, seated between then-Govenor and future U.S. Senator Lamar Alexander, the Republican from nearby Maryville, and Democratic banker/politician Jake Butcher, spoke on opening day. We can only guess at their conversation: Alexander and Butcher had run against each other for governor, three and a half years earlier. The fair's theme structure, the Sunsphere, housed restaurants and viewing platforms accessible by elevator; it's still open to the public today.
Photo Courtesy of Knoxville News Sentinel

Photo by Gary Heatherly

a fatal stabbing in an alley dampened enthusiasm for it. Chili Cook-offs, blues festivals, and barbecue festivals on the fair site itself had mixed success.

None of it lasted. Downtown appeared to be evolving inexorably, almost one-dimensionally, into an office park, directed at the courts, the banks, and TVA's

3,000 employees who reported to work Monday to Friday, nine to five.

In the 1980s, many remarked that downtown looked as if it was arranged as an amenity for TVA. And then, thanks to Reagan-era cutbacks, TVA's downtown presence shrank to one third of its size.

Once-stalwart retailers like J.C. Penney closed their old stores in favor of the suburban malls, and those merchants who remained downtown ceased their evening hours, concentrating on those commuters who could shop at lunchtime. Downtown restaurants emphasized lunch for commuters; most were closed by 3:00 p.m.

After several top-down projects, including an early 1960s "mall" design, old Market Square revived as the result of a serendipitous convergence of individual entrepreneurs and larger organizations like the Chamber of Commerce, which established its headquarters there, all encouraged by a city project to improve its basic infrastructure. A historic overlay calls for a review process concerning major changes to the buildings, but most developers have voluntarily seen the value of developing on a mixed-use model, with retail downstairs and residences upstairs. Today perhaps 100 people live on the square proper.

Photo by David Luttrell

But one unexpected development that pointed toward a different destiny became apparent only when a very old man died.

For almost a century, a common complaint about Knoxville was its dearth of public parks. Even in the Victorian era, some declared Knoxville was the biggest city in America that lacked a city park, and as late as 1980, Knoxville had never deliberately established a public park downtown. That began to change with an unexpected bequest from a quiet and little-known photographer, Knoxville native Charles Krutch, who died in his 90s and left the city a $1 million gift to establish a public park downtown. In 1983, just to the south of Market Square, the city established Krutch Park. About 20 years after the park was established, Krutch Park was extended to Gay Street. Though the reclusive Mr. Krutch certainly never thought of his gesture as part of any sort of a trend, his gift may be considered the beginning of a new era for urban greenery in Knoxville.

Erected by a privately planned effort, partly with state funding the Tennessee Woman Suffrage Memorial draws the attention of Market Square visitors. Originally intended to be a statue of Knoxville's own most famous suffragist, Lizzie Crozier French, in the middle—she often spoke on Market Square, and lived to see her dreams of earning the right to vote realized--promoters learned they could earn state funding by representing notable feminists from Middle and West Tennessee, too.

opes for a more comprehensive downtown sprouted mainly around its edges. A cadre of preservationists, several of whom had been involved in the effort to save the Bijou Theatre several years earlier, began working quietly in a corner of downtown opposite from the fair site, a small warehouse district so forgotten many Knoxvillians didn't even know it existed. The Old City, as it was designated by hairdresser-turned developer Kristopher Kendrick, seemed just a nice idea, at first. Though just four linear blocks radiating from a common intersection, it was perhaps Knoxville's highest concentration of late-Victorian-era commercial buildings, most of them vacant or underused slums. Avoided by most Knoxvillians, it had a reputation for crime.

The first entrepreneur to make it work was a particularly unusual woman who, perhaps, had not lived in Knoxville long enough to believe it impossible to establish a French restaurant in a slum area with hardly any dedicated parking. From England, Annie Delisle, a former professional dancer and ex-wife of novelist Cormac McCarthy, opened Annie's, for several years a crowded destination, especially after it began hosting live jazz.

Several blocks away, two very different projects were simultaneously, but with little fanfare, reviving the idea of upscale downtown living. A block of brick row houses redeveloped by Kendrick (and known as Kendrick Place) quickly emerged as a comfortable home for a few childless professionals. Half a block away, developer Ron Watkins re-imagined the old 1930s TVA headquarters building as a condominium building known

as the Pembroke. For about 15 years to come, these two off-register projects would be oddballs in downtown Knoxville. In the 1980s and most of the '90s, if you were affluent and lived downtown, chances were you lived in one or the other.

Unrelated to the fair, but blooming just after it, was a brash media company called 13-30, later Whittle Communications. The producer of national magazines, at one time owner of *Esquire*, grew astonishingly fast, eventually producing about 25 magazines, several high-profile authors' books, and even some closed-market television programming. Unlike most Knoxville businesses, Whittle hired nationally, hundreds of art directors and editors from other states, many of whom had lived in major cities and were accustomed to urban amenities. Whittle's employees, most of them young and single, flooded downtown's

Photo, previous pages:
One of the Old City's more elaborate historic buildings, the ca. 1890 Carhart Building, designed in the Richardsonian Romanesque style.

Among Knoxville's most unusual re-purposing efforts was this Georgian-style building, constructed in 1991 to serve as the headquarters of an apparently growing magazine and television company, Whittle Communications. After Whittle folded only three years later, it saw an unexpected new use as the federal courthouse.

few bars and nightclubs. Eschewing the westward suburban dynamic, Whittle's affluent employees perplexed the local real-estate establishment by favoring older houses near the central part of town. (One older neighborhood on the north side became known as Little Whittaly.)

For its own recruiting and retention purposes, Whittle got actively involved in promoting downtown through an ambitious plan based on urban-design principles. With city help, in the late 1980s Whittle acquired two downtown blocks near the crippled Butcher towers and commenced building a palatial headquarters designed to look like a 17th-century university: Historic Whittlesburg, as wags called

it when it was completed in 1991.

Meanwhile, across town and down the hill, Annie Deslisle had few neighbors until the latter '80s, when the Old City turned a corner toward mainstream appeal with the long-delayed completion of the area's architectural icon, the circa 1888 corner-turret Sullivan's Saloon. Several other restaurant/bars and boutiques (with evening hours, then extraordinary downtown) opened, along with Java, Knoxville's first espresso-era coffee shop—and Ella Guru's, a basement

Photo by David Luttrell

◄ Photos by Sheena Patrick ◄

fair site, roughly on the site of what had been the Japan Pavilion in 1982. But despite a few monster successes, like a Rodin exhibit, attendance was often disappointing, and the Knoxville Museum of Art rarely had observable effects on downtown itself.

Another longtime lack, remarkable for a city as old as Knoxville, was a permanent history museum. Soon after the KMA opened, a regional group, the East Tennessee Historical Society, had a close look at the long-underused 1874 Custom House, near Market Square. The marble-clad building once used for offices by TVA became home to the county library's McClung Historical Collection, Knox County Archives, and, on its ground floor, a new public attraction, the city's first-ever regional history museum. Open in 1993, the new Museum of East Tennessee History drew only modest visitation in its early

Irish immigrant Patrick Sullivan built this saloon on the corner of Jackson and Central in 1888. Closed by local prohibition in 1907, it was revived as a modern-era saloon in the 1980s, and is often seen as the centerpiece of the Old City.

Below: The Jig & Reel, Knoxville's first Scottish-themed pub, hosts live music several nights a week. Its century-old building was once a Greek-owned restaurant which, during segregation, catered to both blacks and whites.

nightclub offering national music acts, a first of its kind. Its backers included Keith Bellows, a Whittle editor from Montreal—and aspiring promoter Ashley Capps, who would prove to be a significant cultural figure on a regional, even national scale.

In hardly a decade, by 1990, what had been a neglected, dirty, and sometimes scary slum developed a reputation that was trendy, exciting, almost posh.

But the Old City was really just one intersection, small and out of the way. A few new assets popped up here and there. For almost a century, art lovers had been trying to establish a permanent art museum. Since 1960, a pretty old house on Kingston Pike had housed a small collection and occasional exhibits. In 1990, with major help from mobile-home magnate Jim Clayton, the Knoxville Museum of Art opened, opposite downtown on the old

Photo by Stephanie Norwood

days when it was cluttered and eccentrically arranged, but the fact that some big events drew crowds suggested some popular interest in the idea.

Calhoun's, a large and successful restaurant on the long-ignored riverfront boomed in the post-fair era and suggested development

Photo by Stephanie Norwood

potential, with boat-dock parking—but to pedestrians, it was remote from downtown, screened by modern architecture, down a steep hill, and across highway-like Neyland Drive.

As the Old City throbbed in the evenings, the rest of central Knoxville continued its slow slide. Downtown was hemorrhaging offices, as one law firm after another forsook it for the suburbs, touting parking advantages for suburban and rural customers who had become accustomed to adjacent surface parking. After TVA's 70 percent reduction, several Market Square and Gay Street lunch

spots closed or cut back. A major facelift to Market Square improved the looks of the place for a couple of years, but failed to find traction—though during that period it did attract one Iranian immigrant who had an imaginative knack for unusual pizza and sandwiches. In 1990, few could have expected that Mahasti Vafaie's tiny lunch-only Flying Tomato—later Tomato Head—would become important to Knoxville's future.

In 1994, after waves of layoffs, Whittle Communications closed, leaving its huge, two-block long, three-year-old building empty. Though numerically

not as big a loss to downtown as TVA's layoffs, Whittle's collapse may have been a bigger blow. Because they'd been so active downtown, Whittlites, as they were known, had a big influence per capita. When they were gone, everyone noticed. "It left a little bit of a black hole in its wake," recalls Capps. Some restaurants closed as a direct result, as did Ella Guru's.

More retail closed, including the 90-year-old department store, Watson's, as well as downtown's last groceries and drugstores. Knoxville's minor-league baseball team, based on downtown's eastern fringe for almost a century, moved to an interstate exit several miles out of town.

Some highly publicized violent crimes knocked the wind out of the Old City, scaring

suburbanites. One daily newspaper, the *Journal*, closed forever; a few years later, the *News Sentinel*, evacuated downtown, building its plant at a remote site without walking access, a mile away.

Knoxville as a whole wasn't suffering much. Though Knoxville retained its reputation as an unexciting city, some people didn't mind living there. Cable service was good, a fun new chain restaurant opened every few weeks, and the UT Vols, with impressive young quarterback Peyton Manning, were winning football games. The Vols even won the national championship in 1999. Neyland Stadium regularly drew crowds of over 100,000—but only six to eight Saturdays a year.

The suburbs, home to several successful corporations, like Pilot Travel Centers, Bush Beans, the medical-parts manufacturer DeRoyal, and Regal Cinemas (many Knoxvillians don't realize the nation's largest cinema operator is headquartered here), kept booming in their suburban campuses. A new entry to Knoxville's economy arrived mainly in the person of one Ross Bagwell, an eccentric filmmaker who had worked out of Hollywood in the 1960s. In the 1980s, he'd created cable-TV shows like "I-40 Paradise," which has been described as the first made-for-cable sitcom. By the 1990s, his company, Cinetel, the most prominent of a few scrappy video-production companies in West Knoxville, attracted some industry giants, and became the germ of what would become a major economic

presence, today through the work of Scripps Networks Interactive.

No one expected that. Whittle's business model was so unusual that the company's demise might have seemed a permanent end to national media in Knoxville. But as it worked out, a handful of Whittle professionals recruited from elsewhere were able to stay in Knoxville to work for Scripps and other media businesses. By the end of the century, with cable channels like HGTV, DIY, and the Food Network, Scripps became one of the nation's biggest cable-television producers, and built a green, idyllic modern campus in the decidedly suburban Cedar Bluff area, just off the interstate.

For downtown, though, the mid-'90s seemed a dramatic low, a moment for the hero to step in. That didn't happen, exactly, but what did happen may have been better.

Open since 1990, the Knoxville Museum of Art watches over World's Fair Park. The museum hosts ever-changing art exhibits, but also weekly jazz and blues shows, which draw a unique crowd rare elsewhere in town, mature and racially diverse.

Photo by Stephanie Norwood

Photo by C Jill Reed

Photo by David Luttrell

trees in long-disused Market Square while they were waiting for supper on a summer's evening.

The Tomato Head, which in the early '90s introduced sidewalk cafes and freedom from cigarette smoke—still a weird idea when almost all restaurants were still trying to negotiate "smoking sections"—the Tomato Head was the surprise hit of its era, the Knoxville restaurant most often recommended in travel guides, a bright, lively place that re-introduced Knoxville to its own downtown. Breaking the TVA-commuter-lunch mold, the Tomato Head had longer hours than any Market Square restaurant in

The Tomato Head is a small restaurant that casts a big shadow. Opened by an Iranian immigrant in a run-down building in 1990, its innovations established a new standard for Market Square, including outdoor seating, no-smoking dining, and evening and weekend hours—as well as a unique menu that has earned therecommendations of travel writers. To some Knoxvillians, the most astonishing about it was that a new restaurant could succeed with no dedicated parking at all.

Mayor Victor Ashe, who had inherited civic debts dating back to the disappointments of the World's Fair, seemed disinclined to concentrate on downtown, emphasizing instead city services and paying off the debt.

A little frantically, downtown boosters organized a Next Big Steps initiative to review possible strategies, most of them extravagant Hail-Mary passes. One consultant after another came to study the Knoxville problem. Roomsful of gray men in suits and ties harrumphed as one consultant after another proposed a NASCAR museum or a high-tech incubator or an expensive performing-arts center.

Downtown's salvation would not come from one big lion, but from a lot of lambs. Some were new to town and didn't even know the traditional power brokers.

One was Mahasti Vafaie, and her Tomato Head. At first

different only for its innovative sandwich and pizza menu, Vafaie began her luncheonette modestly. But as the 1990s progressed, she began experimenting with evening and weekend hours—almost unheard of downtown, in recent years, especially for a downtown restaurant with no parking lot. First a renter, as her restaurant thrived, she bought her century-old building and commenced an expansive renovation, discovering serendipitous detail, like long-forgotten stamped-tin ceilings. Her customers, some of them newcomers who didn't know not to come downtown in the evenings, found their kids enjoyed playing around the

decades, and broke stereotypes of what it was like to be downtown on a random night after dark.

— • —

In 1994, an energetic couple purchased a defunct furniture store on Gay Street near Market Square and in that cavernous 1890s space with a mezzanine opened Knoxville's first brewpub. Originally known as the Smoky Mountain Brewing Co., it served exotic varieties of beer brewed on the premises. Making use of the old urban-renewal-era "Promenade" parking deck in the rear, it offered free adjacent parking to a city that was then accustomed to nothing else.

Though moderately popular, they weren't able to pay off their investment, and neither were their immediate successors—but after a few articulations, finally known as the Downtown Grill & Brewery, it became one of Knoxville's highest-volume restaurant-bars.

Meanwhile, a similar plan—huge old two-story space, wood floors, long bar, inexpensive food, interesting beer, free parking—applied to a new restaurant in the Old City called Barley's. Originally an Asheville import, Barley's added the extra

attraction of stage-quality live music, usually free, and a family atmosphere that had rarely been an emphasis in the Old City.

That paradigm might have seemed unimaginable to a previous generation: the big family-friendly bar, with patrons under 18 and over 80. The broadening of downtown's demographic appeal is perhaps an underappreciated part of the story. For many years, downtown was on weekdays given over entirely to commuters; rarely seen were children, teenagers, or the old. Nightclubs, bars that offered live music, catered to one of the narrowest demographics: those old

enough to drink, but still single, and overwhelmingly under 35. There are still bars, and nights, where the demographics narrow—but several of downtown's more durable establishments are those where it's not unusual to find either children or the elderly as customers.

— • —

As if borrowing the strategy of the Allies during the first years of World War II, the city didn't attack downtown's problems directly, but around the edges. The 1950s construction of Neyland Drive left hardly any room for riverfront development, just a narrow muddy bank. But

a restaurant built just before the World's Fair, peculiar as it seemed at the time, seemed to be thriving, near downtown if hard to get to afoot. Volunteer Landing, conceived by the Ashe administration in the mid-'90s, put a pedestrian-bike path connecting it to the newly extended Third Creek Greenway, which connected to the city's lonesome 1970s bike trail, and ran deep into Bearden, offering an almost traffic-free bicycle and pedestrian route to downtown from suburban West Knoxville. Along the long, narrow ribbon of riverbank were fountain, wharf, and historic-marker attractions, with a pedestrian bridge over Neyland Drive. A dysfunctional connection that still left a very steep and unguarded walk up the hill to the business district, but a connection nonetheless—and the city's multi-million-dollar investment did signal an interest in investment in downtown. Despite its limitations, Volunteer Landing, adorned with new narrative historical

Planned in the late 1990s, the city's Volunteer Landing improved public access to the downtown riverfront, which had been mostly ignored since steamboat-wharf days. Though it still has significant access problems, and never attracted the retail once hoped, Volunteer Landing does support two large, successful restaurants, and a long marina, where scores of pleasure craft, including some semi-residential houseboats, are moored.

From the river, Knoxville's skyline looks more modern than much of the rest of the city does, dominated by the Sunsphere and modernist office buildings like the 1980 City County Building. Some patrons arrive at Calhoun's restaurant by boat.

Photos this page by Stephanie Norwood

greenways, not just downtown, but all over the city. The city added numerous new suburban parks and dozens of miles of greenways to connect many of them together. To those conversant about Knoxville's deep history in conservation, it seemed an homage to the heroic era of a century before, but greenways would become a major distinction for Knoxville in the 21st century.

— • —

Without fanfare, and frankly without much encouragement from the city, a few affluent people began moving downtown.

A labor of love by a philanthropic railroad man, the Three Rivers Rambler, a real steam passenger train, leaves Volunteer Landing on semi-regular excursion trips into parts of town most have never seen. Near the end of its short trip, it offers a commanding view of the confluence of the Holston and French Broad Rivers, which form the third river, the Tennessee.

Photos this page by Stephanie Norwood

markers, became not only a game-day gathering place, but a venue for riverside wine tastings and other pocket festivals.

Volunteer Landing's least-expected attraction arrived courtesy of Knoxville's only 21st-century railroad baron. Pete Claussen owned a small short-line freight concern in Tennessee and the Carolinas called, despite its Knoxville headquarters and modest reach, the Gulf & Ohio. Originally from New Jersey, Claussen was an attorney who had once worked for TVA. When he began dabbling in trains, he established his headquarters in historic buildings in downtown Knoxville, eventually in one of downtown's only three antebellum houses, the 1830s James Park House, extensively and imaginatively renovating it. Claussen expressed his love of railroads in a fun way that became a popular downtown attraction, the Three Rivers Rambler. Knoxville's only passenger train in decades, the antique steam-powered excursion train leaves semi-regularly

from Volunteer Landing, chugs miles through rarely seen parts of East Knoxville, pauses on a bridge high above the confluence of the Holston and French Broad Rivers—forming a third river, the Tennessee—and proceeds on to an old marble quarry before turning around. Pete and his wife Linda Claussen have become leading philanthropists, especially associated with preserving large-acreage greenways, like the Seven Islands area, east of the city, for public use.

Mayor Ashe's extraordinarily long administration may be best remembered for its new emphasis on

For years, the World's Fair-era Pembroke and Kendrick Place were anomalies. A few old-line apartment buildings, mostly ill-kept old places that attracted struggling older people and daring undergrads, survived. Kristopher Kendrick rehabbed a few old townhouses and small apartment buildings on Fifth Avenue, just north of the highway, and in Maplehurst, the tiny early 20th-century neighborhood on downtown's UT side. But slowly, almost stealthily, affluent people began moving into unlikely blocks in the central business district.

Among the first were Jim and Jo Mason, a successful insurance man and his wife, a wicker-furniture dealer. While running a coffee shop around the corner, they rehabbed a couple of huge late-19th-century commercial buildings on Gay Street's most decrepit block, the 100 block, dominated by pawnshops, thrift stores, Knoxville's main homeless shelter, and huge vacant buildings. They shocked their peers by sleeping, every night, on a block many Knoxvillians feared to visit after dark. But their enormous home, bigger in square footage than most suburban McMansions, was luxurious.

Slowly, at first, they attracted actual neighbors.

Photo by David Luttrell

One of the first to arrive was a young man who had no intention of becoming downtown's maverick savior. In 1992, David Dewhirst was an aerospace engineer, a UT grad and former Defense Department employee who came to town concerning a tech job in Oak Ridge. His years in Washington had awakened a love for urban living and interesting old buildings. Rolling into town off the interstate, he instinctively turned the wrong way on Gay Street, and saw, on a miserable block of empty buildings and dying pawn shops, an old building with the last tenant's slogan: "See Sam / Wear

Diamonds"—and a For Sale sign.

As he was looking at it, he felt a hand on his shoulder. He turned around to see an impeccably dressed stranger who turned out to be neighbor Jim Mason. "You ought to buy that building," he told Dewhirst.

A few minutes later, looking for an apartment to live in right away, Dewhirst met downtown's leading preservationist spirit, Kristopher Kendrick, who would become his mentor. "That was a big day," Dewhirst recalls. Dewhirst bought the forlorn Gay Street building and built a unique home for himself

upstairs, a living room with a wall built like the prow of a boat, and a back porch overlooking a copse of woods invisible from any street and unknown to the public.

"I had no interest in being a developer," Dewhirst says. "I just wanted a cool place to live." Part of his dream for Knoxville was based on his travels abroad. "As I traveled, I got exposed to the real value of buildings." In European cities known for maintaining their distinctive older architecture and historic public squares, Dewhirst wondered about the bland, pragmatic styles of his home country. His thought in Verona, Italy, was, "How cool is this? And why do Americans hate this so much?"

Dewhirst's apartment, which eventually became home to his veterinarian wife

Eccentric hairdresser Kristopher Kendrick saw potential in downtown preservationist development back in the 1970s, before anyone else did. After his work reviving the Old City, Kendrick Place, and several other pioneering projects, he turned his attention to these two late 19th-century buildings on the long-avoided 100 block of Gay Street, together known as the Emporium. But his dreams for them weren't realized until after the aging Kendrick turned them over to his protégé, David Dewhirst. Mostly vacant and underused for years, the block of huge vacant buildings was long shunned, considered a civic liability with no easy solution. Now it's said to be Knoxville's single most popular residential block.

Photo by Scott Busby

and their small children, was famous even among people who never saw it. At the time, most perhaps thought of Dewhirst as one crazy yuppie.

And perhaps a gullible one. After the then-new local alternative weekly, *Metro Pulse,* ran an article about Dewhirst's early renovations, downtown landowners started calling him. He remembers a question he got more than once: "Hey, uh, my family's got a building downtown. Wanna buy it?" Years later, he shakes his head in a sort of grateful disbelief.

"They couldn't wait to get rid of that nasty problem they

had, that building that their family had left them."

Soon, he'd assembled a collection of small buildings, a couple of them on Market Square. "I could only do small buildings," he recalls. "I did them as a hobby. I didn't make any money. The only payday I had was when I sold one. And I just sold them to maintain my habit of rehabbing buildings."

At the time, the city offered no incentives to restore old buildings. The Central Business Improvement District, a dues-based downtown organization, did offer relatively modest $10-15,000 façade grants. Though they constitute a fraction of the total bill of a thorough renovation, Mayor Rogero praises the role of façade grants "to give

the private sector confidence to put their own money in."

Dewhirst's mother Emily, a well-traveled philanthropist, moved into one of the Market Square buildings, becoming the first resident on that ancient square in several decades, and opened an import boutique downstairs.

— • —

For those who didn't notice the potential of the old buildings, downtown seemed to have little to recommend it in the 1990s, as its last drugstore and grocery closed. Contrary to popular exaggerations, the district never "died"—downtown remained the center of most Knoxville political, banking, and legal business, and supported Knoxville's highest density of interesting bars—but visitors

arriving on a Saturday might assume the population had evacuated.

The city's Volunteer Landing didn't blossom as advertised; the restaurants down there did respectable business at lunch and dinner, but new buildings built for prospective retail remained vacant.

One rumor after another of a major corporate headquarters moving downtown—in Knoxville, it was the dream of the 1990s—proved vaporous, as even the district's traditional tenants, like major law firms, kept leaving for suburban office parks, always protesting their clients wanted easier parking.

Downtown's largest single-family residence occupies most of the space in an 1885 building originally erected to house Knoxville's first public library. Later known as the Rebori Building, it became a home for middle-aged professionals Jim and Jo Mason, who lived there for more than 10 years before selling it to another resident.

Photos this page by Gary Heatherly

Photo by Scott Busby

David Dewhirst (third from left) and his team at work in the Holston Building, a 1912 14-story office building that eventually housed, reputedly, Knoxville's highest-dollar condos.
Photo by Sheena Patrick

it as part of Dewhirst's plan for the Emporium. Moving them would save the city money, and also free up the Candy Factory for private development.

Dewhirst now admits he was learning, on-the-job-training style, how to renovate a big building. "We just bulldogged it," he says. A friend, a 20-something landscaper, got a construction license and headed up the project.

"We were committed and passionate," Dewhirst says. "We didn't know what we were doing. Maybe didn't know we should have failed."

With the Emporium, Dewhirst became the face of downtown's private

development, a rare combination of attributes, and maybe just the person a decrepit downtown needed most. Personally energetic and charismatic, committed to the neighborhood enough to live there, Dewhirst was a historic preservationist fascinated with interesting architecture—but still, by profession, an engineer. He couldn't be spoken down to, told that things were impossible. That had been Knoxville's habitual response to most visionary projects for many years. The subtext of downtown's turnaround was that Dewhirst's educated intuitive approach to problems became the new normal.

The city consolidated the Candy Factory's arts organizations—plus a few

Photo by Stephanie Norwood

others, like the Knoxville Symphony Orchestra's offices—into Dewhirst's renovated Emporium. There was some grumbling, at first, but the fairly sudden popularity of the downtown location, especially on First Friday gallery nights, when the Emporium sometimes drew thousands of viewers, won most artists over.

Dewhirst thinks of the city's lease as a turning point. This block hosted a homeless shelter, a failing pawn shop, and several vacant buildings. "It was a sign of commitment from the city," he says, that encouraged others to buy into the once-shunned 100 Block.

Meanwhile, Dewhirst developed the Emporium's upper floors into upscale

apartments. They were almost immediately popular, too.

In partnership with Knoxville developer Cardinal, Chattanooga Mayor Kinsey bought the Candy Factory and rehabbed it for condos, finally realizing a post World's Fair plan deferred for more than 20 years.

The Sunsphere, the icon of the World's Fair and the

most distinctive shape on Knoxville's skyline, had been closed to the public for years. In 2007, the city rehabbed it and leased several floors to Kinsey and Cardinal for development. Though success with restaurants and bars in the unique tower has been mixed, it's open to the public, and offers a strategic view of downtown.

World's Fair Park, reimagined in the 21st century, is home to a ca. 1917 industrial building once produced candy for a national market. After imaginative reuse for restaurants and gift shops during the 1982 World's Fair, plans to convert the Candy Factory to residences seemed doomed for years, as it sat empty, later to be used for city-supported studios and community space. The city eventually divested itself of the building, moving its arts functions downtown to the Emporium. It was more than 20 years after the Fair that it finally became a successful condo project, thanks to a development team that included former Chattanooga Mayor Jon Kinsey.

Photos by Gary Pope ▼ ►

Photo by Gary Heatherly

Photo by Gary Heatherly

Photo by Gary Pope

Photo by Denise Retallack

Several Knoxville leaders refer to Chattanooga as a "laboratory" for interesting ideas. Some of Chattanooga's heralded successes were more relevant to Knoxville's story than others. Knoxville lacked anything comparable to Chattanooga's vigorous pro-urbanist Lyndhurst Foundation. The upstream city's charities were more modest in size, and generally directed toward more specific needs, from cancer research to rural development to various aspects of the university. But in the late '90s, Knoxville accrued a new and unusual philanthropic venture called the Cornerstone Foundation.

Avoiding spotlights, Cornerstone began as a frankly faith-based organization, but it's hardly evangelical in character. It concentrated on community development by a definition so broad it embraced music venues and nuclear-science laboratories, quietly funding projects deemed to be community assets through its ongoing community-research reports. Downtown became a recurring theme.

Its director was one of Knoxville's many unlikely champions. Originally from Nashville, Laurens Tullock had been an attorney in the U.S. Air Force's celebrated JAG unit, later in the U.S. Attorney's office. He came to Knoxville when he was assisting the prosecution in the long and complicated bank-fraud case against the Butcher brothers in 1984.

Open in 2010, the innovative, modernist Knoxville Transit Center offers a café, lounge, and other amenities to city bus riders well into the night, with separate bays for each bus route. Partially built on a bridge across a multi-lane highway, James White Parkway, the project effectively reclaimed a little bit of downtown space previously surrendered to through traffic—and perhaps helped reconnect traditional downtown with attractions on the other side, like the Civic Coliseum.

Photo by Jacques Gautreau

He got an apartment in one of the only two build-

> *"The historic core was retained, but rather than a slum, it had become a vacant movie set."*
> — Laurens Tullock

ings that would have been agreeable to professionals, Kendrick Place. "That's when I got to love downtown Knoxville," he says. But he noticed its problems. "The historic core was retained," he recalls, "but rather than a slum, it had become a vacant movie set. Knoxville had moved to the suburbs, and just left vacant buildings behind. I thought, this has the most amazing potential I've ever seen in my life. Somebody's just got to populate this. It was a walkable, compact downtown—and it's got character to it because it sits on a hill the way it does."

Mayor Ashe appointed Tullock Director of Community Development, a post he held for several years. But after some differences with the administration about how to address the problems and potentials of downtown in ways he thought were fruitful, he quit.

As director of Cornerstone, Tullock kept aiming at the same goals he'd never quite achieved in city government. One of Cornerstone's first major efforts borrowed a page from the Chattanooga revival story. Cornerstone invited urban-visioning expert Gianni Longo, whose work in Chattanooga was often credited for directing philanthropic funds toward that city's downtown and riverfront. Longo came to Knoxville to see what he could do.

The Knoxville model was different, much broader than Chattanooga's concentrated urban effort. When polled, Knoxvillians chose to spread the idea around a nine-county uber-metro-area, and drew suggestions and concerns from across that mostly rural region. Known as "Nine Counties. One Vision.," its broad focus disappointed some, who assumed such a huge effort would spread itself too thinly to yield anything noticeable. It did yield one surprising result. Miles beyond city and county limits, East Tennesseans expressed an interest in reviving downtown Knoxville.

The Nine Counties group eventually recruited prominent Portland, Oregon, firm Crandall-Arambula. In 2003, after months of research, the firm presented a complex view of Knoxville's ideal future.

The plan never had the clout of adoption by city government, and almost none of Crandall-Arambula's specific recommendations had come to fruition a decade after the plan was laid out in colorful charts. But it's remarkable

> *"The more govern-ment gets involved the more the odd isn't favored."*
> *—David Dewhirst*

how often the plan is mentioned by influential people, as an inspiration, a different way of looking at the Knoxville problem.

David Dewhirst generally opposes mandated urban designs. Dewhirst nurtured

his ideals of what a functional city should be while traveling in idiosyncratic towns in Italy, and in Knoxville he has wrestled with some torturous engineering codes that he, as an engineer himself, thinks are unnecessary and sometimes ridiculous. "The more government gets involved," Dewhirst says, "the more the odd isn't favored."

However, he calls Crandall-Arambula a "mind-stretching exercise," perhaps comparable to his own trips to Verona. "It mostly got you out of Knoxville, Tennessee, to say, 'This is what you're capable of becoming. How lucky you are to have this, over a lot of communities.' When you're just sitting here, you don't get it."

The plan's emphasis on connectivity, in particular, is credited for the city's re-siting of its long-agonized-over transit center: not in the center of town, but in the space over a highway, along a viaduct on the dysfunctional east side. That amenity, which serves mainly as a headquarters and central station for the city bus service, was Knoxville's first attempt to build in air space over a highway—completed in 2011, the imaginative modern facility spans about a dozen lanes of James White Parkway and adds some liveliness to what was once a lonesome and some times spooky viaduct connecting the business district to the Civic Coliseum complex.

And the buses using the station are reportedly more full than ever before. Thanks to Knoxville Area Transit improvements, more people may be using public transportation in Knoxville than since the days of streetcars.

— • —

Major top-down projects had effects, if not always exactly the ones intended.

An expansively ambitious Justice Center proposal, led by the county sheriff, resulted in the acquisition and demolition of a large historic industrial building being rehabbed for residences—and then came to nothing. But the proposal was so unpopular it may have helped the downtown effort by organizing the opposition, which formed a chat group called K2K. Maybe unique among open-chat groups, it became, for the most part, a well-intentioned and well-informed daily public discussion of a great variety of downtown issues. Many of its participants, among them architects, lawyers, developers, professors, and politicians, began meeting in person at Gay Street's brewpub. Even the mayor was a regular.

Though conservative in most regards, Ashe was curious about urban solutions, and his administration was a never-ending pageant of consultants. One proposed, as feasible, an idea that seemed to have died decades earlier: the downtown cinema.

To most, it perhaps seemed absurd, that downtown cinema might return. But what had died, back in the '70s, was not the downtown cinema, but the single-screen cinema, which had previously been downtown's only model of a cinema. The old economic model for cinemas, showing a new film to a big house for just a few days, was no longer profitable. Due to Hollywood's business plans, it made more sense to show films to small houses for several weeks. Hence the Cineplex, which first blossomed in the suburbs, because that's where there was land to build them.

But new urban cineplexes had recently proven

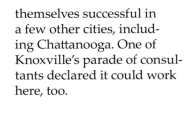

themselves successful in a few other cities, including Chattanooga. One of Knoxville's parade of consultants declared it could work here, too.

— • —

The American convention center was a late 20th-century urban cliché that nonetheless offers some usefulness, and it became a priority for the Ashe administration. Harrison "Buzz" Price, the noted Disney World consultant, had advised against investment in a convention center just after the World's Fair, but he returned in the '90s and reported that it now seemed like the time to strike.

Ashe surprised many associates by shifting decisively from a long-discussed downtown minor-league baseball park to a state-of-the-art convention center for downtown's old dilemma, the World's Fair Park.

Mike Edwards, chief of Knoxville's Chamber Partnership, is one of the few born-and-raised Knoxvillians

"My charge was to put together a convention center that would fix downtown," recalls Mike Edwards. "That was sort of naïve."

in the city's leadership. He's worn a lot of hats in urban and suburban development, but in the '90s, he was in charge of public buildings. "My charge was to put together a convention center that would fix downtown," he says. "That was sort of naïve."

Its planning drew in the learned jury known as the

KNOXVILLE CONVENTION CENTER

Photo by Stephanie Norwood

Urban Land Institute—which startled some by noting a convention center alone couldn't attract conventions, insisting on the importance of improving downtown, and specifically developing Market Square as a convention-related attraction. Market Square was potentially interesting enough, they claimed, that it could be a reason convention planners might choose Knoxville.

To make the convention center work, as Edwards recalls the logic of the day, Knoxville needed a better downtown, with more shopping, "all the stuff that wasn't there." The convention center was intended to make downtown better—but to succeed, the convention center needed a better downtown. "The fix to the fix was silly," Edwards says.

The convention-center project, which included a redo of much of the World's Fair site— including the

relocation of an electrical substation, a project deemed too expensive when planning for the World's Fair—expanded into a nine-figure proposition. Despite a price tag as big as those of some of the world's international modern landmarks, the committee-designed building itself was unlikely to interest architectural critics. Traffic at the convention center itself was disappointing—it hosted only a few of the high-tech, nationally consequential conventions promised, but became a more regular venue for high-school reunions, religious conventions, and weddings.

The redesigned park itself was more obviously successful. The redesign of the central part of the old World's Fair site as an appealing park with multiple uses, from interactive fountains popular with kids on hot days, to a solemn war memorial, to a flexibly empty South Lawn (immediately useful for the popular annual beer festival,

the Knoxville Brewers' Jam). For the first time in the 20 years since the Fair, the problematic gulley between downtown and the university looked like a destination.

But the Knoxville Convention Center's biggest positive effect on downtown may have been the way it was financed. The state Convention Center Financing Act of 1998 assured the sales-tax revenue from the central business district would be dedicated to paying off the convention center. Tullock sees that act as the convention center's greatest legacy. The city of Knoxville had never had such a strong financial incentive to focus on the success of its own downtown.

It also brought old Market Square closer to the front burner. Previously, Market Square had been an Ashe-administration priority, albeit a rather vague one. Various proposals called for reimagining the square.

Completed in early 1982, barely in time for Knoxville's six-month World's Fair, the 266-foot Sunsphere, symbolizing the origin of all energy on Earth, has become the most distinctive feature of Knoxville's skyline. However, most of the Fair's other construction has since been removed. The look of World's Fair Park, like the artificial creek near Cumberland Avenue, and the 2003 Knoxville Convention Center, is mainly a 21st-century design, funded by a nine-figure project that gives downtown a unique amenity, but also left the city with long-term debt.

One of only two remaining structures built expressly for the 1982 World's Fair, the Tennessee Amphitheatre is an unusual auditorium, sheltered from the rain but open to breezes. Designed with tensile fabric with the help of noted international engineer Horst Berger, it was used for 16 years after the Fair for events ranging from rock concerts to Shakespearean plays. Closed in 1998 due to rust-related structural problems, it was almost demolished, but encouraged by local architects, who praise it as one of Knoxville's most innovative modernist structures, Mayor Haslam found funds for a major rehab. It was ready in time to host Haslam's second inauguration in 2007.

Photos by Gary Pope

Residents of Market Square enjoy a unique urban vista. This 1860s building houses busy shops on the first floor. For decades, lunch spots and small shops occupied the first floors, while many of Market Square's second floors were vacant or used for storage. Now many are residences, just as they were in the 19th century.

Photo by Gary Heatherly

In the mid-'90s, the square enjoyed a tantalizing flirtation with high-tech fame when one of its old brick wholesale-grocery buildings unexpectedly hosted Cyberflix, a sophisticated and briefly famous alternate-reality CD-ROM computer-game company with sales in the millions. It was a moment of unexpected tech glamour in an unlikely place, as Cyberflix's generous parties in their dramatically lit multi-level offices gave envious Knoxvillians ideas. The example suggested a high-tech future for the square, and the city talked of it as a "Digital Crossing" center for new-technology start-ups. Knoxville's first cyber café opened in an old Market Square storefront, and soon an offbeat video-production company opened in a walk-up nearby. But Cyberflix dissolved, and soon so did dreams of Digital Crossing.

Other ideas proposed enhancing the square's "programmability," to host an ever-revolving series of little festivals. When advocates proposed removing the square's trees, they found little support. Some called for opening the square to automobile traffic, citing studies and consultants claiming that pedestrians-only squares never worked for long.

In the late '90s, one private firm laid out an extraordinarily ambitious project to reinvent about one quarter of downtown. The plan, called Renaissance Knoxville, was hailed by the mayor as the biggest thing since TVA.

RK offered several promising and imaginative ideas, including a "winter garden" on World's Fair Park, to highlight the region's botanical diversity; retail built into a bridge over problematic Henley Street, Ponte-Vecchio style; and a Cineplex. However, downtown was showing some early signs of life that seemed incompatible with certain heavy-handed

Most notoriously, the first version of the plan called for a weatherproof dome to be built over the pedestrian area.

aspects of the plan, especially when it came to ancient Market Square. The plan demanded a single owner-operator instituting strict "covenants" for vetting businesses permitted on the Square, as well as required hours of operation, which they claimed were essential for the viability of a pedestrian square. Most notoriously, the first version of the plan called for a weatherproof dome to be built over the pedestrian area.

Its influence may have been galvanizing the opposition. Hundreds appeared at public meetings concerning the project. Opponents, most of them under 40, liked the "organic" attractions that had begun springing from the city's old hulk—like Tomato Head, the brewpub, and a unique business around the corner called Yee Haw, an unconventionally artistic print shop that used antique machinery. Yee Haw, unapprovable under the covenants of RK—it kept peculiar and unpredictable hours, and it was, in part, a "T-shirt shop," a term frequently mentioned as the bane of a successful downtown—developed a national reputation, touted in the *New York Times* as one of the best reasons to visit Knoxville.

Also, residences were sneaking in, one by one, in interesting upstairs spaces. David Dewhirst's globetrotting mother, Emily, ran an import/gift shop beneath her upscale condo.

Even more vigorously than they opposed the jail project, K2K criticized the big top-down Renaissance Knoxville project, in meticulous detail, and proposed alternatives. Many of the people who would be influential in positive developments downtown in years to come first encountered one another through their opposition to Renaissance Knoxville.

Eventually bereft of mayoral support—it turned out it would cost the public more than expected—Renaissance Knoxville quietly withdrew. But the plan marked the beginning of serious developer interest in a downtown Cineplex—and it attracted more interest to Market Square, its problems and potential. The city's efforts in renovating downtown had previously been modest fix-ups around the edges of downtown. But with the big-hitter private developers out of the picture, the city moved into Market Square and, with an $8 million investment— modest compared to many modern cities' urban projects— accomplished a major months-long subterranean rebuild of the old square's infrastructure. The city also built a large, multi-level parking garage, adjacent to the square. Paying heed to urban-design professionals, the city made room in the design for something else in the parking-garage footprint, some new residential development with retail space.

Photos by Gary Heatherly ▼ ▶

At the same time, wielding both the carrot of modest façade work and the stick of imminent condemnation, the city persuaded Market Square's many owners to get to work or get out. Originally from Memphis, Bill Lyons was a political-science professor at UT who was known for his classes in urban politics

when he became chairman of Knoxville's Community Development Corporation. The city's quasi-independent housing authority and development agency had previously been charged mainly with slum clearance and subsidized housing. The city found it expeditious to expand KCDC's role in the

Beginning in the late 1990s, Knoxvillians surprised themselves with their own eagerness to come to Market Square in the evenings to relax and here a show. Some rock shows have attracted more than 10,000. On the stage on a lower-key evening, late saxophonist Rocky Wynder performer alongside fellow local musician Chico Crawford.

Photo by Jacques Gautreau

case of Market Square, especially through the authority of Lyons, who served as a sort of diplomat between the city, the square's property owners, and the ever-more-interested public at large. Lyons commenced a series of vigorous public and private meetings concerning the square.

He recalls downtown's advocates in the '90s were divided between the impatient who demanded, "Do something!" as if anything would be better than the status quo, and those who demanded, "No, don't do it wrong!"

That anxious urgency existed alongside a cultural reality. "There's a pretty strong independent culture here that resists telling people what to do with their property," Lyons observes.

It was a complex problem, but Lyons' basic tactic was pretty simple. "Let's have lots and lots and lots of engagement with property owners," he says, both asking for ideas and, eventually, nudging property owners into a spirit of cooperation.

The prevailing feeling was to keep the pedestrian plaza and, after some modest city-sponsored improvements—major subterranean infrastructure improvements, minimal façade redos, moving the stage closer to the end of the square. Complaints that the stage's roof blocked residents'

views—hardly anticipated when the previous stage was installed in the '80s—showed, in itself, how much the square had evolved in a few years.

And though some of the square's owners supported some ultimately rejected proposals, like the idea of an organized redevelopment through a single authority, or restoring automobile traffic to the square, they all got heard. Unexpected passion for the square's existing trees distracted the conversation, but ultimately resulted in preserving most of them.

A 675-space city-sponsored parking garage, built over what had been a surface lot just behind one side of the square, eased the parking concern and also ushered in a new policy for all city public parking garages: they'd charge competitive rates in the daytime, but parking at all city garages would be free at night and on weekends. Some claim that one generous gesture, in parking-anxious Knoxville, was heavily responsible for downtown's revival. But it coincided with the emergence of a great many other reasons to visit the neighborhood.

Though the parking garage itself was not built on the much-touted mixed-use model, as the previous Locust Street garage had been, it was maybe the next best thing, coordinating with an adjacent mixed-used retail/residential building, another Kinsey Probasco project, with street front retail space and 24 residential units above. Completed in 2007, that relatively modest project known as the Residences at Market Square constitutes the only new-construction residential project downtown since some subsidized housing in the 1970s—a fact that demonstrates how heavily downtown's residential resurgence, which has garnered more than 1,000 new residential units,

has leaned on historic preservation alone.

In the end, the city was able to rely entirely on carrots, not sticks. Eminent domain was hardly even a threat except in the case of one building with an impossibly complicated ownership history.

Stroud Watson himself came to conduct Chattanooga-style charrettes about the fate of adjacent Krutch Park, which was redesigned without an exterior wall. It was a controversial choice, and an expensive one. Many still miss the original park's quaint old walls, but there seems no question that the now-open park is used much more by the public at large than it ever was before.

"Everything was sorted and sifted and talked about," says Lyons. "People started seeing that good ideas would be listened to. Even people who failed felt they got listened to."

At the same time the city was reconsidering Market Square, with all its conflicting ideas and passions, another downtown icon was getting a makeover, a little more quietly.

The Gay Street Bridge, a half-mile-long steel span over the Tennessee River built in 1898, is exactly the same bridge over which Wild West train robber Kid Curry

escaped from jail on a sheriff's stolen horse in 1903. By 2000, it was determined to be potentially unsafe. Many assumed it would be dismantled and replaced.

A 2001-04 federal project enabled by Congressman Jimmy Duncan repaired the original bridge, making it safe for heavy automobile traffic, but also adding, for the first time, comfortably shielded pedestrian walkways.

Upon completion the bridge opened almost as a new amenity, inviting lunchtime walks, which afford an interesting view of the city and its river—but upon reaching the south side, pedestrians could hardly avoid noticing that district's scarcity of basic amenities like sidewalks—and, for that matter, of attractive destinations. Hilly and overgrown where it's not heavily industrial, South Knoxville, hardly a ten-minute walk from downtown, seemed a lost opportunity.

The neglected south side would soon get the attention of a new mayor.

Opposite: The Gay Street Bridge, seen from the south side of the river. Built in 1898 before the era of automobiles, it has lasted into a new century. Though authorities considered demolishing it, federal funding was secured to restore it with structural improvements in 2004.

A positive legacy of the defunct Universe Knoxville proposal was that it left the whiff of a Cineplex in the air, specifically as a potential savior for Market Square. At least one major national cinema chain with experience in downtown theaters expressed interest in building a theater, via Kinsey-Probasco— but it wasn't Knoxville's Regal Cinemas, which publicly denounced the whole idea of a downtown cinema as unfeasible and potentially disastrous.

Following the lead of Chattanooga, which had successfully combined a parking garage and public transit connection with a downtown theater complex, Ashe contemplated combining the theater project with a federally funded transit center project. It made sense at first, but after one problem after another, it became clear that it wouldn't be easy.

Developers watched the cinema proposal closely, especially on Market Square, which saw it as a perhaps necessary catalyst, and as months turned into years, they began to wonder whether it would ever happen.

Coinciding with downtown's physical improvements was a sort of municipal cultural renaissance that likely played a role in stoking interest in the city. Asked to describe "Knoxville culture" in the 1980s, a local might suggest something about Volmania, and perhaps the Appalachians, leave it at that, and be grateful for a change of subject.

But people's take on what Knoxville was began to change, significantly, late in the century, and it's hard to point to any one source for it, or to suggest that it was anything more than serendipity at work.

A national interest in America's musical roots sometimes led to a rediscovery of Knoxville's mid-century live-radio heritage, which included country icons Roy Acuff and Chet Atkins, and a few blues icons like

Singer/songwriter R.B. Morris, a recording artist whose songs have been recorded by Marianne Faithfull and others, has played an unusual role in reintroducing Knoxville to itself--through his songs and performances, which are often very specifically about local institutions, and through his work to build a small park in honor of Knoxville native James Agee.

Brownie McGhee and Ida Cox. And that was before an unpredictable British postpunk revival of the weird old murder ballad "Knoxville Girl." It was all bubbling back up just as several new rock bands and songwriters were earning unaccustomed national attention, at least in alternative circles.

Seemingly coincidental was an unprecedented new interest in local literature. In 1979, author Cormac McCarthy had published the most Knoxville-specific novel in history, the dense and darkly humorous narrative *Suttree*. Though it's hardly a complimentary book, its almost too-vivid evocation of Knoxville's underbelly in the early 1950s was compelling, and drew comparisons to James Joyce's ambivalent but fascinating depictions of his native Dublin. Though not an immediate

> *R.B. Morris... performed an unauthorized one-man play about Agee... near Agee's childhood home... an unusual collaboration between the city of Knoxville and the University of Tennessee.*

hit, Suttree grew in popularity in the 1980s and '90s, as McCarthy's later novels became bestsellers and inspirations for movies. By the century's last decade, both tourists and Knoxvillians came downtown, albeit in small numbers, trying to find the settings of scenes in Suttree.

Partly in response to national and even international currents, Knoxville was also rediscovering an already well-known author, James Agee, author of "Knoxville: Summer 1915." He'd died back in 1955, but his autobiographical novel *A Death in the Family*, set in Knoxville, was the subject of prime-time, big-star television adaptations in 1981 and

2002. A critically acclaimed 1985 biography of Agee made the long-dead Knoxville native sound dangerous, sexy, and relevant. In 1995, the BBC came to Knoxville to tape an audio documentary about Agee; broadcast globally, it won international awards.

By the late '90s, Mayor Ashe was reportedly telling his staff they needed to read Agee. Quotations from Agee, McCarthy and other Knoxville writers like Nikki Giovanni appeared inscribed in stone along the city's 1998 Volunteer Landing project. Later Agee, McCarthy and others would be quoted in the pavement of Market Square.

Singer-songwriter R.B. Morris, long a proponent of Agee's work—he'd written and performed an unauthorized one-man play about Agee—formulated a plan for a small park in a vacant lot in Fort Sanders, near Agee's childhood home. Agee Park, an unusual collaboration between the city of Knoxville and the University of Tennessee, opened in 2003.

Morris, whose songs have been recorded by Marianne Faithfull and others, was among the first popular rock or folk musicians to begin writing and singing songs specifically about Knoxville, perhaps dooming their chances for national radio play. By the end of the century, the Knoxville song was almost a subgenre, one favored by the more daring performers. Songwriter Scott Miller's song about a peculiar Knoxville nightclub, "Ciderville Saturday Night," was a minor radio hit in Australia.

It was more evidence of a new interest in the city as a setting. In 2012, a new Gay Street bar called Suttree's was immediately popular, as the

city announced long-range plans for a Suttree Park on the south side.

Several other unexpected developments, most of them originating well outside the city, added pieces to the puzzle of Knoxville. National home-improvement shows highlighted previously obscure Victorian-era architect George Barber, whose mail-order designs guided construction of houses all over the country; he was based in Knoxville, and left dozens of houses here. And European scholars expressed interest in Knoxville-raised director Clarence Brown, whose films became available, via DVD and the Internet.

Two very different prime-time PBS documentaries in 1985 and 2002 heralded extraordinary jazz/country/bluesman Howard Armstrong, whose eclectic but ultimately obscure career seemed to symbolize the city where he'd first recorded and broadcast. A 1998 biography exalted locally forgotten Knoxville native Beauford Delaney, the Harlem-Renaissance era artist whose modern paintings were selling in the six figures in big cities on both sides of the Atlantic. A 2004 biography of Frances Hodgson Burnett, whose novel *The Secret Garden* had recently been made into a major motion picture, shone new light on the English author's surprising Knoxville youth. The term Secret Garden began to appear in various contexts, and perhaps seemed a metaphor for a city's own hidden appeal.

Taken altogether, it seemed to suggest that maybe Knoxville had something like a culture, and was worth a second look.

— • —

Something was in the wind. Before 2000, Knoxville repeatedly attempted to launch festivals centered around barbecue, chili, music, St. Patrick's Day, literature, or the holidays. Some were more successful than others. Knoxville had proven it could sustain an annual Greek festival, held in a suburban church parking lot to celebrate the city's significant Hellenic population. But attendance at downtown festival events was often disappointing, some such flops they left organizers with the impression that Knoxvillians were inherently unfestive. The city's hallmark springtime Dogwood Arts Festival had evolved into a sober and underwhelming daytime affair that seemed aimed mainly at rural audiences; some likened it to an annual garage sale. Some denounced it as embarrassing, more a liability than an asset.

The culture began to change in the late '90s, perhaps with some free-music events on Market Square. The fact that hundreds, even thousands, of young people might come downtown on a Thursday night startled some. A regional beer festival, later known as the Knoxville Brewers' Jam, held on World's Fair Park, started respectably strong in 1997 and grew each year to prove a dependable draw.

But the biggest shock came in the spring of 2002, when the Knoxville Opera sponsored—out of the blue—a festival in honor of Italian composer Giaochino Rossini, with multiple opera performances and an "Italian Street Fair." The city's Italian population is slight, and the total number of Knoxvillians who attend an actual opera in any given year may be as low as 3,000. But locals seemed to respond to the very outrageousness of a celebrating a composer who never visited America and died in 1868. With Italian food, wine, street arias, and swordfights, concentrated mainly in a few hours on a Saturday afternoon, the first Rossini Festival drew tens of thousands, jamming Gay Street for several blocks. It came to seem the best street festival in memory.

In years to come, other festivals, like the Latino festival Hola, and the International Biscuit Festival, would approximate Rossini's success with a large and concentrated number of diverse offerings, with both family diversions and alcoholic beverages. Even Dogwood caught the same wind, becoming at once

The Rossini Festival, sponsored by Knoxville Opera, was a surprise hit from its inception, featuring a surprising variety of attractions, including, occasionally, medieval combat on Gay Street.

Photo by Gary Heatherly

more sophisticated and more popular.

Knoxville's annual festival days still account for only a few weekends a year, but they serve a major purpose in

▼ *Some Market Square events are extraordinarily popular--even prompting criticism that they're so popular that local businesses' regular customers have voiced their ire at the inconvenience.*

Photos by Gary Heatherly

introducing the city to itself, and bringing many suburbanites into intimate contact with downtown, which seemed more interesting and less intimidating than they'd assumed.

— • —

Knoxville had never been known as a city of statues, which might be seen as another barometer of a city's cultural health. In 1990, downtown Knoxville had hardly four or five statues, most of them around a century old.

It may suggest something about Knoxville's reawakening sense of itself that beginning in the 1990s, statues began springing up around downtown, mostly as a result of independent and coincidental efforts. An oversize bronze "rowboat man" materialized as part of a private bank/office complex at the corner of Gay and Church. The city's Volunteer Landing project installed an interesting marble statue depicting the 1791 Treaty of the Holston, representing obviously ambivalent Cherokees.

Then, after the death of sometime Knoxville resident Alex Haley, friends funded a very large statue of the

popular author on the edge of Morningside Park, just east of downtown. The work of noted sculptor Tina Allen, upon its completion in 1998, the 13-foot seated bronze with a lap that invites climbing, it was the nation's largest sculpture of an African-American—before the Martin Luther King statue on the Washington Mall.

A Rotary Club installed a statue commemorating its members' efforts to eradicate polio, and installed it in Krutch Park. Nearby, some feminist professionals commissioned a partly state-funded statue of three of Tennessee's most influential suffragettes for Market Square.

Perhaps the oddest and least anticipated statue was the work of Russian sculptor Viktor Bokarev, who never visited Knoxville, but wished to place his large statue of Sergei Rachmaninoff in the city where he performed his final concert, in 1943, and that happened to be Knoxville. But both the city and the university, where the pianist-composer's concert had taken place, declined the gift. The only statue of Rachmaninoff in America stood unbronzed and unwanted in Jim and Jo Mason's condo on Gay

▼ *World's Fair Park is home to America's only statue of Russian pianist-composer Sergei Rachmaninoff, who performed his last show in Knoxville in 1943.*

A vigorously reborn Dogwood Arts Festival commenced an Art in Public Places project, which places striking modern statuary around downtown pedestrian areas. Every spring, at the time of the festival, they're swapped for new ones.

▲▼ Photo by Gary Heatherly

Street for years, until a group of local philanthropists took it over, bronzed it, and had it installed in World's Fair Park in 2003.

As if inspired by the city's unexpected accumulation of interesting statues, the Dogwood Arts Festival commenced its Art in Public Places program to install a yearly changing array of modern sculptures around downtown, chosen by a jury-based competition.

A major makeover of 1930s landmark Neyland Stadium even included a large statue of the Vols' most successful football coach, the mid-20th –century genius of strategy General Robert Neyland.

One of Knoxville's best-known statues symbolizes female basketball players across the generations. It's at the Women's Basketball Hall of Fame, a national institution suggested by the success of Pat Head Summitt's Lady Vols. America's most successful basketball coach in history led UT's most famously successful sports team to eight national championships. The Hall was a public-private project completed on the east side of downtown in 1999,

and features what's claimed to be the largest "basketball" in the world, a 30-foot, 10-ton architectural feature that almost mirrors the Sunsphere's golden globe on the other side of downtown. Though it does draw visitors from across the country and serves as a venue for weddings and other grand events, it's perhaps not the major tourist attraction its backers once hoped it would be, but it has become a conspicuous landmark anchoring downtown's eastern edge.

Reflecting the new interest in local and regional culture was a major addition to the old marble Custom House. Designed in like character by old-line architectural firm Barber McMurry, the extension greeted Gay Street, forming a much-bigger building collectively called the East Tennessee History Center. A collaboration between Knox County and the regional East Tennessee Historical Society, the building completed in 2005 doubled the unusual reference library known as the McClung Historical Collection, and enabled an expanded, professionally organized and curated permanent museum on the ground floor. Its permanent "Voices of the Land" narrative exhibit opened in 2008, with,

among hundreds of other icons, Davy Crockett's rifle, and is a regular destination for school field trips. With a gift shop and auditorium space, it draws regular traffic daily— and on some evenings, when

▼ *The nationally recognized Women's Basketball Hall of Fame, opened in 1999, was inspired mostly by the success of Coach Pat Head Summitt's Lady Vols, winner of eight national women's basketball championships.*

Photo by Stephanie Norwood

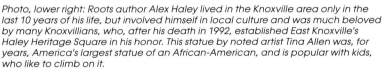

Photo, lower right: Roots author Alex Haley lived in the Knoxville area only in the last 10 years of his life, but involved himself in local culture and was much beloved by many Knoxvillians, who, after his death in 1992, established East Knoxville's Haley Heritage Square in his honor. This statue by noted artist Tina Allen was, for years, America's largest statue of an African-American, and is popular with kids, who like to climb on it.

◄ Photo by Gary Heatherly

◄ Photo by Gary Heatherly

Photo by Gary Pope ▶

◄ Photo by Sheena Patrick

▶ Photo by Gary Heatherly

Photo by Jacques Gautreau

it hosts receptions, book signings, lectures, and semi-regularly, rare films of historic interest, which sometimes draw standing-room-only crowds.

The historical-center development might seem purely coincidental with all the other fresh hubbub on Gay Street; the historical society, whose members live and work throughout the region, had little direct engagement with the other developments downtown, but the neighborhood's ever-more-obvious revival certainly made the multi-million-dollar investment, stretching toward re-energized Gay Street, seem like a better investment than it might have 15 years earlier.

— • —

The copacetic new view of downtown didn't work in every realm. At the turn of the 21st century, the Knox County Public Library seemed confident about building a new main library, downtown. It had been more than 30 years since the main library had been designed. Even at the time of its completion in 1971, planners assumed that the library would soon be expanded, both onto an adjacent lot obtained for the purpose, and by adding another floor. But the expansions never came, even as the county's population swelled by more than 100,000. Numbers seemed to prove that Knox County library patrons were underserved, at least in the size of their main library.

The library had opinion polls showing more than 80 percent of the county population approved, and there were interested architects and developers, some of them inspired by the amazing new neo-beaux-arts Nashville library, a palace of learning that was becoming a key to that city's growing downtown. Most importantly, there was at least theoretical funding in

place for a new Knox County library, largely by way of a $30 per year increase in the county wheel tax. But that final item didn't sit well with some citizens in rural and suburban quarters, who saw the "downtown library" as a bit of subsidized favoritism toward urban elites. A counterproposal called for placing the main library in suburban West Knoxville, with lots of free parking. Organizing a revolt, the antis defeated the tax in 2004, in a polarizing red-blue county, and the already disheartened pro-library faction withdrew. At least two later attempts to locate and build a new main library have ultimately come to nothing, and today, a county of over 400,000 still works with an aging 1971 library built for a county of 275,000.

The county library debacle, roughly coinciding with growing public disgruntlement over the city's unprecedented investment in a convention center with decades of debt and disappointing returns, alongside a new era of state and federal stinginess, seemed to guarantee that government would not play a very generous role in downtown's revival.

And not all historical-renovation efforts were successful. At the height of the condo boom, attempts to talk a downtown bank into either selling or fixing up a 1904 beaux-arts apartment building called the Sprankle failed. The bank demanded the right to tear down the building it had purchased, describing its needs for expansion and advertising plans for a new bank building on the site. After being stalled by an extraordinary mayoral historic-zoning gesture, the bank finally demolished the building in 2005. At this writing, the site of the Sprankle remains only a private parking lot.

In the '90s, one would-be developer bought the enormous late-Victorian McClung Warehouses on West Jackson, an almost-deserted corner of downtown then untouched by downtown's renaissance. He announced that, rather than renovating them for the upscale condo market, they'd be mixed-income apartments, enabled by federal low-income tax credits, and began work on the project. But after about nine years of delays, things seemed stalled. When the city and Knox Heritage tried to force his hand, to finish the project or sell, the owner became a property-rights cause célèbre. He had the right to proceed at his own pace, some politicians claimed on talk-radio shows. He even had the right not to proceed at all.

> *In early 2007, a fire broke out in the buildings, the largest fire seen downtown in several decades.*

In early 2007, a fire broke out in the buildings, the largest fire seen downtown in several decades. It destroyed the largest and oldest of the buildings, along with a fire truck, buried in a wall collapse. After a bankruptcy and six more years of lawsuits, two remaining buildings appear to be on their way to revival.

— • —

New term limits, advocated by K2K and other downtown advocates, transformed Knoxville's old-school City Council almost overnight, bringing in generally younger and more progressive members. Term limits also ended Victor Ashe's unprecedented 16-year reign as Knoxville's mayor in 2003. Though his first few years are remembered with frustration by advocates of downtown

◄ *The ruinous McClung Warehouse fire of 2007 destroyed several large late-Victorian industrial buildings that had been promised to be a major residential project. Though it presented a major setback, the block of West Jackson were it happened is showing new life.*

development and preservation, he had become a true believer in both in his later years, and downtown's revival got a solid start during his watch.

Ashe's legacy as a proponent of greenways is less complicated. No mayor had ever proposed that the whole city might someday be linked by pedestrian greenways, and Ashe, especially through his restless and persuasive greenways coordinator Donna Young, a former landscape-architecture professor who'd previously worked on the Atlanta Olympics, made major headway, adding dozens of miles to create a genuine municipal greenway system. Neither the rotund Ashe or the severely asthmatic Young, both in late middle age, ever seemed outdoorsy, but recognizing long-term value for the city, worked to overcome Knoxville's century-old park deficiency, and perhaps push it beyond what anyone expected.

The race to replace Ashe pitted former union organizer and community advocate Madeline Rogero, favored by most of the young downtown activists—she announced her candidacy in a Market Square café—against Bill Haslam, the little-known youngest child of prominent billionaire

travel-center magnate Jim Haslam, long considered Knoxville's most powerful individual.

The closeness of the race surprised some, but Haslam won, as Ashe left local politics to become U.S. Ambassador to Poland. The untried Haslam astonished his opponents with his leadership abilities and with his vigorous pro-downtown initiatives.

He was inaugurated mayor right on Market Square, the fastest-changing acre in Knoxville. With the city's obvious investment, numerous new shops and restaurants sprang up on the Square, and a few dozen people moved into the spaces above the street level. Several new businesses were surprising for one reason or another—a cyber café; a brightly lit, no-smoking bar.

Several of its developers were non-developers. Andie Ray, a young admirer of jazz-age fashions, had been a librarian and a paralegal; she bought a Market Square building, painted it bright yellow, opened a retro dress shop and moved in upstairs.

One of the square's first post-renovation shops, opened by a sophisticated young

couple. Scott Schimmel and Lisa Sorensen, bloomed as a bright, imaginative gift shop called Bliss. Changing its stock so often it seemed a different place every week or two, Bliss became a rare retail destination, not just for people who happened to be downtown already.

John Craig, suburbanite and former hospital-contract manager, bought a Market Square building after learning his great-grandfather had once run a prosperous furniture company there. Following the mixed-use model, he transformed the small building into retail, office, and apartments with modern roof decking.

Craig, who became involved in the leadership of Knox Heritage, later led the redevelopment of the problematic art-deco icon the S&W Cafeteria—and, a big surprise to himself, launched a couple of major festivals, including the International Biscuit Festival.

— • —

But nothing turned more heads than the activity on the square's east side, where Scott and Bernadette West, previously the power couple of the Old City, opened several businesses and began major work

Below: Mayor Madeline Rogero shares observations with live-music guru Ashley Capps, Knoxville's most influential music promoter and co-founder of the monster festival Bonnaroo.

Below, right: Market Square—this eastern side hosts some of the Square's oldest buildings, like the 1860s buildings on the left, but attracts some of the newest ideas.

Photo by Gary Heatherly

on the square's most difficult buildings.

Previously, downtown developers were sometimes diverse in age and background, but most were affluent members of the professional class who recognized each other at receptions and zoning-commission meetings. Scott West, a flamboyant, longhaired rock guitarist, and his flight-attendant wife Bernadette, both of them artistic photographers, were talented outliers. In Knoxville they lived simply, like college students, but thanks to Bernadette's airline career, they had opportunities to travel the world.

They seemed unlikely developers, intuitive in their approach. In the Old City, their efforts had included an environmental-themed gift shop and framery, Earth to Old City, which proved so successful it opened branches in other towns. Less successful were an old-fashioned ice-cream parlor and a slightly bizarre intellectually themed bar called the Thinq Tank, known for showing movies on its back patio. As the Wests gave up on the idea of intellectuals gathering by the hundreds to drink beer, they sensed the next big thing might be Market Square.

Most prospective developers waited to see how the city's proposed rebuild of the square would work out, but the Wests struck right away, opening an extravagantly decorated saloon called Preservation Pub. Cultivating a relationship with public radio station WDVX, the bar gained a reputation for interesting live music, eventually boasting close to 100 acts each month. When the square was a fenced-off construction site, its few businesses accessible only by planking, Pres Pub was the only place open late at night. Most astonishing was the fact that the Wests pledged that all profits from Preservation Pub would be donated to local preservationist projects.

The Wests took on Market Square's biggest problem, a block of adjacent buildings owned by a landlord who for more than a decade had refused to sell or repair his buildings. Neither the city's carrots and sticks nor would-be developers' offers impressed him. But the Wests took the recalcitrant land-owner out to breakfast several times and talked about his buildings and dreams, and softened the old man's heart. One by one, he sold them to the Wests.

Market Square's Preservation Pub has hosted a steady stream of several live bands every week since it opened in 2002. Despite a turbulent history, it remains one of downtown's most popular attractions, and now features bars on three floors, including a rooftop deck.

Photo by Gary Heatherly

Some had already lost their roofs and were nearly ruined inside. They were, by any official standards, unsafe, but the city had been reluctant to condemn them for fear of undermining the historic character of the square.

Shunning the guidelines that came with historic tax credits, the Wests rebuilt modern, steel-framed buildings within the shells of the old ones, keeping the Victorian facades but redesigning the interiors with elevators and modern upstairs apartments with a roof deck.

Later the Wests opened an unusual pasta restaurant, Knoxville's first wine bar, an extraordinary art gallery/bar

The Aveda Institute, a lively and comprehensive beauty school and shop, is the unlikely heir to the large and elaborate 1937 art-deco cafeteria once known as the S&W.

Photo by David Luttrell

combined with a subterranean nightclub designed to look like a grotto, with an adjacent massage/yoga parlor, and Earth to Old City, moved with the same name from its namesake neighborhood.

— • —

As unlikely as hairdresser Kendrick or aerospace engineer Dewhirst, or the bohemian Wests, was a dapper, compact Englishman named

Jeffrey Nash, a longtime importer-exporter of women's fashions based in Spain and the United Kingdom. He came to Knoxville following his American wife, handbag designer Patricia Nash. He'd lived briefly in Nashville, and was "disappointed" in the state

of Knoxville as he found it in 1999. It reminded him of East London after the war. "It was hit the hardest by the Luftwaffe. I spent my youth playing in brick ruins, running through old buildings just left standing there."

But he also remembered how all that changed. He remembered being warned away from neighborhoods: "Don't go there, you'll be raped and pillaged. They're now prestigious, popular places to be." Nash played a small role in London's revival,

renovating a few buildings, himself.

But in '99, his move to Knoxville "seemed like a real retrograde step, in moving backwards," he admits. He says his friends at home were "appalled" to hear where he'd landed. But, he says, the more time he spent downtown, the more he liked Knoxville. "It was a mix of different people from all over the U.S., people from Europe, people whose parents were scientists at Oak Ridge, ex-UT students who never left. The demographics here had such an undercurrent of different types of people, income, backgrounds. It was very Londonlike. It's lovely to have this mixture of cultures even today."

He bought one building, a failed diner, and though it wasn't much, it gave him some status. "I had an ear here," he says. He found people who would listen to his ideas.

He's especially proud of the mixture of people who

come to his pride and joy, Tennessee's first "gastropub," the Crown & Goose. Nash opened it in 2008 when he joined two old saloon spaces together in the Old City with a "beer garden" in back that offers a rare look at the interior of an interesting block.

It followed several small historic-building condo projects in the center of town. A larger old apartment outside the downtown area, on riskier North Central, helped focus the city's attention on what became known as "Downtown North."

His Courtland Group has emerged as one of the more prominent new-urbanist residential firms. In 2012 he fixed up a badly abused jewelry shop on Gay Street as his wife's boutique, with small office and residential space above and below.

Now at an age when many are retiring, Nash keeps an eye out for the next opportunity, but spends much of his time chatting with customers

at the bar in the Crown and Goose. "The sign outside says 'You're local.' That's what a pub is. Pubs are your living room. It attracts suits and ties, jeans and T-shirts. It's not a place of rich people, or young people, or white people," he says, and looking around on most nights, it's easy to prove. The pub does attract lots of Europeans, but it may also be the most popular downtown destination of local blacks, especially those over 40, who come on jazz nights.

He's seen a change in America, just in his 15 years here. "American loves great big houses, lots of land, lots of cars, lots of dogs." But he says many are turning toward the stimulation of downtown for residential and recreational purposes.

"People like to live," he says, almost as if maybe it's a new idea in his adoptive country.

Opened by former Londoner Jeffrey Nash, the Crown & Goose was Tennessee's first "gastropub"--that is, a British-style pub with much better fare than their old reputation suggested. It has become a popular bar and restaurant with an unusual rear beer garden on the interior of a very urban block of the Old City, the surprisingly intact Victorian saloon district that in the 1980s became one of Knoxville's first urban-revival efforts.

Photo by David Luttrell

Photos by David Luttrell

Mayor Haslam, a lifelong Knoxvillian associated with one of the city's most successful businesses—Pilot started as a chain of gas stations—might have been expected to be mainstream or conventional in his approach.

He showed his commitment to bring about the long-doubted downtown cinema, but startled developers by making it a local project. With the assistance of a few other downtown-friendly allies, he brought downtown-skeptical Regal aboard. Other theater chains may already be interested in the downtown-cinema revival, but it would serve Knoxville best, Haslam said, to be able to show off one of the city's major businesses, right downtown.

Haslam also oversaw a complicated effort, led by Knox Heritage and other design volunteers, to preserve some interesting historic buildings that had been in the footprint of early cinema designs. One was a 1937 art-deco cafeteria; another was a pair of Victorian commercial buildings. One of those buildings, Haslam remarked when he made the surprising announcement that they would be saved, was one he had a soft spot for. It had once been an athletic store where, as a kid, he bought baseball equipment. The team found a way to wedge an eight-screen cineplex behind historic storefronts, leaving space for new individual businesses.

In saving the buildings as agreed, Kim Trent observes, the cinema's designers were forced to push its necessary windowless walls away from Gay Street. The once-endangered buildings became homes to a sandwich shop, a gelato shop, and offices, including an innovative architect's studio. The meticulously restored art-deco S&W cafeteria eventually became an especially elaborate, multi-story Aveda beauty school with a mezzanine and sweeping spiral staircase.

Mast General Store opened in downtown Knoxville in 2006, and it quickly became one of the small chain's busiest. Selling modern outdoor-oriented clothing, kitchenware, toys, and candy in a disarmingly retro atmosphere, Mast is a year-round favorite. The store has an unusual strategy of moving into traditional downtowns and rehabbing old buildings; in this case, a ca. 1900 department store.

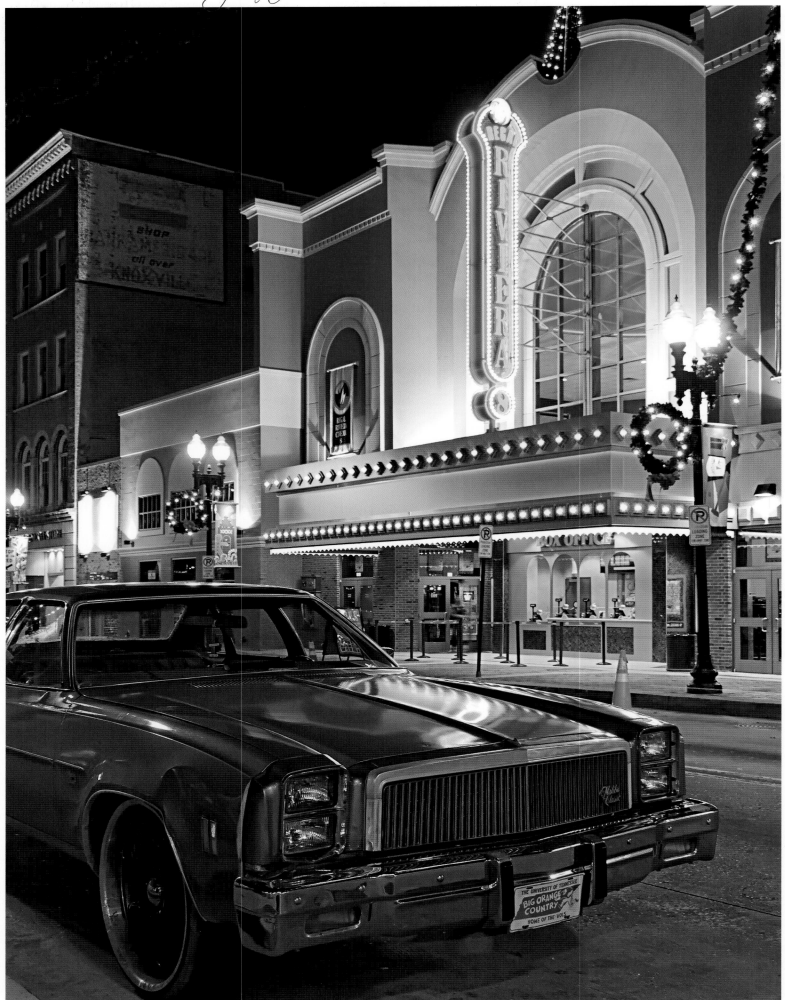

Photo by Jacques Gautreau

Long before the new cinema sold its first ticket, the mayor's commitment to the idea encouraged business development. Another Haslam effort was recruiting Mast General Store, the North Carolina-based department store's first effort in Tennessee. "I was convinced the movie theater was a no-brainer, because of the energy around downtown," says Haslam. "Mast was a little harder."

The small chain carried a retro theme and an unusual policy of opening stores only in hardwood-floored old buildings in downtown centers, and with city help they found a former supermarket's space in a century-old building, empty for 20 years and almost forgotten. A vigorous public-private effort paved the way for Mast which, the day it opened in 2006, became central Knoxville's highest-volume retailer, the first of its size in several decades; it was almost instantly successful, becoming, in particular, a holiday-shopping destination.

Mike Edwards notes that Mast provided two results, providing a retail destination downtown, but also introducing the downtown neighborhood as a retail market.

Related development by local developers rehabbed the same building's upper floors as creative upscale condos. Condos were opening all around; in 2006, local developer Cardinal, whose previous work had been mainly in the suburbs, but who had done construction work with Kinsey-Probasco's downtown projects, opened the 12-story Burwell Building, which since 1908 had never been anything but an office building. Diagonally across the street, Dewhirst transformed the larger Holston Building, a 1912 bank-related office building overlooking Krutch Park, into 15 floors of condos,

among them Knoxville's most expensive.

In the end, it took an unprecedented $2 million personal investment from Haslam himself to make the cinema complex happen. In 2007, the Regal Riviera became the first downtown cinema in 30 years—and the first new downtown cinema since the Herbert Hoover administration. The eight-screen Riviera, built on the site of a long-vanished 1920s icon also called the Riviera, silenced cynics with its instant success.

Some visitors are inclined to attribute downtown's new excitement to that one project, and it certainly didn't hurt. The new cinema complex made downtown a dependable every-night date attraction, something restaurants could count on.

But it would be hard to prove that any one thing revived Knoxville, circa 2007; the construction of the Regal Riviera coincided with several other developments, among the biggest of which was a nearby project both more expensive and more unlikely, the extravagant rehabilitation of the Tennessee Theatre. The painstaking, almost fastidious renovation restored the 1928 movie palace's sumptuous Faberge-egg interior to a degree that surpassed all previous renovations, and expanded the theater into something akin to a performing-arts center.

The Tennessee's generous backers weren't the new downtowners who packed the bars and funky apartment projects. They were old-line philanthropists, many

of them elderly, who lived in the suburbs and loved the Tennessee and its potential for the symphony, the opera, and other fine-arts performances. Though the city and county supported the Tennessee, its relationship with downtown's residential and nightlife rebirth seemed partly coincidental. But they each added a lot to the new party.

Two blocks away, the 1909 Bijou got a less-extravagant rehab. The two theaters, once considered rivals, had rarely thrived at the same time, even in their earlier decades. But now, both run by the same downtown-Knoxville-based company, AC Entertainment—just becoming known for its annual mega-festival, Bonnaroo—they complemented each other, and made their

The new cinema complex made downtown a dependable every-night date attraction, something restaurants could count on.

host city one of very few mid-sized American cities with two historical performing-arts theaters on the same street.

"I know of no comparable situation in the United States, or the Southeast, at least" says Capps.

Capps says his company's unusual management strategy—"the operators, managers, and marketing people are the same people"— makes them "two of the most successful live-music theaters in the country. These are magnets that bring thousands and thousands of people downtown night after night after night."

The two theaters may also be the most conspicuous demonstrations of the important role that historical preservation was playing in downtown's revival.

The Regal Riviera, built by the world's largest theater chain—which happens to be headquartered in Knoxville—was enabled by Mayor Bill Haslam. Though entirely new construction, the eight-screen theater is on the site of the long-since demolished 1920 Riviera Theatre. Though many were skeptical about whether cinema could return to downtown, where it had died in the 1970s, it has become one of Regal's most popular theaters in the region.

Photo by Stephanie Norwood

The 1928 Tennessee Theatre, originally a silent-era "motion-picture palace," closed for 18 months in 2003-05 as it got a mostly privately funded multi-million-dollar rehab. When it was all over, it had become something like a performing-arts center. With a capacity of 1,631, it hosts rock concerts, Broadway road shows, symphony and opera performances--and, occasionally, old movies. Its exotically sumptuous interior is justly famous.

Photo by Jacques Gautreau

In many cases, old buildings, with their modest size and sidewalk visibility, support urban life much better than most modern styles do, as urban theorist Jane Jacobs noted more than half a century ago: new businesses need old buildings. Preserving old buildings plays a role well beyond making downtown look better, by encouraging a diversity of small businesses on a single block.

In fact Knox Heritage, whose role is ostensibly to save old buildings, has been involved to various degrees in launching most of the new businesses downtown, and in almost all of the residential conversions, both by campaigning to save threatened buildings and by helping owners and developers negotiate the confusing thickets of historic tax credits. The nonprofit, once an idealistic band of sentimental old-building lovers, has become a force to be reckoned with, with a full-time staff, hundreds of volunteers, and membership in the thousands. KH works usually behind the scenes, making calls, doing paperwork, supporting historic rehabs, but sometimes takes center stage, especially when a historic building's survival is at stake.

Several times a year, the nonprofit seems determined to rattle popular assumptions about historic preservationists when it proves itself one of Knoxville's liveliest party hosts. Each year, KH hosts multiple fundraising events—walking tours and imaginative historic meals hosted in downtown buildings, Victorian mini-palaces,

or unusual 1950s "mid-century modern" ranchers, rarely the same place twice. Though they're all fundraisers, and fairly expensive to attend, the Summer Suppers series have become popular social adventures, selling out months in advance.

> "...sometimes, honestly, it seems more like fate, as if it was meant to happen."
> —Kim Trent

Kim Trent, Knox Heritage's longtime executive director and the dynamo

behind much of its modern success, has earned national status based on her work in Knoxville, including board membership on the National Trust. She is often in awe of her adoptive city, especially its downtown, where she lives and raises two children. "Sometimes I can't believe how lucky we are, that all these people are here, doing the right thing at the right time. But sometimes, honestly, it seems more like fate, as if it was meant to happen."

— • —

Fate has taken a hand in downtown's revival in lots of unpredictable ways.

The scale of the Wests' work on the east side of Market Square flabbergasted neighbors who wondered where the offbeat, bohemian couple, who lived in their own apartment development and spent many evenings partying with their patrons at the crowded Preservation Pub, found the capital to do such ambitious rebuilding.

The answer came in 2006, when a raid of federal agents on Market Square produced evidence that the Wests had been involved in a complex money-laundering project for an international marijuana-smuggling network. The Wests both went to prison, and had to surrender their buildings to the federal government, which auctioned them off to the highest bidders.

It says something about the Wests' values that the prosecution never found the Wests had spent significant money on personal luxuries, funneling it all toward improving buildings on Market Square. And it says something about the Wests' persistence that most of their offbeat businesses survived their arrests and convictions, and prison time. The buildings' new owners allowed the Wests to maintain their businesses, in absentia and via their hard-working families. After a total of six years, between them, in federal penitentiaries, the Wests returned as some of Market Square's liveliest promoters. Their Preservation Pub has expanded to three floors, including a rooftop deck, often hosting more than one musical act at once, and almost always, it's packed.

The square, historically remarkable for its diversity, drew all sorts. A few doors away from the Wests' offbeat triumphs, another problematic building with ownership complications eventually became the property of the faith-based Cornerstone Foundation, which designed its upper floors to house collegiate students in a Christian urban-studies program, but laid out the lower floor in accordance to needs the community at large had expressed, some of it via Cornerstone's periodic surveys: in addition to a restaurant, 4 Market Square became home to a bakery and coffee shop with a large performance space, in size deliberately filling a niche between existing nightclubs and auditoriums. Though the space is used for religious services on Sundays, much of its activity is secular. It serves alcoholic drinks and has hosted a wide variety of attractions, as a choice venue for jazz and bluegrass as well as lectures along the lines of international trends like TEDx talks and the rapid slide-show phenomenon known as Pecha Kucha.

If the Wests were outliers, so was hairdresser Kendrick and aerospace engineer Dewhirst and nearly every developer who took a chance on downtown

Knoxville. That's the remarkable thing about downtown's story: most who made it happen were not professional real-estate developers, and almost none of their approaches were conventional.

"All these guys were just able to see something that others couldn't."
—Mike Edwards

Mike Edwards has more business experience than all downtown's developers combined, at least when they started their downtown ventures—but he's impressed. "All these guys were just able to see something that others couldn't."

— • —

At the same time as the Tennessee and Bijou were raising the curtains on their second acts, a more offbeat show-biz attraction landed farther down Gay Street, when an unusual deal between the city's relocating tourist bureau and maverick public-radio station WDVX—a grassroots operation that emphasized bluegrass, old-time, and Americana music—resulted in the construction, in a radically renovated old building, of a live-audience radio studio. WDVX, something of a legend in the Americana community, had begun life on a shoestring, broadcasting from a camper van, out in the country. Moving downtown, they began a daily lunchtime show, the Blue Plate Special, inviting the public at large to watch live performances by traveling artists for free. The unpredictable hourlong show, typically six days a week, brings in audiences of 30 to 150 is one

Opposite page: The Square Room was one of the out-of-the-blue surprises of Market Square's revival. Planned and financed by the Cornerstone Foundation, it's part of a complex that includes a bakery, a restaurant, a quiet coffee lounge, and a dormitory for a faith-based urban-studies program, all at the same address. The Square Room, meant to fill a niche between auditoriums and bar-oriented nightclubs, with seating for about 400, has hosted a wide variety of shows, from live-radio programs to church services to well-known musical acts.

Photo by Scott Busby

"The Blue Plate Special," a free daily live-radio show that's earned an international following, attracts performers from all over the country, both famous and unknown. Offbeat public radio station WDVX, which specializes in Americana music, partnered with the Knoxville Visitors Center to produce this listening room, where performers, announcers, and audiences are all within view of the Gay Street sidewalk; the same big room doubles as a gift shop and tourist-information center. Red Hickey, center, is the colorful host of the show, which was inspired by the influential noontime live radio shows on Gay Street in the '30s and '40s. The happy persistence of live-audience radio is one of Knoxville's rarest distinctions.

Photo by David Luttrell

Knoxville attraction that may be genuinely unique.

And—meanwhile—still another initiative with little direct relation to deliberate city planning or other development took root. Market Square's physical restoration happened to coincide with the national organic and locovore food movement. The very few aging old farmers who had previously sold occasionally on Market Square—by 2002, there may have been only two or three—seemed disinclined to wait out the year of construction.

But after the square's new concrete was set, a group of enthusiastic young people led by 23-year-old former Memphian Charlotte Tolley began selling local and organic foods on old Market Square on Saturday mornings. It became more popular with each passing season, and by 2010, the Market Square Farmers' Market, strictly limited to local growers, had grown to about 70 vendors, and regularly attracted crowds in the thousands—especially in high tomato season, where the market sometimes displayed as many as 60 heirloom varieties.

"It's definitely a catalyst," says Carol Evans, executive director of the relatively new foundation Legacy Parks. Originally in television production, she'd lived on both coasts, doing time as a Fairbanks, Alaska, weather girl, before she arrived in Knoxville in the 1980s, working for the Lady Vols as Pat Summitt's first marketing director. She's enjoyed several mini-careers since then, but seems to have found her dream job as a promoter and developer of privately endowed greenways and parks. She oversees a new sort of annual festival, the one-of-a-kind Outdoor Knoxfest, an annual weekend of extreme sports, much of it across the river at Ijams and the new mountain-biking trails. But she's usually easy to find striding around the business district.

"It's pretty astonishing to come here on a Saturday," Evans says, to see the happy crowds and colorful activ-

> *"Knoxville is a place where you can kayak in a river and, a couple of hours later, be having dinner on Market Square, on your way to a show on Gay Street."*
> —Carol Evans

ity. Market Square's Saturday market, she says, is another outdoor adventure that has a "ripple effect," even over to her more athletic projects.

To Evans, whose spare, open office is symbolically right between the business

Originally from Memphis, Charlotte Tolley was the young maverick behind the successfully revived Market Square Farmers Market, which has already become a Saturday tradition, drawing thousands to the open Square to appraise the produce and meet the farmers, as buskers entertain. Though the market has a reputation for the organic, the main rule is that everything sold there has to be produced locally.

Photos this page by David Luttrell

LOCAL!

From Timberlake Farmers Co-op – Jefferson County

GYPSY SWEET PEPPERS

$4.49/lb

district and the river and greenway, downtown is part of the whole outdoor experience. She frequently refers to Knoxville as a place where you can kayak in a river and, a couple of hours later, be having dinner on Market Square, on your way to a show on Gay Street. She's heard a new term,

plain-looking 1920s Daylight Building, a block away from Market Square, did not interest preservationist developers, even the wonder-working Dewhirst. But Kim Trent at Knox Heritage was determined to save it, and talked him into it. Dewhirst bought and renovated the building,

Haslam proposed no master plans for downtown, but did emphasize several principles, some of them expansions of initiatives started in the Ashe administration. He hired Lyons to be full-time director of development. Ashe had experimented with tax-increment financing. Under

"local tourists," to describe people who have begun to enjoy new adventures in their own city.

Tolley and some of her farmers' market colleagues got together and founded a permanent year-round business, Just Ripe, a combination organic grocery and café. Even that's an unusual example of historic preservation at work. Long owned by a conventional local developer, and long expected to be demolished for any of several big projects that didn't work out, the

and in so doing discovered several secrets, like vaulted ceilings, rare woodwork, second-floor skylights, and most surprising of all, extensive copper work on the exterior, painted over decades ago. The long-ignored Daylight Building is now home to four thriving retail businesses, including Just Ripe and Knoxville's only independent bookstore, and 40 efficiency apartments. There's a waiting list.

— • —

Haslam, Lyons says, "we made a systematic process for it, more aggressive use of TIFs [tax-increment financing], with specific criteria." They updated codes, dropping the 1960s-style parking-lot requirement for many downtown businesses, and worked with a proposed wine-and-liquor store after it was discovered that Knoxville's 50-year-old blue laws, designed for the suburbs, effectively prevented such a project in the business district, where every address was too close to a park or a church.

: Once a TV "weather girl" in Alaska, Carol Evans is the vigorous director of the ambitious nonprofit Legacy Parks, a private foundation that acquires and develops wild land for public recreation. Its most challenging project may be an effort to link three historic Civil War earthworks along the river bluffs with other attractions, including a stunningly beautiful quarry, an offbeat cabin community called Log Haven, and Ijams Nature Center; much of it's already completed.

Photo by David Luttrell

By 2005, the city had launched a first-ever Design Review Board for downtown buildings, sometimes cited as a legacy of the Crandall Arambula plan. Though it has little punitive power and no hard-and-fast urban plan to work from, the board engages publicly with developers, offering encouragement, criticism, and other options. It can at least delay projects that seem reckless or hasty.

acknowledged respect for existing buildings, and the idea that mixed-use development—including residential, office, retail, and/or restaurants, should be encouraged and not constrained by postwar-style codes concerning parking or setbacks.

The south side of the river, hardly half a mile from downtown via two bridges, remained a stubborn problem,

been the main view from the mayor's office for a quarter century hadn't had much effect. But a federal reconstruction of the century-old Gay Street Bridge with much-better pedestrian accommodations, as well as a couple of speculative south-side condominium projects, got people talking.

Vigorously in his first years, Haslam laid out an ambitious 20-year plan to develop the mostly blighted south side, along the mixed-used model. In the ideal, it would look something like a cleaner, newer mirror reflection of downtown's revival, with lots of residences as well as offices, greenways, shops, parks, cafes. Hiring an urban-design professional to head up the project, Haslam intended to base downtown's trans-riparian annex on sound new-urbanist

Of all Knoxville's historic rehabs, none was more unexpected than Union Avenue's Daylight Building. Once a drab, ignored, and underused office building, slated for demolition with little protest, the Daylight surprised many during Dewhirst's thorough redo which disclosed a previously unknown copper façade and several other appealing details from its 1920s origins. It drew this lively complex of unusual shops, including a locovore grocery/bakery called Just Ripe, and most surprisingly in an era when the independent bookstore is alleged to be a thing of the past, an independent bookstore. Union Ave Books has defied the odds. Above and beneath the stores are efficiency apartments.

Photos by David Luttrell

A new term, "form-based zoning," was creeping into the development lingo.

And by then, a new term, "form-based zoning," was creeping into the development lingo. That new concept, which was in some ways a very old concept,

part industrial eyesore, part overgrown kudzu forest, with a declining commercial area, poorly planned streets, an obsolete hospital, and crumbling sidewalks. The fact that it had

principles. And, this being property-rights Knoxville, he promised not to resort to eminent domain.

Though the plan was met with much excitement and speculation on both sides of the river, a few residents bitterly resisted it, and some large industrial concerns refused to budge, even for the well-connected mayor. Haslam reflects almost fondly on the challenges of diversity, evident at the first public meeting concerning the proposal. "One thought the whole thing should be a giant butterfly garden," he recalls. "Then one said, God made riverfronts for a purpose, and it should be all industry."

Photos these pages by Stephanie Norwood

Knoxville

Almost every year brought clusters of new central-city residences. With each renovation, more and more people were moving into downtown permanently, generally young professional singles and, in smaller numbers, older retirees, plus a handful of families with children. By the time the Riviera opened, the residential population seemed to have reached a critical mass for some basic retailers. A few stepped forward to address downtown's lack of a grocery store with small food and convenience shops. Success was mixed, but a couple lasted.

The housing-related recession of 2008 put the brakes on condominium development. But residential development continued unabated, shifted toward rental-apartment projects, almost all of them in old buildings that had been built for other purposes. Recession or no, supply had not yet reached the demand for downtown residences; in some regards, the neighborhood seemed almost recession-proof.

The same was not true for the not-yet neighborhood across the river, Haslam's dream. The city project had been slow to gain traction in that famously independent-minded part of town, and had made only a little preliminary progress before the recession of 2008 put the project into deep freeze. Though it's still on the current

mayor's agenda, the south bank looks little different from the neighborhood that greeted Haslam's gaze in 2003—perhaps worse in one regard, since mammoth Baptist Hospital, the largest presence there, closed in 2008. At this writing, an out-of-state developer's proposal calls for demolishing most of the old hospital buildings for a major residential and hotel development.

In his second term, Haslam had hired his former opponent, Madeline

greenness that may be harder to come by. Knoxville offers sometimes astonishing green urban vistas and recreational opportunities, but connecting them with real green options for sustainable living have proved elusive for years.

Commuting was a major incentive for the development of Knoxville's 58 miles of greenways, which sometimes received government funding based on the premise that they would reduce automobile traffic congestion, and air pollution. Though a

improvements, Knoxville's air quality, as judged by ozone levels, is relatively poor.

Much of the problem reflects multi-generational low-density development patterns concerning especially where people have chosen to live over the years. "Regional planning is difficult," says Rogero; from that trained urban planner, it's an understatement.

For now, the mayor is concentrating on smaller-scale projects. One Haslam-

Photo by Sheena Patrick

Photo by Sheena Patrick

Photo by David Luttrell

Long frustrated by damage presumably caused by careless skateboarders, the city tried another tack under Haslam's administration, in establishing the Knoxville Skatepark. Adjacent to historic Tyson Park, near UT about mile west of downtown, the skatepark was a state-of-the-art model, professionally designed and popular since its opening.

Haslam's opponent in 2003, community organizer Madeline Rogero eventually worked in Haslam's administration--and in 2011, was finally elected mayor herself.

Rogero, as director of community development. In 2010, she was elected to replace him, Knoxville's first female mayor, but significantly also the first Knoxville mayor in some 70 years who had been raised outside of Tennessee. Pleased with Haslam's policies, she continued most of them in her administration, especially concerning center-city development.

Rogero has put greater emphasis on green development, and green technologies. Knoxville has plenty of literal greenness, but it's the figurative, transformative

committed minority does use the greenways for practical transportation, theoretically driving less, most use them only recreationally.

As a regional long-term five-county research and advisory project known as Plan ET (for East Tennessee) points out, less than two percent of commuters in that region use transportation other than gasoline-powered automobiles—and Knoxville-area residents spend more than twice as much of their household income on transportation than the typical American does. Despite some recent

Rogero initiative applies new-urbanist principles to the campus area's recklessly developed commercial strip, western Cumberland Avenue, with form-based zoning. Cumberland, four lanes wide as long as anyone can remember, and often jammed at that, will be just three lanes. The idea, borrowed from Portland, Oregon, which pioneered it, is that slower traffic will be more appealing to pedestrians and will enhance business. New urban-style residential construction is underway there.

An unexpected large private development promises to enhance Cumberland's economy and convenience. A flattened factory site amidst the western part of UT's campus is on its way to being the unusual home to a supermarket and a smaller urban-scale Walmart. Because developers took some care to present it as an appealing and potentially pedestrian-friendly project, and an imaginative remediation of a potentially toxic industrial site, it has not garnered the condemnation it might have otherwise. And central Knoxville has very few sources of appliances, hardware, inexpensive clothing, and simple home furnishings of the sort for which Walmart is famous.

One of famously Republican Mayor Bill Haslam's most surprising efforts was adding the city's substantial imprimatur to an effort to build a state-of-the-art skateboard attraction on an old softball field on the edge of Tyson Park, near UT, a concrete-sloped wonderland designed by a nationally known skate-park architect. The Knoxville Skatepark's half-million bill was paid by the city and county, with help from some private donations.

It seemed to mark a sea change in city attitudes toward a perceived threat; in the 1990s, a grim City Council had banned skateboarding from some public areas, including Market Square, without offering alternatives. Completed in 2008, the Knoxville Skatepark has seen almost constant use.

— • —

Despite its proximity, for most of its history the University of Tennessee never maintained any sort of a presence downtown. But in the 1990s, facing development pressures on its traditional campus, and interested in access to downtown's existing hotels, the university moved dozens of offices, including its non-credit programs and its publishing arm, UT Press, into a recently emptied 1956 department-story building on the western edge of downtown, and named it the UT Conference Center. For the first time ever, some university employees joined downtown's daily mix.

Since then, the university has also opened an architectural design studio in an old store space on Gay Street, where selected students work during the school year.

As if inspired by that example of higher education in a downtown setting, Lincoln Memorial University, whose main campus is 60 miles north of Knoxville, near Cumberland Gap, opened its first law school in downtown Knoxville in 2009, with encouragement and help of Congressman Jimmy Duncan. Chosen as its location was one of downtown's most revered locations, the hilltop 1848 building that had successively housed the Tennessee School for the Deaf, Knoxville City Hall, offices of TVA, and the Knoxville Chamber of Commerce. The law school has struggled with accreditation issues, with a total enrollment of only a couple hundred, but it has become another unlikely piece of the puzzle that is downtown Knoxville.

Another piece is just across the busy intersection of Henley and Summit Hill, another large, iconic building that for years had no clear plan for the 21st century. The ornate 1905 L&N

Photo by David Luttrell

The L&N train station, built in 1905, greeted its last passenger train in 1968. After a long period of vacancy and neglect, it became an anchor for the 1982 World's Fair, and hosted a series of restaurants and offices—until 2011, when it was converted into a specialized public high school, Tennessee's first STEM Academy.

Station had not welcomed a passenger train since 1968. In the decades since, when it wasn't vacant, the L&N had mixed success hosting restaurants and offices, rarely to full advantage. Its location, on World's Fair Park but separated from downtown by noisy, broad, highway-like Henley Street made it a long shot to share in downtown's pedestrian-driven revival.

However, with a mixture of city, county, state, and corporate help, the Knox County School System obtained the building, and in 2011 opened it as the state's first STEM

Academy, a public high school for students gifted in the sciences.

— • —

A city emphasis on Happy Holler, an old mill-town commercial area about a mile northwest of downtown, has shown progress, as a destination adjacent to an already reviving historic neighborhood. The city attempted to push downtown's liveliness north past I-40, the region's busiest highway, using the attractions of carefully administered façade grants, new bicycle lanes, and other encouragements. North Central, which could once seem dangerous when it wasn't empty altogether, is livelier than it's been in decades.

With the help of Knox Heritage, it seemed as if every aspect of downtown development caught on to the winds of preservation. The regional homeless shelter, Knoxville Area Rescue Ministries obtained the old Fifth Avenue Motel—a badly deteriorated hostelry considered to be one of Knoxville's most dangerous—and recovered its almost-hidden interior 1913 brick rowhouse complex called Minvilla. Using financing advantages including the same historic tax credits used to rehab upscale condo buildings, KARM rehabbed the eyesore into a strikingly handsome supportive-housing development. Open in 2010, it became a positive inducement for the temporarily homeless, and subsequently won a National Trust/HUD award for preservation.

— • —

Haslam's hubbub on the south side may have gotten some ideas flowing. Nothing that has happened in Knoxville this century has been more surprising than the private philanthropic proposal known as Legacy Parks. Announced to a happily stunned outdoor luncheon in

One of Knoxville's most astonishing developments of recent years was the expansion of Ijams Nature Center. A modest riverside bird sanctuary for almost half a century, Ijams became the beneficiary of two major limestone/marble mining sites, including some quarries which had been abandoned for so many decades they almost resemble natural features or ancient aboriginal ruins. About 275 acres in itself, Ijams connects to other greenways and wildlife preserves, resulting in close to 1,000 acres of recreational public land. At right is a view of a farm east of Knoxville, visible across the river from the original part of Ijams.

Photos these pages by Sheena Patrick

2009, the idea would include a unique ridge-top greenway connecting the ruins of three Civil War forts, the charmingly peculiar refuge known as Log Haven, interesting caves, and rarely seen bluff-top property, along a hiking and bicycling trail.

The proposal already had some momentum when it got an unexpected assist from the new Aslan Foundation, a charity formed by the will of wealthy Knoxville lawyer Lindsay Young. Aslan bought Log Haven, saving it from threatened development, and secured Fort Higley, a Union redoubt never easily accessible before. A much larger river-bluff park nearby is being developed as a city park.

The Legacy Parks trail would eventually connect, if all went well, with Ijams Nature Center, which was experiencing a seemingly unrelated renaissance. For many decades a modest bird sanctuary established during the original conservation era by illustrator-ornithologist Harry Ijams (the j is silent; it rhymes with rhymes), was well known to birdwatchers and school children, occasionally as a place for a daring

wedding—but in a combination of luck and careful stewardship, beginning in 1990 it exploded in size and scope, acquiring more riverfront land, then first one and then another adjacent marble quarry, including many parts that had been so little used they had returned to nature in unusual ways. By 2010, Ijams was up to 275 acres, 16 times the size the nature center had been for its first 80 years. The new acreage yielded an astonishing array of landscapes, from a craggy, narrow canyon, to a pocket desert (a couple acres of limestone dust, the result of decades of industrial dumping) to a dark, moist jungle, to a beautiful and very deep green pool—all of it within about two miles of downtown. In the 21st century, Ijams still

attracts birdwatchers, but also a new generation of athletes, from rock climbers to mountain bikers.

In its almost weird diversity of landscapes in a small space, Ijams, which is privately owned but open to the public, and run by a non-profit, may well be unique in the world.

Opposite: One of the newest additions to the Old City, Boyd's Jig & Reel is a Scottish-themed pub, with Scottish liquor, Scottish beer, Scottish music, and even Scottish food. It has surprised some skeptics, and perhaps even its owners, with its popularity.
Below: Another bucolic view across the river from Ijams just moments from downtown.

Photos these pages by Sheena Patrick

In its almost weird diversity of landscapes in a small space, Ijams, which is privately owned but open to the public, and run by a non-profit, may well be unique in the world. English-born executive

director Paul James was here for most of its expansion, and likes to think it's the long-deferred fulfillment of Harry Ijams dream, of 1,000 acres of bird preserve (combined with some adjacent city and state parkland and wildlife preserves, it's close to that size). Ijams is unusual in its combination of natural history and local human history.

In the 1920s, Harry Ijams' spread was a regular gathering place for several of the organizers of the Great Smoky Mountains National Park, among them people who have mountains named for them, like David Chapman. "Knoxville's lucky to have a place with so many

connections to Knoxville's history," James says.

Many Knoxvillians say they love the Smokies, James has observed, though they may visit the mountains only two or three times a year. To get to the Smokies from Knoxville can be a couple hours' round trip, and a tank or two of gas. "But Knoxville almost has its own little national park, a mini national park," James says of Ijams. "And you can go to Ijams daily. It's right there!"

Ijams is more popular than it has ever been, and James thinks the revival of downtown has helped. Previously, people in the

far-flung residential suburbs, like Farragut, complained that Ijams was too distant to visit often. But as they become more acquainted with downtown, Ijams, just two miles from there, seems not so far away.

Inspired by Ijams's astonishing trails, a group of mountain-biking enthusiasts blazed a new 12-mile trail through South Knoxville, connecting some neglected parks by way of some undeveloped gulleys and hillsides in a green forest, much of it looking as wild as anything in the Smokies.

At the helm was community organizer Carol Evans, executive director of Legacy Parks, which in 2012 opened a permanent attraction on downtown's Volunteer Landing, an Outdoor Adventure Center, where customers may shop for outdoor gear and rent canoes, kayaks, and waterboards. Ijams, upstream and across the river, is the most popular destination.

"We're lucky to have it by default," Evans says, comparing South Knoxville to the story of the Ugly Duckling. Much of it was too rugged to attract developers, it remained lush and unspoiled. "It's very interesting, beautiful land. You would not believe you're in the middle of a city."

"I think we have a swagger, a little bit," says Evans, of the city and her part in it. "We're past the place that we're trying to be something else. Finally, we are comfortable in our own skin."

Rather sudden in the world of urban planning, Knoxville's surge in outdoors attractions has already attracted national applause.

"This is working because it's authentic," Evans says, and not imposed by top-down planners. "It makes us different." She doesn't think

the city needs an urban plan, at least not from her vantage. But then she stops for a moment, and says, "but we have a plan—like England has a constitution. It's all very collaborative. If you come in new, it's hard to understand the structure, but it's all working."

Downtown keeps evolving. Overlooking Market

charm is its freedom from the national mundane.

Dewhirst continues to develop downtown's most surprising block. The formerly run-down, taboo 100 block of Gay is now reputedly the highest-density residential block in metro

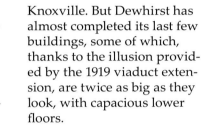

The formerly run-down, taboo 100 block of Gay is now reputedly the highest-density residential block in metro Knoxville.

Square, Knoxville's "first skyscraper," the seven-story 1906 Arnstein Building is another of Dewhirst's painstaking renovations: a perfect mixed-use project, with retail on the ground floor, architectural offices above, and upper floors reserved for upscale residences. Dewhirst calls the old department store (it closed in 1928) his favorite building in East Tennessee. The ground floor—actually an imaginatively designed multi-level interior—opened in 2013 to house Knoxville's first Urban Outfitters.

Though generally greeted with excitement, its arrival has caused some anxiety about what it might suggest for the future character of downtown. Urban Outfitters is the largest national-chain retail store downtown since the mid-20th-century days of J.C. Penney's. Though downtown tolerates a few small chains, a Lenny's, a Subway, a Rita's Italian Ice, downtown has mostly thrived off the radar of the most garish sorts of national-chain expansion, and so far, downtowners have been happy about that. A large part of downtown's

Knoxville. But Dewhirst has almost completed its last few buildings, some of which, thanks to the illusion provided by the 1919 viaduct extension, are twice as big as they look, with capacious lower floors.

Dewhirst's latest project is as ambitious as any on his resume. He purchased the 1885 White Lily Flour factory—it was still producing the famous product until it closed in 2005—and is converting it into apartments. The development's significant because it crosses the Southern train tracks, a symbolic northern boundary of the Old City, and of the traditional central business district. It may open a relatively ignored mostly decrepit industrial area across the tracks for further development.

Buzz Goss, an architect originally from Florida who has worked on downtown projects for a quarter century, including many of Dewhirst's early conversions—he's especially known for his imaginative historic-preservation designs in the Old City—has turned developer, a partner in downtown's first large

new-construction apartment building since the 1980s, a 300-resident development on an underused parking lot near both the Old City and Market Square. Despite its size, it's actually a downward-revised version of a much more various mixed-use plan he'd announced four years earlier.

Downtown's developers keep emerging from unpredictable quarters. One of the latest is Randy Boyd, who has made a career in invisible fences for pet owners. In 2011, he and his wife Jenny bought a defunct corner bar in the Old City, thoroughly renovated it, and called it Boyd's Jig & Reel, Knoxville's first Scottish-themed pub, inspired by their own trips to Scotland. Some worried about a couple who thought a place with a framed portrait of Robert Burns, regular Celtic music, and "Scotch eggs" on the menu would work, but the place often flirts with the fire marshal's limits for crowds. In 2012, Randy Boyd, who also serves as an educational consultant for Governor Haslam, bought the Old City's high-Victorian centerpiece, Sullivan's Saloon, with intentions to fix it up.

Chapter 10

Photo by Sheena Patrick

Today, downtown Knoxville's still artificially constricted, hemmed in by highways and literally smaller than it was in the late 19th century. One of those barriers arguably got worse, in the midst of downtow n's revival, as the state widened I-40, leaving a bigger and noisier underpass underneath, where busy city blocks used to be, further separating downtown from its not-quite-forgotten northern quarter. It's a frustrating limit to growth, as the city discusses various ideas—murals?—none of them an obvious solution. But the north side has found ways to thrive on its own, as Downtown North, including the old commercial center Happy Holler, has formed a nascent downtown. There, interesting businesses, including Knoxville's only co-op supermarket, Three Rivers Market; the regionally famous specialty bakery, Magpie's; and the industrial art studio known as Ironwood suggest a new gravity along a street where legal activity once ended at 5:00.

Other, farther nodes show long-term promise, like West Knoxville's Bearden, an old commercial strip with downtownish potential, with a few of Knoxville's best regarded restaurants, and, soon, the metro area's first Anthropologie. On a good day, the far north's Fountain City, which has established one of the city's loveliest and best-used public parks, near a couple of blissfully independent restaurants, can seem like a charming small town. Even extreme suburban Farragut, which has recently expressed interest in renovating one of its few historic buildings, sometimes exhibits early symptoms of developing a walking downtown.

And, of course, as the economy improves, the South Side development may yield some fruit. Long-ignored South Knoxville, suddenly getting almost daily attention thanks to Ijams' astonishing attractions, Legacy Parks'

promise, and the greenways connecting them all, seems on the brink of some positive change. "The basics of the place are good," says Haslam. "Madeline and others will make it work."

Cornerstone, in its latest initiatives, is emphasizing pushing downtown beyond its boundaries, even in ways that might someday intersect with their ongoing interest in one of Knoxville's strengths, UT/ORNL research, calling for a "Joint Institute for Radiological Sciences and Advanced Imaging" at Cherokee Farm, UT's developing research facility across the river. Perhaps inspired by the downtown experience, Cornerstone offers specific recommendations that scientists should have a public place, perhaps on that campus, to get together and discuss their work.

The artificial constriction, though, may be one of the

Cherokee Farm viewed from across the river.   Photo by Stephanie Norwood

Photo by Jacques Gautreau

leaders regret the lack of a hardware store, a pharmacy, a cell-phone store. Some are confident these things will arrive when the residential concentration reaches a critical mass.

And what of the future? At the moment, downtown Knoxville's success can seem serendipitous, dependent on about 40 energetic, enlightened, and well-placed individuals, independently doing the right thing. There's nothing wrong with good luck, except that its success can seem tenuous. Knoxville's morbid have been known to remark that the wrong plane crash could bring it all to an end. Though Dewhirst and others think they have a long way to go before downtown Knoxville can be declared an unqualified success, they're also convinced that its magnitude of residential commitment makes it unlikely to backslide, due to the existing density of residents, both rental ones and a few hundred who are invested as owners. "I don't have any concern that downtown will continue to be interesting and unique," without a plan, and without any given developer, Dewhirst says. Downtown lacks several amenities, like that elusive drugstore and the mainstream grocery. Some of

be other people stepping up. The market is there."

Knoxville has always been unpredictable. For much of the latter part of the 20th century, the city seemed to be getting gradually blander, blanker, more spread out, less distinguishable from the

Photo by Gary Heatherly

rest of middle America. In the 21st century it is, of its own accord, growing denser, more diverse, more complex. In ways that can sometimes dumbfound historians, it's coming to resemble, more than anything else, the city it was built to be in the half-century after the Civil War, the 24-hour city it was—circa 1900, perhaps—when most people walked from home to work, when Market Square was a place to encounter foreign languages and fresh vegetables, when the city was proud of itself and not exactly like any other place in the world.

secrets of downtown's bloom, in ways pruning can enhance the concentrated vigor of some flowers. It's been easier for a healthy-sized metropolitan area to enliven that one interior urban spot, hardly more than a half square mile. Beyond those boundaries, success looks spottier.

Mike Edwards compares Knoxville's problems with Chattanooga's. The latter city's downtown is comparatively vast—and serves a smaller metropolitan area than Knoxville's. Tearing down to build big doesn't make sense in downtown Knoxville. "It's a postage stamp!" says Edwards. "Working with what we've got, that's what makes sense."

Speaking of the 100 block of Gay Street, the block where Mason and Burch and Dewhirst got started, where Haslam, in one of his last downtown initiatives as mayor, planned utility and road

improvements, broad sidewalks and benches and planters, Edwards says, "That's a plan. It's not an Albert Speer type plan, but it works." (Evoking the Nazi planner may suggest an attitude toward the comprehensive top-down planning shared by both liberal and conservative Knoxvillians.)

> *"There's no such thing as a good plan, just good planning. Nothing is static. Nothing remains the same."*
> *—Dwight D. Eisenhower*

Eisenhower said, "There's no such thing as a good plan, just good planning. Nothing is static. Nothing remains the same."

A comprehensive city plan might have found a way to wedge in certain much-missed amenities. Several

those nuts have been tough to crack. "But you know who does want to come downtown?" he asks. "A city full of crazy people who want to live here."

Mayor Rogero seems to agree. "There are some big players," she says. "There'll

Fin

Knoxville Views

Photo by Jacques Gautreau

Though bicycling was all the rage among young people in Victorian-era Knoxville, it might once have seemed a long shot for a revival in a city long known for its oblivious automobile traffic, stultifying humidity, and steep hills, but thanks to both the city's greenway system and to the development of center-city residences, two-wheeling has caught on to such a degree that in good weather, bicycles, parked and ridden, are almost omnipresent in downtown Knoxville. This couple enjoys a ride on Jackson Avenue, in the Old City.

Photo by Stephanie Norwood

Knoxville

Inset, Old City's venerable coffee shop, Java. The distinctive round brick window is an architectural theme of the tiny neighborhood, which differs from the rest of downtown in several respects.

Photo by Stephanie Norwood

A remnant of Knoxville's Victorian-era saloon district, the Old City is a longtime work in progress. Sullivan's Saloon, opened by an Irish immigrant in 1888, is the neighborhood's historic anchor, and has been renovated since the 1980s to house a restaurant and nightclub. But until recently, everything just beyond it, across the railroad tracks to the north, was industrial, and much of it run-down. The cream-colored building in the background is the once-famous White Lily Flour factory, which milled high-quality baking flour for 120 years. Abandoned after a corporate takeover, the original factory is being renovated as a 42-unit apartment building, part of a concerted effort to push the boundaries of downtown's revival to the north.

Photo by Stephanie Norwood

Photo by Jacques Gautreau

Photo by Jacques Gautrea

Perhaps more than most cities, Knoxville's height variations, tendency toward lushness, and variety of architecture promotes lots of startling vistas. Visible through a copse of trees in World's Fair Park is part of the Knoxville Museum of Art. And against a blue sky, the Hilton is one of three hotels built for the 1982 World's Fair.

Knoxville

Photo by Jacques Gautreau

Photo by Jacques Gautreau

Whether deliberately intended or not, Knoxville's most peculiar landmark, the Sunsphere, pops up in lots of photographs of the city. At right, the edge of Old Gray Cemetery, Knoxville's Victorian garden-style grave-yard on the northwestern corner of downtown. This mournful tombstone, carved from marble mined at the famous Carrera quarry in Italy, belongs to Eleanor Deane Swan Audigier, a prominent patron of the arts who died in Rome in 1931.

115

Knoxville

Photo by Jacques Gautreau

Old Gray, established in 1850 and named in honor of Thomas Gray, the English poet who wrote "Elegy Written in a Country Churchyard," is the final resting place of thousands of Knoxvillians, including many veterans of both the Union and Confederate causes in the Civil War. This statue, Old Gray's only sculpture of a male—most of Old Gray's statues memorialize young women--represents a Confederate soldier on a family plot where two rebel veterans are buried. During the Victorian era, when Knoxville lacked a sizable public park, Old Gray was a popular destination for walks and even picnics.

Knoxville's up-and-down topography is rarely more obvious than on Jackson Avenue, where a brick-lined ramp leads up to Gay Street. When this viaduct, which carries traffic over the old Southern Railway yards, was constructed in 1919, it covered the first floors of a block of buildings on Gay Street. Some of the old street frontage is still visible, within basements. Long-term plans call for resurrecting parts of it, along subterranean corridors.

Photo by Jacques Gautreau

Knoxville's nightlife is no longer as easy to describe as it was in the 1970s, when R.B. Morris and Hector Qirko first performed for Knoxville audiences. Songwriter Morris and guitarist Qirko have achieved some national and international recognition, recording several albums, together and separately—but they still perform semi-regularly in downtown venues. At right, another singer-songwriter, Lydia Salnikova, draws an altogether different following. A Russian immigrant who has performed all over the western world, she's a regular at Market Square's Preservation Pub.

Photos these pages by David Luttrell

Knoxville

Photos by Gary Heatherly

In the 1980s, only a handful of affluent professionals lived in downtown Knoxville, which had been shedding its middle-class population by degrees beginning with the first "trolleyburbs" in the 1890s. As late as 2000, the downtown resident had a reputation as eccentric and daring. But today, more than 1,000 live in the half-square-mile known as downtown Knoxville, and they range from college students to octogenarian retirees, with, in the middle, even several families with small children. And at this writing, the number is still rapidly climbing. But because downtown spaces tend to be a little different, downtown residents may still be a little different, too.

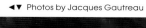

◄▼ Photos by Jacques Gautreau

Based on comments from some visitors, Knoxville may be notable for the sheer tonnage of brick in its older buildings. Since the 19th century, brick was industrially manufactured in Knoxville, and found its way into lots of exterior walls. At left, with some terra-cotta flourishes, is the side of the 1886 Knox County Courthouse; though most court and clerical functions have been moved to the huge, modernist City County Building, the old courthouse still hosts some courts and offices. In the background is the 1991 Whittle Building/Federal Courthouse, designed in a retro 17th-century Georgian style by trendy New York architect Peter Marino.

At right is UT's Ferris Hall, a 1930 engineering building on the side of the university's iconic Hill. Its designer was Charles Barber, a prominent Knoxville architect who rejoiced in the Gothic.

Photos these pages by Gary Pope

Knoxville

With the Sunsphere in the background, the Knoxville Convention Center, finished in 2003 with an associated revamp of World's Fair Park, was controversial for its expense. In its first decade it has hosted national bowling tournaments, international scientific conferences, and some episodes of PBS's Antiques Roadshow—as well as dozens and dozens of weddings and reunions. Though critics say the KCC has underperformed, its debt burden concentrated city attention on downtown as never before.

Photo by Gary Pope

Knoxville

Knoxville's downtown, which until the 20th century, constituted most of the city, combines more than two centuries of building styles. At left, glassy 1970s Plaza Tower is still East Tennessee's tallest building flanked by the pseudo-planetary orbits of the city's two most whimsical public structures, the Sunsphere (center) and Womens' Basketball Hall of Fame (bottom). At right, brick-dominant Market Square features mostly late-19th and early 20th-century commercial architecture.

Knoxville

Photos by Gary Heatherly

◄▲ Photos by Stephanie Norwood

Knoxville is known in some quarters as Big Orange Country, a term coined by the late basketball coach Ray Mears in the 1960s. As the story goes, UT's football team picked its gridiron colors back in the 1890s, inspired by the proliferation of daisies on College Hill. Originally more of a yellowish orange, the color turned a brighter and brighter pure orange as the decades passed. But even without the Tennessee Vols, it might be hard to recognize Knoxville without the color orange. It's the hue of much of the thick clay just beneath the topsoil in the upper Tennessee Valley, and the color of the city's hundreds of brick buildings, many of them built from the products of local brick factories, which have made good use of that local clay for two centuries. It's also the color of several indigenous trees, like oaks and especially sugar maples, in the autumn. And on a Victorian house, like this one on the fringe of Fort Sanders, orange makes a nice contrast.

▲ Photos by Stephanie Norwood

Photo by Sheena Patrick ▼

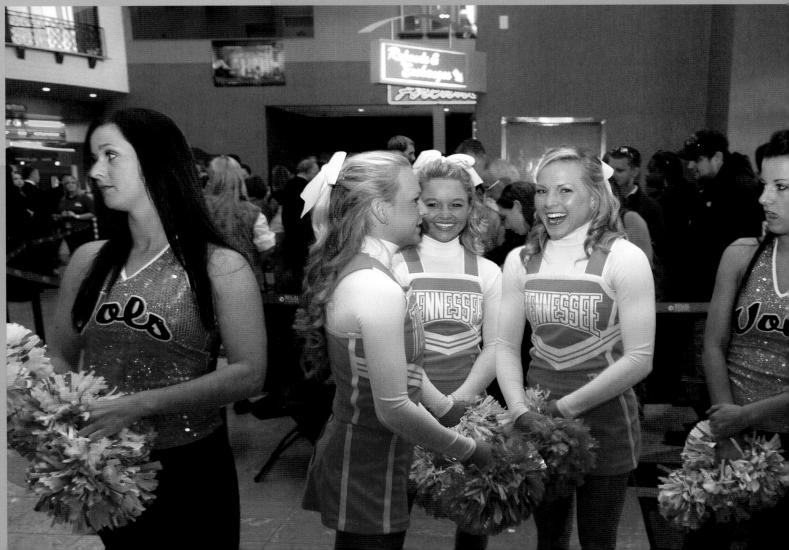

STADIUM
TKINS FIELD

Photo by Gary Pope

Knoxville

The UT home football game has become something like a de-facto community festival, with its own time-honored rituals.

Photos by Gary Heatherly

UT's more modern buildings range from the stark "brutalist" style of the 1981 Art & Architecture Building, left, to the 1987 "ziggurat" more formally known as the Hodges Library.

▲▼ Photos by Gary Pope

Much of UT's mid-20th century architecture revels in the ornate styles of the "collegiate gothic" style.

The 1934 Alumni Memorial Hall was the site of Sergei Rachmaninoff's final concert in 1943. Today it holds the music hall, Cox Auditorium.

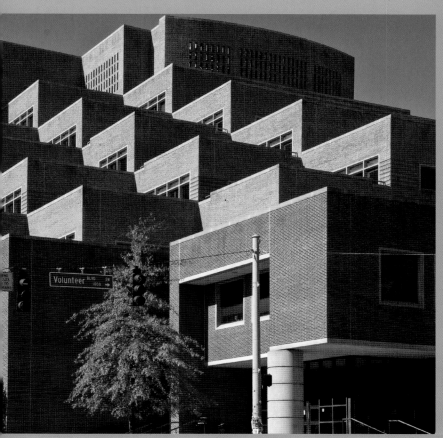

133

Photos this page by Gary Pope

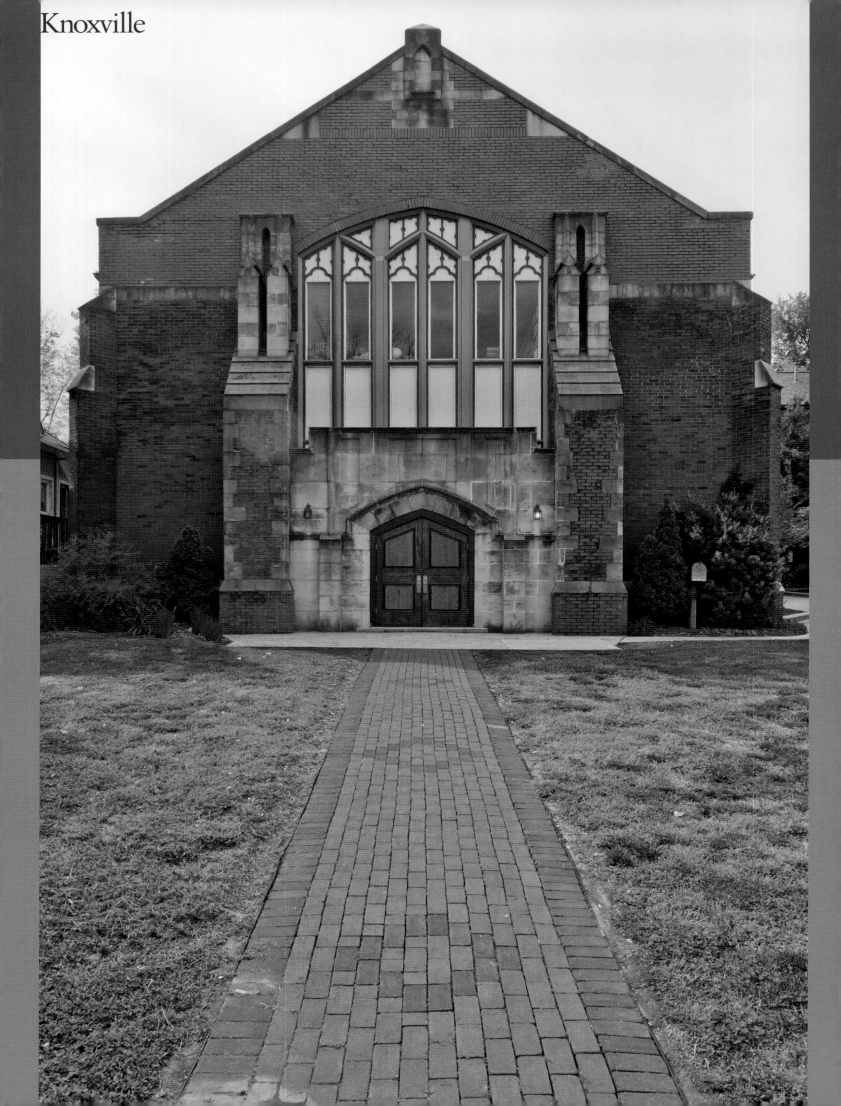

Adjacent to both downtown and UT, Fort Sanders is named for the Union stronghold that repelled a Confederate onslaught in November, 1863. The 20-minute battle was East Tennessee's fiercest and bloodiest in the war. The old earthworks are long gone; whether some trace of them is discernible, in the peculiar contours of certain yards, is a matter of sometimes heated dispute.

The neighborhood has been home to many artists, musicians, and writers, but no one has immortalized it like James Agee, whose prose poem "Knoxville: Summer 1915"--later included in his Pulitzer-winning novel, A Death In the Family—describes its "middlesized gracefully fretted wood houses built in the late nineties and early nineteen hundreds, with small front and side and more spacious back yards, and trees in the yards." A block from the site of his family's long-vanished house, a small park commemorates Agee's memory.

Despite major changes wrought by a rapidly expanding hospital, an encroaching university, and the dozens of modern collegiate apartment buildings that have rendered Fort Sanders East Tennessee's most densely populated census district, some of the once-graceful neighborhood's old character remains.

Photos these pages by Gary Pope

Several of Knoxville's close-in historic neighborhoods have been reviving to one degree or another—Fort Sanders, Parkridge, Island Home, Mechanicsville, Old North, they all have different stories, with some successes—but none has bounced back quite as dramatically as the little neighborhood, just across the highway from downtown, known as Fourth & Gill.

This Victorian-era "trolleyburb" developed in the late 19th century, constructed mostly of wood houses built close together, often in styles borrowed from Knoxville's own residential architect, George Barber, as a refuge for many of the city's successful professionals and downtown shopkeepers. After interstate construction severed and destroyed parts of it beginning in the 1950s, it might have appeared to be a goner, a derelict and crime-ridden fire trap riddled with vacancy, and seldom seen by suburban Knoxvillians. However, beginning in the 1970s, idealistic homeowners began buying into the neighborhood, house by house. The piecemeal redevelopment, eventually helped along by historic zoning, took decades, but today it's a showplace, and many of its homes are more expensive than the suburban average. Once considered a daring place to live, Fourth & Gill has become such a family neighborhood that its community Halloween parties have become an attraction for families who live miles away. Photos these pages by Gary Heatherly

Knoxville

For most of the 20th century, one of Knoxville's most-often-bemoaned lacks was that of a civic art museum. In the early 1960s, art lovers established a small gallery in a house on Kingston Pike, but major funding for a more significant museum came by way of mobile-home magnate Jim Clayton. Designed by well-known modernist Edward Larrabee Barnes and completed in 1990, on World's Fair Park—on the site of what had been, eight years earlier, the Japan Pavilion. Nearby downtown and UT, the Knoxville Museum of Art has become a familiar institution, hosting both academic art shows and crowd-pleasing jazz and blues concerts.

Photo by Gary Pope ▲

Photos by Sheena Patrick ▼▲

138

Photos this page by Sheena Patrick

▲▼ Photo by Gary Heatherly

Photo by Stephanie Norwood

Visual art had not been a major part of Knoxville's cultural life until the coalescing of galleries downtown, especially in and near the Emporium on the 100 block of Gay Street. A former 1890s department store, the Emporium has become a multi-purpose arts mecca, with multiple levels of galleries, studios, offices of arts and cultural organizations (like the venerable Knoxville Symphony Orchestra) , and an intimate performance space used for small jazz, poetry, and even hip-hop events. Even with all that, the old building's upper floors are devoted to residential apartments. Once a month, First Friday openings attract thousands of strollers to downtown's museums, galleries, and art studios. Even the university, has a permanent presence with its Downtown Gallery, which often gets more traffic than its older, larger gallery on campus. At left a musician plays his pipe to the night at an open space on Market Square.

Photos this page by Gary Heatherly

Ensconced among hills, with lots of hidden places developers never got to—and also industrial areas so long abandoned they have begun to return to nature--Knoxville has rediscovered its great outdoors, especially on the south side of town, where two deep quarry lakes, leftover from long-ago marble and limestone operations—present scenes no one would expect to find in a city.

Established more than a century ago, Ijams Nature Center, in particular, may be unlike anywhere in the world. Originally a modest wooded bird sanctuary by the river, founded by a professional illustrator who was a member of America's original conservationist movement, it has exploded in size in recent years to include two large former quarries that happened to be close by, leaving an extraordinary variety of scenes, including open fields, weird canyons, deep jungles, and even an odd, dusty, desert-like slope, within a concentrated area.

Photos these pages by Sheena Patrick

Knoxville

Photo by David Luttrell

Photo by Sheena Patrick

Photo by Scott Bu...

A lot of Knoxville's recent excitement has to do with food. The national locovore movement happened to coincide with the rebirth of Knoxville's long-dormant (but never quite dead) Market Square. Since 1854, the old square has favored local producers, usually by policy, but Charlotte Tolley, the young former Memphian who helped revived the farmers' market, is the first in decades who has made it stick. Regional food suppliers Cruze Dairy and Benton's Bacon, which have received national press, are enthusiastic participants.

▲▼ Photos by David Luttrell

▲▲ Sheena Patrick

Cruze Dairy
A Farm F...

Light

$2.00 BUNCH

CR
SAUTEED, STEA

www.Cruzeda...

ton Bank

CruzeFa
A Far...

CruzeFa

CRUZE DAIRY

WELCOME TO
CRUZE FARM
MILK BAR
COME GET SOME
SPECIAL JERSEY COW MILK
AND
AWESOME DELICIOUS
INDIAN FOOD AND
MADE BUTTERMILK BISCUIT
AND CORN BREAD !!

IMPORTANT !
VERY DELIC

FROM
CHEF MANJIT

ONE
WAY

WHOLE   LIGHT   CHOCOLATE   BUTTER   COFFEE   WHITE...

CRUZE DAIRY

Photos by Sheena Patrick ▶▶▶

Knoxville

Part of what's new in Knoxville is its discovery of its creative past. The city's particularly well known for its role in nurturing the development of folk, country, and bluegrass music, beginning perhaps with the blind buskers who played at the old Southern station more than a century ago, but eventually including major figures like Roy Acuff, Chet Atkins, and Dolly Parton, all of whom started their professional careers in downtown Knoxville. Hank Williams, the subject of the plaque below, wasn't as fortunate with the city; he spent the last evening of his life, New Year's Eve, 1952, at Gay Street's Andrew Johnson Hotel. The next morning, he was dead at age 29.

CRADLE OF
COUNTRY MUSIC TOUR

No. 3 ANDREW JOHNSON HOTEL

The Andrew Johnson Hotel's top floor was the original site for WNOX's live country music variety show *The Midday Merry-Go-Round*. An early star of the show was a little known fiddler named Roy Acuff. The rowdy fans and musicians who crowded the hotel's elevator and lobby brought complaints which forced WNOX to hold its live shows elsewhere.

On New Year's Eve, 1952, Hank Williams checked into the hotel for what would be the final hours of his life. Though he was pronounced dead in West Virginia, many believe Williams was dead before his teenaged chauffeur carried him out of this hotel.

Photo by Gary Pope ◀

▲▼ Photo by Scott Busby

KNOXVILLE'S MARKET HOUSE

Knoxville's first Market House, opened on Main Avenue between Walnut and Market Streets in 1816, and the second and third on this square in 1854 and 1897, long served for the sale of farm products, colorful center of ... 64 the Market ... powder magazine ... of citizens. Th... ...ced by th...

NaNNaNNaN
NaNNaNNaN

NaNNaNNaN

Knoxville

Most of Knoxville's architecture dates from after the Civil War, but a few remnants of a much-earlier era remain here and there, visible to those who know what to look for. The Bijou, open in 1909 and one of Tennessee's oldest theaters, has hosted performers ranging from the Marx Brothers and John Phillip Sousa to Tony Bennett and Joan Baez. Barely two blocks away from another historic theater, the Tennessee, the smaller Bijou typically puts on a couple of shows every week.

Most who visit the Bijou know the theater itself is old, but may not realize the front part of its building, which houses the lobby and the restaurant known as the Bistro, is nearly twice as old as the historic theater. One of Knoxville's oldest buildings, the Lamar House, as it was known, is one of only three dating from its state-capital era. Constructed as a residence by Irish immigrant Thomas Humes in 1816, it served as a hotel for most of the 19th and 20th centuries. An uphill battle to save it from demolition coalesced the vigorous nonprofit known as Knox Heritage.

The Bistro at the Bijou occupies a space that has been used by several restaurants and bars since the 1850s. The current management celebrates Knoxville's lively musical history; former Knoxvillian Roy Acuff, who began his career fiddling for audiences on Gay Street in the 1930s, later created a country-music empire in Nashville. Today, other young performers, including occasional fiddlers, perform in this room, the oldest room in Knoxville that's regularly open to the public.

Photo by Gary Pope

Photo by David Luttrell

In the latter 20th century, some festival organizers bemoaned the assumption that Knoxville was inherently unfestive, unlikely to come out for festivals that didn't involve football games. That seems to have changed somewhat, as the city's annual Knoxville Brewers Jam, held every October on World's Fair Park, seems to demonstrate. Breweries from across the Southeast bring their best ales, as Knoxville's best local bands perform. The city once had plans to build its new convention center on this grassy patch known as the South Lawn. However, the Urban Land Institute, in town to advise on the convention center project, happened to be here the evening in 1999 when rock legend John Fogerty played to a huge crowd on the South Lawn, under a full moon. The consultants advised the city to move the convention-center project elsewhere; in their opinion, live music for big crowds on the grass was the highest and best use for the site.

Photos these pages by Gary Heatherly

Knoxville

The city continues to breed performers, like singer-song-writer Mic Harrison, left, who has earned some national acclaim; the band known as Guy Marshall, which is really husband-wife team Sarrenna and Adam McNulty; and Jack Rentfro, a former journalist who has carved his own niche as a far-offbeat spoken-word poetry-and-jazz performance artist. At right is a whimsical sculpture by Knoxville's own glass artist Richard Jolley.

Photos these pages by Gary Heatherly

Knoxville

A legend to a certain generation of Knoxville's counterculture, singer-songwriter Maggie Longmire picks up new fans every time she performs. She was once a lead singer for the alt-country group the Lonesome Coyotes, who had some national success in the 1970s, and still re-unite on a semi-regular basis.

Photos these pages by Gary Heatherly

Page 156: The 1928 Tennessee Theatre, capacity 1,600, is a favored venue for many sorts of acts, from rock and country performances to traveling Broadway shows to symphony concerts and opera productions. It shares its host building, the 1908 Burwell building, with upscale condos and a few offices.

Page 157, above: A public magician performs on Market Square, one of many unplanned results of the old farmers' market's revival.

Page 157, below: In Knoxville's most unusual performance space of recent years, the cave-like nightclub called the World Grotto, an avant-garde musician performs on a didgeridoo. The room has since been remodeled as a more conventional space, but still hosts live music.

Foreground, below: rock-jazz-country impresario Ashley Capps, booker of downtown's historic theaters and one of the founders of the enormous festival Bonnaroo—and writer Jack Neely—in an outdoor audience some years ago.

Photo by Scott Busby

157

Photos by Gary Heatherly

Photo by Jacques Gautreau

Photos these pages by Jacques Gautreau

Knoxville

At the time of the Civil War, Knoxville was known mainly for its past as Tennessee's former capital. But thanks in large part to its natural resources and rail connections, the city bloomed as an important industrial center in the half-century after the war, and much of its architecture reflects that era of factories and wholesale houses. Downtown's pre-1930s buildings are especially prized. On previous pages, some of the ca. 1890s wholesale houses of Jackson Avenue, now in the Old City, and the 1905 L&N station, now a specialized public high school. Knoxville's eclectic culture makes room for bohemians and Kerbela Temple Masons.

Photos these pages by Jacques Gautreau

Knoxville

Photo by Jacques Gautreau

Always a city of contrasts, Knoxville sometimes presents too much to take in at once.
On Gay Street, the entrance to Yee Haw, a
print shop that specialized in 19th-century
letter-press equipment, shows a forgotten retailer's old entry mosaic, as across the street,
an optimistic developer's banner heralds
a residential project that never quite happened. Meanwhile, next door to the left,

Photo by Gary Heatherly

Mast General Store has proved itself more successful than even its boosters expected. Nationally known for posters, magazine illustrations, and prominent album covers, Yee Haw is now known as Pioneer House.

Above, an illusory, twin office building seems to frame an old and familiar celestial object.

Knoxville

Photo by Gary Heatherly

Gay Street was East Tennessee's highest concentration of theaters in the 19th-century vaudeville era, and it's maintaining that tradition. At left, the breathtaking Tennessee Theatre—more than one performer on its stage has likened it to a Faberge egg—has been Knoxville's fanciest theater since 1928, but a recent multi-million-dollar renovation

166

Photo by Stephanie Norwood

brought out rococo detail even the old-tim-ers had forgotten about. At right, the Regal Riviera, an eight-screen cineplex on the site of a 1920s theater by the same name is just half a block from the Tennessee. Both draw crowds every week, and are credited with sustaining business in the vicinity, especially restaurants.

Knoxville

Formed by the confluence of the Holston and French Broad Rivers just a couple miles upstream from downtown, the Tennessee River was Knoxville's life blood when the city was founded in 1791, and in the 19th century was important to industry, as stern-wheel paddle boats took freight as far as New Orleans. By the 20th century, more and more ignored, even avoided for its associations with waste, stench, and crime. In the 21st century, though, clean-water practices and riverfront development have made it a more appealing river for recreation, attracting pleasure boats, excursion boats, and recently even canoeing, kayaking, and paddle boarding.

Photos this page by Stephanie Norwood

Photo by Gary Heatherly

Knoxville

Photo by Gary Pope

Knoxville's architecture offers a little bit of everything, from the glassy heights of the modernist and post-modernist Plaza Tower and Riverview Tower, built successively by the colorful Butcher brothers, known for their controversial banking practices; to the nude caryatids of the 1905 Miller's Department Store (now an office building) to the late-1920s moderne lines of the Medical Arts Building, now residential.

▲ ▲ Photo by David Luttrell

Photo by Gary Pope

It may say something that the most prominent survivor of the 1982 World's Fair is one of its oldest buildings, the 1905 L&N railroad station, now a selective public high school specializing in science and technology. Flags in the foreground commemorate international participants in the exposition. The stone structure just beyond the flags is the East Tennessee Veterans' Memorial. Most of the old fairgrounds is now a public park.

◀ Photo by Gary Heatherly

Photo by Jacques Gautreau ▶

Knoxville

Photo by Gary Pope

Photo by Jacques Gautreau

Knoxville

No longer a city that shuts down after dark, downtown Knoxville hosts dozens of bars and restaurants that compete for the night-owl crowd well past midnight. Fireworks aren't an everyday thing, though. Knoxville makes a big deal for the Fourth of July, but an even bigger deal for the Labor Day weekend event known as Boomsday, one of the largest annual fireworks displays in the South, it attracts an estimated crowd of 400,000—not counting those who watch from home in the suburbs.

Photo by Gary Heatherly

Knoxville

from a photo by Gary Pope of the Sergei Rachmaninoff sculpture   178

Profiles in Excellence

Profiles appear in the book in the order in which the organizations were established in Knoxville.

UNIVERSITY OF TENNESSEE SYSTEM

Educating. Discovering. Connecting.

The University of Tennessee System is composed of campuses at Knoxville, Chattanooga, and Martin; the Health Science Center at Memphis; the Space Institute at Tullahoma; and the statewide Institute of Agriculture and Institute for Public Service. Between UT Extension offices in each of Tennessee's 95 counties,

A UT education helps students plan for the future.

regional AgResearch and Institute for Public Service centers, UT Martin's off-campus centers throughout West Tennessee; and medical, dental, and pharmacy clinical rotation sites, the University of Tennessee System is a critical resource to every part of the state.

A MISSION TO EDUCATE

Approximately 50,000 students are enrolled at University of Tennessee campuses, which produce almost 10,000 new graduates annually. The University of Tennessee boasts three of the top four graduation rates among public higher education institutions in Tennessee. The UT System Administration's Strategic Plan, developed and implemented under the leadership of UT President Joe DiPietro, aligns university priorities with the 2010 Complete College Tennessee Act to ensure ever-improving outcomes in student retention and graduation. Success in

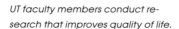

UT faculty members conduct research that improves quality of life.

achieving the Strategic Plan's goals will grow economic opportunity for all Tennesseans by enhancing the state's workforce – a key priority of Tennessee Governor Bill Haslam – and competitive positioning for jobs of the future.

A MISSION TO DISCOVER

The University's partnership with Oak Ridge National Laboratory (ORNL) sets UT apart from most public universities nationwide. More than 100 UT faculty members have joint appointments at ORNL, and their discoveries create intellectual property jointly owned by UT and ORNL. UT and ORNL also have five joint institutes concentrating on advanced materials, heavy ion research, biological sciences, neutron sciences, and computational sciences, and ten world-class scientists have been appointed as UT-ORNL Governor's Chairs. Alternative energy is one of the main thrusts of UT System research efforts. The university has an established history of work in this sector and in turning that

research into economic development gains for the state.

A MISSION TO CONNECT

Outreach and service to all Tennesseans comprise the third part of the UT System's three-part mission to educate, discover, and connect. Hundreds of adults and children statewide are helped every year by medical and dental clinics of the UT Health Science Center. UT Extension made more than 5.3 million contacts in providing assistance to Tennesseans with financial and crisis counseling, nutrition, and combating diseases like Type 2 diabetes. The Institute for Public Service (IPS) assisted on projects that led to more than $420 million in economic impact for Tennessee in the last year.

Because of the fundamental role of UT in Tennessee's economic vitality and quality of life, the University of Tennessee and the state of Tennessee enjoy mutually determined success.

UT students touch lives while receiving hands-on experiences.

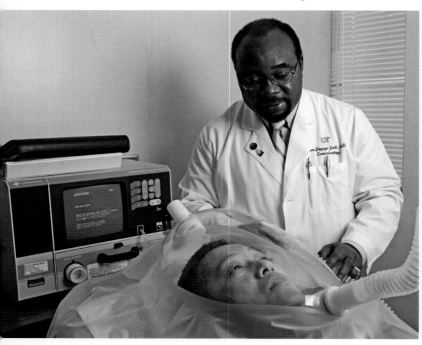

THE UNIVERSITY OF TENNESSEE, KNOXVILLE

History Emanates From the 'Hallowed Hill'

The more than a quarter million graduates of the University of Tennessee, Knoxville, may have arrived at the university with their own individual dreams and ambitions, but they left with a common focus and much more than a diploma. From their first days on-campus, students are filled with the passion that the school's faculty

and staff have for advancing the mission of the university: to move forward the frontiers of human knowledge and enrich and elevate the citizens of the state of Tennessee, the nation, and the world.

An untold number of the university's alumni have done just that. Armed with their degrees from more than 300 programs offered by the university's 11 colleges, these leaders have helped write history as they excelled in fields such as medicine, business, agriculture, engineering, law, public service, and athletics.

UT Knoxville is recognized as the preeminent research-based land-grant university in Tennessee. The university embodies the spirit of excellence in teaching, research, scholarship, creative activity, outreach, and engagement attained by the nation's finest public research institutions.

ROOTED IN THE PAST, FOCUSED ON THE FUTURE

UT Knoxville was founded as Blount College in 1794, just 11 years after the last British troops left the newly independent United States and two years before Tennessee became the 16th star in the American flag. Over the next half century, the fledgling school endured the growing pains of adolescence that led to several closings and name changes. In 1826, the school moved to its present site on "the Hill" and 53 years later was designated by the state legislature as Tennessee's federal land-grant institution.

The twentieth century saw unprecedented growth and expansion with UT Knoxville's colleges of law and medicine and the beginning of its storied athletics program. The university is working toward an aggressive

goal of becoming a Top 25 public research university in the next decade. The strategic goals and their momentum are transforming the campus, enhancing the student experience and broadening the university's research, outreach and economic impact throughout the state.

"By identifying our top priorities and metrics for success, we strengthen the university for the benefit of our students, all Tennesseans, and the world," Chancellor Jimmy G. Cheek said. "Performing quality research is critically important to becoming a Top 25 institution. The money invested advances knowledge and builds our economy through new jobs and innovation."

Fueling these efforts is its management partnership with Battelle Corp. to run the Oak Ridge National Laboratory, the nation's largest government science and energy lab. The lab is central to the state's technology – and science-driven economy and brings together world-class scientists to tackle the mysteries of the universe. UT students benefit from a wide array of research opportunities.

Big Orange pride runs deep throughout the community, and UT students, faculty, and staff live the Volunteer Creed by serving others. From non-profit fundraisers to houses, students serve in schools, churches, and social service agencies throughout East Tennessee. Faculty lend their expertise in many ways that include leading health clinics,

tackling chronic homelessness, contributing to urban design and overseeing community-based school programs. The 560-acre campus also serves as the community's cultural hub for the arts by sharing numerous music, theater, and fine arts offerings throughout the year.

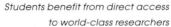

Students benefit from direct access to world-class researchers

KNOXVILLE CHAMBER
Driving Regional Economic Prosperity

I t came as little surprise when the American Chamber of Commerce Executives recognized the Knoxville Chamber as the National Chamber of the Year in 2011. For more than 150 years, the Knoxville Chamber has been the clarion voice speaking on behalf of the business community for Knoxville and the surrounding area. Over this century

and a half of service, the organization has never deviated from its mission of "Driving Regional Economic Prosperity."

"When you boil down our essence as an organization to its simplest form, it can be described with one word – jobs," Mike Edwards, Chamber president and CEO, said. "Our mission of Driving Regional Economic Prosperity begins and ends with making sure the area's residents are provided opportunities to prosper and contribute to the greater good of the community. That means we wake up every day striving to help retain and grow the businesses that already call our community home and

inspired to identify and recruit new business to the area."

Under the direction of the 45 business leaders who make up the Chamber's Board of Directors, the Chamber's 28 full-time professionals provide a broad range of services to its 2,200 members as well as the community at-large by supporting existing business, recruiting new companies to the region,

Knoxville Chamber offices on Market Square ▲

Photos by Laddy Fields

Knoxville Skyline ▶

striving to establish a world-class workforce, and advocating for business-friendly government. Chamber members receive access to cutting-edge services and programs designed to support business growth and make Knoxville America's Best Business Address®. Chamber member companies range from large corporations to small start-ups and micro-businesses. Small businesses make up more than 80 percent of the Chamber's membership.

The Knoxville Chamber sets itself apart from other business organizations in the area by leading

a regional economic development initiative, Innovation Valley. Experience shows that a regional approach to economic development offers the most advantages to businesses planning a corporate relocation or expansion and the communities involved. The Chamber's partnership with other area economic development agencies strengthens the region's collective assets.

"I appreciate the work of the Knoxville Chamber in recruiting new jobs to Knox County," remarked Knox County Mayor Tim Burchett. "Their work helps

ensure that we have a strong local economy that not only attracts new industry, but also helps our existing businesses grow in this community."

Market Square ▲

Photo by Laddy Fields

The Sunsphere was built for the 1982 World's Fair and is now an iconic symbol for the city. ▼ Photo by Laddy Fields

City of Knoxville Mayor Madeline Rogero also recognizes the important role the Chamber plays in the community's economic development. "The Knoxville Chamber is our go-to partner on numerous projects, from multi-million dollar developments to a business accelerator for budding entrepreneurs," she said. "The Chamber understands that in order to attract, develop and retain business we must have a stellar quality of life. Clean water, transportation options, recreational activities and environmentally sound practices all contribute to a great quality of life and help to make for a green and healthy community. I am confident that the Chamber's practical approach to help make Knoxville a green city and its number one mission of creating jobs will benefit generations to come."

AN HISTORIC PAST EQUIPPED FOR THE FUTURE

Considering that the business roots of Knoxville run deep in the downtown heart of the city, it is perhaps fitting that the Chamber now calls the city's historic Market Square district its home. In the mid-1800s the establishment of a Market House on the Square provided farmers from across East Tennessee a venue for selling their merchandise, establishing the Square as Knoxville's early commercial center. Today, the Chamber is housed in an historic building that has been completely refurbished to offer state-of-the-art facilities for the area's business community to convene. The Chamber is justifiably proud of the fact that its move to Market Square in 2005 helped spur a renaissance of the once neglected Square. Residents from throughout the region now recognize downtown as a desirable place to live, work, and play.

Nestled in the heart of the Smoky Mountains, the city of Knoxville has served as a regional hub since its founding in 1791. Firmly entrenched in the best of its Appalachian roots – strong work ethic, family-centered community, and intense respect for the surrounding natural beauty – the city is poised for its future in the technology-based world of business.

Home to the University of Tennessee-Knoxville and Oak Ridge National Laboratory, the region's diverse employer base fosters innovation and entrepreneurialism. Several well-known corporate brands also call the area home, including Scripps Networks Interactive (HGTV, Food

University of Tennessee, Ayers Hall ▲
Photo by Laddy Fields

Network, DIY, Cooking Channel, Travel Channel, and GAC), Bush Brothers & Company, Clayton Homes, Pilot Flying J, Regal Entertainment Group, Jewelry Television, and Radio Systems Corporation, just to name a few.

The quarry at Fort Dickerson, a crown jewel of Knoxville's Urban Wilderness, is located less than two miles from downtown. ▼
Photo by Laddy Fields

Donwtown Knoxville nestled in the foothills of the Smoky Mountains ▼   Photo by Laddy Fields

ROWE TRANSFER

Moving American Industry Since 1883

Buffalo Bill Cody was premiering his "Wild West Show" in Omaha, Nebraska and the Brooklyn Bridge was opening amidst Presidential fanfare in New York City in 1883 when entrepreneur David Rowe first opened the doors to the business that would bear his name in Knoxville. Rowe founded a transfer company that he operated

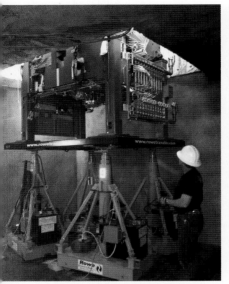

A 30-ton particle accelerator is lowered 20-feet below the streets of Birmingham, AL.

A 1966 photo shows part of a Saturn rocket being transported over the winding roads of middle Tennessee.

In the early 1900s horse-drawn carriages provided transfer within the city.

out of the Knoxville train station and used horse-drawn wagons to move products and supplies for businesses such as Knoxville Iron Works, Dixie Cement and Knoxville Woolen Mills, among others. The flood of new residents moving to the Knoxville area and clamoring for jobs with these companies would boost the city's population from 5,000 in 1860 to more than 32,000 by the turn of the century. Rowe Transfer took great pride in moving many of those new arrivals and their possessions to burgeoning neighborhoods throughout the Knoxville area.

More than a century later, the professional staff at Rowe Transfer continues to provide much more than moving services. The company has evolved into the "go to" solution provider for all types of rigging, crating, warehousing, and transportation projects. Specializing in the relocation, rigging, and installation of medical and industrial operations, Rowe is the one-stop turnkey logistical center for moving everything from a single MRI machine to relocating an entire manufacturing plant.

ON TIME SERVICES . . . GUARANTEED

Rowe Transfer maintains its own fleet of trucks and a large variety of trailers to accommodate almost any type of cargo. Rowe's professional drivers complete stringent safety and training programs to ensure they meet all DOT requirements. In addition, specially trained and certified drivers can be relied upon to provide the highest quality of services for unique projects. They specialize in rigging medical imaging and radiological pharmaceutical equipment. Rowe has been the name that satisfied customers have turned to with confidence for moves across town, across the country, and across international waters.

"We have diversified over the years and developed into a very specialized niche in the industry," states Bart Browning, Sales Representative with Rowe. "We're now known for moving American industry. Each of our employees takes great pride in what we do and enjoys providing solutions to the many challenging projects we've undertaken over the years, whether it's moving a PET-CT or MRI machine for a hospital in Knoxville, a 100,000 pound cyclotron, or a manufacturing plant to India."

In 1966 Rowe Transfer moved the third stage of NASA's Saturn rocket through the mountains of eastern Tennessee. Regardless of what a client needs, whether it's a long haul or just down the street, Rowe provides individually tailored solutions to meet those needs on time and within budget.

Meeting the needs of their clients requires Rowe to offer a number of highly specialized services:

▶ Crating/International Packaging—Rowe's fully stocked packaging department is capable of creating any size container needed.

▶ Rigging/Machinery Moving—Rowe professionals can move a single piece of equipment or completely disassemble an entire assembly line.

▶ Transportation—Drivers are specially trained to haul machinery, equipment, large objects, medical equipment, or almost anything that clients can't put in a box and ship themselves.

▶ Flat Bed/Heavy Haul—Rowe can load and haul heavy commodities as large as self-contained buildings.

▶ Warehousing—Rowe maintains a 50,000 square foot climate controlled warehouse for storage of clients' goods.

The provision of these specialized services requires careful coordination and spot-on timing by the Rowe team. We understand the urgency of time-sensitive projects and maintain a tight focus on our clients' expectations. The company employs the latest technology, such as GPS truck tracking systems, to accurately calculate delivery time and maintain schedules.

Hyperbaric Chamber similar to one placed at the University of Tennessee Veterinary Hospital.

An MRI building weighing 55 tons is readied for its journey to Milwaukee, WS from Johnson City, TN.

In addition, Rowe has had extensive experience meeting the special needs for a variety of different types of equipment. Because everything moves in different manners, and people want equipment in hard to reach places, we develop customized solutions and innovative ideas for the unique requirements of each individual customer.

The consistently efficient implementation of these services has led to numerous industry awards, including the Longevity Award from the Specialized Carriers and Rigging Association, for which Rowe Transfer is justifiably proud.

FOCUS ON KNOXVILLE

David Rowe would certainly be proud of the fact that the company he founded in 1883 has evolved today into a leader in one of the most highly specialized niches in the transportation and relocation industry. He would also certainly nod with approval of the role the company plays in improving the quality of life in Knoxville through the sponsorship of local organizations such as the Fellowship of Christian Athletes, Barefoot for Haiti Relief Fund, and the Shriners.

"Going forward to the 21st century, we feel we are in a good position to handle the rapidly changing markets," stated Dan Kaman, the President of Rowe Transfer. "From the original concept of helping people move from one place to another, we have strategically grown to accommodate most any need our clients have for bringing products to market. Sometimes it takes remembering where you were in the past to move through the tough times of the future. Our goal is always to provide excellence in service to any of our clients no matter how large or small."

Heavy Haul of A 55-Ton section of a trenching machine built by Astec Industries in Loudon, TN.

THE KNOXVILLE NEWS SENTINEL

Community Service for More Than a Century

News, it's said, is the rough draft of history. In that capacity, the News Sentinel has been sketching the history of Knoxville for more than 125 years. It was on December 23, 1886, in the middle of a raging snowstorm, that Kentuckian John Tevis Hearn printed the first edition of The Knoxville Sentinel on a steam-operated press from his office above a Gay Street liquor store.

After learning that Knoxville had two morning newspapers but no evening edition, Hearn determined to fill the journalistic void. "Believing that Knoxville has a future," he said, "we shall use every effort to advance the material interests of Knoxville and East Tennessee."

"GIVE LIGHT AND THE PEOPLE WILL FIND THEIR OWN WAY." *NEWS SENTINEL*

WOW! THAT'S A LOT OF LIGHT.

YEAH...IT'S A BIRTHDAY CAKE WITH 125 CANDLES.

► *Charlie Daniel incorporated the company's motto and light-house logo into his cartoon celebrating the News Sentinel's 125th anniversary.*

Hearn is credited with transforming the newspaper industry in Knoxville. Instead of paying a weekly salary, Hearn sold his papers to newsboys who re-sold them to their own customers, thus allowing them to run their own businesses.

A competing newspaper, The Knoxville News, was established in 1921 by Robert P. Scripps and Roy W. Howard. The paper crusaded for the establishment of Smoky Mountains National Park, attacked the state's anti-evolution laws and supported the creation of a modern form of city government.

Knoxville embraced the News. Its circulation grew, and in 1926, Scripps bought the Sentinel and merged the papers. The combined newspaper demonstrated its community leadership during the Civil Rights Movement, when editor Loye Miller's editorial to "Make Knoxville an 'Open City'" helped bring about the peaceful desegregation of the city's businesses.

The Knoxville News-Sentinel published as an afternoon paper until 1986, when it switched to a morning publication. The Knoxville News-Sentinel continued its leadership role in the community and the industry. In 1994 it was among the first newspapers to establish its own website, Knoxnews.com.

In 2002, the paper moved into a new facility with a new, state-of-the-art printing press. That same year, the paper dropped the hyphen from its name to become The Knoxville News Sentinel.

A CLARION VOICE

The Knoxville News Sentinel of today is a multi-media company unmatched in delivering valuable information and services throughout East Tennessee. The News Sentinel aims to be the number one source for news and information in the region and delivers content in print, online, and via mobile and tablet devices.

The company also provides community news through the weekly Shopper-News publications and alternative news through the Metro Pulse. The Greater Knoxville Business Journal reports monthly on the community's economic news, and its Book of Lists is an annual directory of the region's

leading business enterprises. The News Sentinel produces major local events such as Women Today and the Auto Show and manages the Scripps National Spelling Bee for the Southern Appalachia region. The News Sentinel also maintains a growing commercial print and distribution business.

In addition to Knoxnews.com, the newspaper's family of websites now includes GoVolsXtra.com, featuring coverage of University of Tennessee sports, and Knoxville.com, highlighting entertainment news and things to do.

From its inception, the News Sentinel has never aligned itself with any single political party. The paper's hallmark has been that of an active voice in the community opposing corruption and advocating for transparency and fiscal responsibility in government. In 2007, the newspaper filed suit against Knox County government, alleging violations of the state's Open Meetings Act. The lawsuit resulted in 12 politicians being removed from elected office and the county being ordered to obey the "Sunshine Law." The newspaper received several national awards for its effort, including the Associated Press Managing Editors First Amendment Award, the Scripps Howard Foundation's National Journalism Award for Distinguished Service to the First Amendment and the National Headliner Award for Public Service.

In recent years, the newspaper has won several national awards for its digital content, including two Edward R. Murrow Awards for Online Video Documentary, the Online News Association Award for Best Breaking News, the EPpy Award for Best Sports Website and Digital Edge awards for Best Overall Newspaper Website, Best Use of Interactive Media and Best Site Design.

As The Knoxville News Sentinel has been shaped by the community, so too does the

community continue to be shaped by the paper. For more than 100 years, the Sentinel has provided food to families and toys for children at the holidays through the News Sentinel Empty Stocking Fund. This program and the Milk Fund — which assists with nutritional and medical needs for disadvantaged kids, elderly and ill individuals — are managed through the charitable arm of the company, News Sentinel Charities, Inc.

The News Sentinel also produces the News Sentinel Open golf tournament, which is an annual stop on the national PGA Web.com Tour. The News Sentinel Open positively impacts the local economy and donates funds to many local charities.

In addition, the News Sentinel donates more than $1 million in contributions and complementary advertising annually to a variety of civic and charitable organizations which are helping make East Tennessee a better place to live.

President and Publisher Patrick Birmingham keeps in mind the Sentinel's long history of journalistic excellence, advocacy and community service in looking toward the future. "We take our responsibility to serve the public very seriously," he notes. "The News Sentinel has always been a strong advocate for the greatest good. We are an integral part of this community, and we look forward to serving East Tennessee for many years to come."

▲ *The News Sentinel offers award-winning local news coverage in print, online, and via smartphone and tablet.*

▼ *The News Sentinel Empty Stocking Fund provides food baskets to 3,600 families at the holidays. Each basket contains approximately 40 items, including a turkey, fresh produce, canned goods and holiday staples.*

Green by Nature

189

WILLIS OF KNOXVILLE

Solutions for a Risky World

Willis of Knoxville develops and delivers professional insurance, risk management, and human resource consulting for corporations, public entities, institutions, and individuals in East Tennessee and surrounding states. The roots of Willis of Knoxville are woven deep into the fabric of the lives of the people and businesses of the Volunteer State. The Knoxville office can be traced back to 1897 and has grown substantially during the last decade. Willis has a significant presence in Tennessee with over 700 employees and offices in Memphis, Nashville, and Knoxville.

LOCAL COMPANY, GLOBAL REACH

"Clients across the United States in the retail, manufacturing, healthcare, construction, transportation and mining industries turn to us with confidence to serve their needs. Our global resources are delivered locally to help clients realize their highest risk management and business objectives regardless of geography" states Ron Alexander, President and CEO of Willis of Knoxville.

Willis' Knoxville office is part of Willis Group Holdings, a leading global insurance broker that offers its clients the unparalleled resources of a major global company while maintaining a local focus on the people and businesses of eastern Tennessee. Willis has over 400 offices and 17,000 associates worldwide. Willis North America has more than 100 offices and 6,000 associates.

Many of these employees attended local universities and have now made their homes and raised their families in local communities. As such, they are stakeholders in the improvement in the quality of life in these communities through the provision of services integral to the success of private businesses and public entities in today's global climate. The company is a long-time and active Knoxville Chamber member. "Willis and its employees are proud to be a Premier Partner of the Knoxville Chamber," Alexander adds. "We believe in working with our clients and the Chamber to promote economic growth in our region."

COMMITMENT TO SERVICE

Willis of Knoxville's goal is to create a long-term partnership with its clients to provide the protection they and their families need today and in the future. The company specializes in the mining, construction, life sciences, environmental, higher education, transportation, retail and manufacturing industries. Willis is a leader in transparency and continually considers its

Above: Terri Johnson, Receptionist

Below, pictured left to right: Tiffany Harris, Assistant Client Services; Cindy Powell, Assistant Client Services; Connie Gotham, Sr. Client Services Specialist; Francis Horn, VP, Willis National Legal Research Practice; Nicole Rioux, Principal, Client Services; Christine Reid, Sr. Client Services Specialist

clients' best interests throughout every aspect of the business.

Willis' associates have a relentless commitment to service excellence. They begin by listening and acquiring a thorough understanding of client needs in their respective industries. Willis works with clients to provide solutions for expense reduction, cash flow improvement, financial protection and decision making insight. To meet that challenge for its clients, Willis of Knoxville is organized into four divisions.

Willis Human Capital Practice offers a comprehensive suite of brokerage and consulting services to proactively work with organizations to design and deploy key human resource initiatives. Rocky Goode, Andy Rader, John Milam and Nicole Rioux lead the company's local employee benefit and human capital consulting division.

The Property Casualty division specializes in large risk program design and innovative risk transfer programs. The company's local team of Dee Anderson, Alan White and Steven McGhee collaborates with Willis' industry specific resource personnel to develop cost effective solutions for its clients. Willis also affords clients industry specific loss prevention and claims consulting resources.

Bill Hamilton leads the Construction Division which specializes in providing insurance and surety programs to the region's leading general contractors and subcontractors. In addition to insurance, risk management, and surety, Willis offers loss control and OSHA training for clients.

The Mining division of Willis of Knoxville provides insurance and surety programs for the mining industry. Tracy Tucker, Fred Smith III, Fred Smith IV and Mike Ford lead the Mining Division. Willis has developed customized property and casualty coverage for the mining industry through collaboration with Willis' London and Bermuda associates. In addition, the division's team members develop custom surety programs and are considered the North American experts in commercial surety and reclamation bonds for the coal mining industry. Rick Rose, Jeremy Rose and Janice Fennell lead our Commercial Surety Division.

Willis of Knoxville is very proud of the fact that many of the company's associates share their belief in giving back to the communities in which they live. Willis strongly believes in supporting the community by volunteering and contributing to nonprofit organizations and other organizations that work to improve the quality of life and economy of East Tennessee.

Office Leadership from left to right: Alan White, SVP; Fred Smith IV, VP; Rocky Goode, Sr. EVP; Dee Anderson, EVP; Ron Alexander, CEO; Jeremy Rose, VP; Andy Rader, SVP; Bill Hamilton, EVP
Not pictured: John Milam, EVP; Tracy Tucker, EVP; Fred Smith III, SVP and Rick Rose, SVP

JOHNSON & GALYON CONSTRUCTION

Innovation & Integrity Since 1914

A centennial anniversary is always a much-anticipated event regardless of whether the celebrant is a person, an organization, a school, or a business that has endured for 100 years. A rock solid focus on quality, integrity, and innovation has made possible the marking of a century of providing the finest in construction services by the tradesmen and professionals at Johnson & Galyon.

UT Strong Hall completed in 1925.

Cherokee Country Club completed in 1928.

Europe had just been plunged into World War I in 1914 when A.H. Whisman first opened the doors to the business that would become Johnson & Galyon Construction. Whisman remained at the helm of the business until his death in 1936 at which time W.K. Johnson, the company's former bookkeeper, and J.E. Willard, a respected civil engineer, assumed the leadership role. E.L. Galyon joined the company in 1942 as an estimator and the company later evolved into Johnson & Galyon Construction.

Over its century of serving East Tennessee, Johnson & Galyon built a reputation based on tradition and innovation while completing projects on schedule and within budget. Realizing that trust is the all important factor in selecting a contractor for a construction project, each member of the Johnson & Galyon team continues to work hard to earn the trust of new clients while, at the same time, focusing on maintaining the business relationships which the company has valued for decades.

"As a 100-year old company, we've been here long enough to have worked on additions, expansions, and renovations to projects we initially completed years ago on a handshake," states Jim Bush the Chairman of the Board of Johnson & Galyon. "Our company is built on repeat business with several relationships spanning more than 50 years. About 75 percent of our business comes from satisfied repeat clients. That's the highest compliment we can get from clients attesting to the quality of our work. It's something we think about every day, and we work hard to retain that trust."

EXCEEDING EXPECTATIONS

The materials, technology, and tools that the professionals at Johnson & Galyon used to complete the many projects that now bear the firm's name have changed dramatically over the years. But the company is keenly aware that materials, technology, and tools don't construct buildings. People construct buildings. For that reason, the approximately 100 members of the Johnson & Galyon team today make the same commitment to exceed the expectations of their clients that was made by their predecessors a century ago. They embrace the same quality craftsmanship, honorable values, and successful projects that identified the firm in its earliest days while employing today's latest cutting edge technologies and innovations that will better serve their clients. The team's safety and quality control programs are now models for the construction industry.

Serving clients primarily in East Tennessee, Johnson & Galyon provides construction management, general contracting, and design-build services to the healthcare, higher education, religious, manufacturing, and commercial office building sectors. On many occasions, clients have approached the company with only an idea or building concept. They have relied on the talented Johnson & Galyon team to bring their dream to life, working closely with them at each stage of the project to develop strategies that provide reliable budgets, enhanced quality, and lower costs, resulting in outstanding structures.

Below–Lobby of the Eash Tennessee Children's Hospital.
Below Right–University of Tennessee Medical Center

UT Neyland Stadium Peyton Manning Locker Room.

Knoxville Station Transit Center.

"Johnson & Galyon has had a long and productive history with East Tennessee Children's Hospital," states Keith D. Goodwin, the hospital's CEO. "Almost without exception they have been the construction experts we have looked to when we needed to build or renovate facilities. Their understanding of our business, their ability to find efficient solutions to challenging facility challenges, their historic understanding of how we got to where we are and their sensitivity to our pediatric patients and their families make them the partner of choice."

Johnson & Galyon has quickly become a leader in Green and LEED-certified building construction. Developed by the U.S. Green Building Council, LEED (Leadership in Energy and Environmental Design) sets a benchmark for design, construction, and operation of high-performance green buildings. LEED certification provides independent, third-party verification that a building, home, or community was designed and built using strategies aimed at achieving high performance in key areas of human and environmental health.

The team at Johnson & Galyon is accustomed to working with designers and owners to improve a building's efficiency and document the required processes for LEED certification. The team is skilled in LEED construction and commissioning, and has recently completed seven LEED projects for both government and private sector owners, including platinum, gold, and silver level certifications.

Over its century of operation, Johnson & Galyon has taken great pride in its assistance to helping the Knoxville community thrive. That commitment is reflected in the firm's history of community involvement through our time and resources. "Our company's participation with United Way, East Tennessee Children's Hospital, the Emerald Youth Foundation, Boy's and Girl's Clubs, Scouts, and many other community organizations is driven by the culture developed over the last 100 years. Giving back is what East Tennesseans do and we're an East Tennessee company," commented Doug Kennedy, Johnson & Galyon's CEO.

Howard Baker Federal Courthouse, formerly Whittle Communications,

Below–Tennova-North Knoxville Medical Center.
Below Left–Covenant Health's Parkwest Medical Center

BarberMcMurry Architects
Passion, Integrity, Dependability and Service

The King Family Library Grand Reading Room
PHOTO BY JEFFREY JACOBS

George F. Barber arrived in Knoxville from his native DeKalb, Illinois in 1888, a time when areas of the former Confederacy were in the midst of physically rebuilding. An experienced builder and architect, Barber founded his primarily residential architectural practice in Knoxville, and quickly developed an international following with his series of "plan books" created by his Knoxville studio staff. Those homes can be found around the world today.

Birth of a Family Business

George Barber's son, Charles, followed him into the practice. After completing the acclaimed "Beaux Arts" tour of European architecture, Charles chose to remain in Knoxville where he partnered in an architectural design practice with E.A. Seahorn, Dean Parmelee, and his cousin, David West Barber. In 1915, Ben F. McMurry joined Barber in establishing Barber & McMurry Architects. The partners launched into an active practice of recognized styles of design and quickly gained a reputation as leading residential architects.

Beginning in the 1920s, Barber & McMurry expanded its practice to include the design of educational facilities, churches, commercial office properties, and multi-family residential. The firm developed an especially impressive portfolio in the field of educational architecture, most significantly with the University of Tennessee. It was not long before many of the buildings on the Knoxville campus bore the distinctive Barber & McMurry signature. In the 1940s and 1950s, the firm acquired a reputation throughout the Southeast as a specialist in the design of churches. During the same time period, Barber & McMurry began to produce healthcare architecture. They designed many of the new hospitals, medical office buildings, and related facilities for regional healthcare systems headquartered in the area. In 1964, Barber & McMurry was commissioned to design the first regional hospital dedicated to serving children. The firm proudly continues to work at East Tennessee Children's Hospital today.

A Century of Service

Few firms have the distinction of practicing architecture for nearly 100 years, so the people rooted in the Barber McMurry tradition understand the value of long-term relationships. More than 85 percent of their work is from repeat clients. The many long-term relationships BMa enjoys are a reflection of their dedication to delivering outstanding service with passion and integrity.

The firm is now known simply as BarberMcMurry

Two Rivers Church main entrance and steeple, at sunrise
PHOTO BY JEFFREY JACOBS

BarberMcMurry office, downtown Knoxville
PHOTO BY DENISE RETALLACK

architects or BMa. The merging of these two names reflect the singular unified approach BMa takes for every project. That is to aggressively pursue innovative solutions to each client's most fundamental challenges. BMa believes that the best ideas evolve from an engaged and collaborative design process with their clients, their consultants, and within their own firm.

BMa strives to produce meaningful architecture that inspires the lives of their clients and community. Their design is well-crafted, both aesthetically and functionally. BMa's service is client focused and responsive, and they believe in a working partnership where effective collaboration helps their clients achieve their goals and objectives.

BMa's portfolio today comprises a well-rounded base of experience. While the firm's scope of services has expanded and the technology its professionals employ is cutting edge, the philosophical fundamentals of Charles Barber almost a century ago remain unchanged – "Every building must express character in its design and in its effect upon those who use and experience it."

A Quality Approach

BMa's project leader is always an equity partner in the firm who is committed to client accountability and responsiveness. A seasoned project manager is teamed with an intern architect to provide a fresh outlook on the design process. This combination creates an environment that leverages each person's passions and unique perspective. The result yields common ownership, a fresh attitude to problem solving and seasoned practicality - a realistic approach to design that BMa clients have come to appreciate.

All BMa employees invest in the firm's resources through continuing education and peer review sharing. A formal lessons-learned process assures that valuable experiences gained in the design of one project or project type is shared with others. This circulation of ideas helps BMa continually elevate the level of design strength.

BMa participates in a semi-annual gathering of peer firms from around the country called the Design Network. They meet to exchange best practices and new ideas in client service, technology, and employee development. This exchange provides extremely valuable information that directly benefits BMa clients.

Sustainable Practice

BarberMcMurry architects incorporates proven sustainable design techniques and practices into each project the firm undertakes. Many of the firm's staff have achieved LEED Accredited Professional status, a designation that underscores a commitment to positively contributing to the built

Church of the Ascension interior column capital detail
PHOTO BY JACK PARKER

environment by embracing sustainable, energy-efficient design, and encouraging clients to build with enduring materials that minimize life cycle maintenance costs. The preservation of the natural resources with which the region is so richly blessed is an integral part of each design solution that BMa carefully crafts

for its clients. The firm remains committed to working toward a sustainable future through the implementation of design concepts and business practices that improve the social and environmental well-being of each community.

The University of Tennessee Medical Center, Heart Hospital   PHOTO BY JEFFREY JACOBS

East Tennessee Children's Hospital, Main Lobby
PHOTO BY JEFFREY JACOBS

COMMUNITY INVOLVEMENT

BMa's philosophy regarding community involvement is rooted in "responsibility." The firm has created a charitable giving fund equal to roughly 25 percent of its annual profit. In addition, BMa is committed to the One Percent Initiative, a program to encourage architects to donate on an annual basis one percent of their time to pro bono services for non-profit organizations in need of architectural services. In addition, BMa is proud of its 100 percent employee participation in the United Way campaign and the community service performed by the entire staff.

ACCOLADES:

HISTORY OF SUCCESS, GROUNDED IN THE PRESENT, POISED FOR THE FUTURE

Being the oldest and one of the largest architectural firms in East Tennessee, is in itself an impressive tribute to BMa's past, but it is the firm's long list of signature projects that truly

The new University Center at the University of Tennessee
RENDERINGS BY BARBERMcMURRY architects

identify the impact on the city and the region. As impressive as the firm's portfolio may be, an even greater reward is having a panel of their peer judges highlight their projects as exceptional. That recognition has come in numerous awards from diverse groups. Among the most noted designs of current projects include:

► The Residences at Eastport:
 • LEED Platinum
 • 2013 Tennessee Historical Commission Certificate of Merit
 • U.S. Green Building Council —East Tennessee Chapter Green Project Award

The Natalie L. Haslam Music Center, the University of Tennessee, Knoxville   PHOTO BY DENISE RETALLACK   *Church of the Ascension*

- Tennessee Housing Development Agency Best in Innovation Award
- Knox Heritage | Knox County Mayor's Award
- East Tennessee Preservation Alliance Award
- Keep Knoxville Beautiful Orchid Award

► University of Tennessee Medical Center Heart Hospital: International Acclaim

► Le Conte Medical Center: Healthcare Design Magazine Project Awards

► King Family Library: Southeast Central Construction Institute Award of Merit

► East Tennessee Children's Hospital: AIA East Tennessee Award of Merit

► Pellissippi State Community College Magnolia Campus: AIA Gulf States Award of Merit

► Webb School of Knoxville: American School and University Award of Honor

► University of Tennessee—Music Center, Student Center, Joint Institute for Advanced Material Sciences: LEED Silver

► Past projects that have achieved landmark status include:

► Tennessee General Building

► Smoky Mountains National Park Headquarters

► Church Street United Methodist Church

► Holston Hills Country Club

► Blackberry Farm

► Tennessee Smokies Stadium

Church Street United Methodist Church, as seen from Henley Street in Downtown Knoxville
PHOTO BY JACK PARKER

"Great success renders great responsibility," says Chuck Griffin, AIA, the President of BarberMcMurry architects. "Each of us at BarberMcMurry realizes the importance of our firm's legacy. Our commitment to service, and being a trusted advisor to our clients, is and will continue to be the focus of our firm."

"Our goal at BMa is to deliver thoughtful design solutions created with passion to help our clients achieve their goals…in the end, our client's needs must be our first priority," adds the firm's Senior Vice-President Kelly Headden, AIA.

PHOTO BY JACK PARKER

ZEBRAlliance (Zero Energy Building Residence Alliance) homes, Oak Ridge National Laboratory

PHOTO BY JEFFREY JACOBS

COVENANT HEALTH

Excellent. Together.

From battleground to operating room and from atom bomb to gamma knife, Covenant Health hospitals have been central figures in battles of life and death for nearly a century.

Covenant Health was created in 1996 when Fort Sanders Health System of Knoxville and MMC HealthCare of Oak Ridge consolidated, uniting hundreds of doctors, hospitals and facilities in an alliance to improve the health and quality of life in East

RIVERSIDE-FORT SANDERS HOSPITAL, KNOXVILLE, TENN.—40

Above: A color postcard from the 1940s of Riverside-Fort Sanders Hospital, one of the founding organizations of Covenant Health.
Below: Parkwest Medical Center, West Knoxville's premier medical facility and one of Covenant Health's seven acute care hospitals.

Tennessee. The founding organizations believed that by combining forces, they could do more to safeguard the health of the community, a value deeply entrenched in their respective historical roots.

A SITE FOR HEALING, 150 YEARS AFTER CIVIL WAR

In 1919 Knoxville's second hospital opened in the Fort Sanders community. It was a citadel of peace and healing, where only a few years earlier stood a fortress of war and death. On November 29, 1863, Confederate troops attacked the Union fortress, but failed to break through defensive lines. The bloody battle of Fort Sanders was a fast but furious fight, and a decisive engagement for the siege of Knoxville. When the firing stopped, 826 Americans lay dead or wounded on the muddy, blood-soaked Fort Sanders hill.

Today, battles for life are fought by armies of doctors, nurses, and other health care professionals working together at Fort Sanders Regional Medical Center, Patricia Neal Rehabilitation Center, Thompson Cancer Survival Center and other Covenant Health facilities.

A CALL TO ARMS FOR THE BEST MEDICINE

"The best and the brightest medicine can offer ..." That was the charge in 1943 when the U.S. government recruited physicians to provide healthcare services for the best and brightest men and women in science. Their move to Oak Ridge for work on the top-secret Manhattan Project also brought an unprecedented number of highly acclaimed physicians and nurses to the city. During this time Oak Ridge was the fifth largest city in Tennessee and home to the largest building in the world, but it wasn't on any maps.

After the war, civilian work on peacetime uses for nuclear energy was initiated, and the need for superb medical care continued. Nearly seventy years later, that reputation for medical excellence flourishes at Methodist Medical Center and other Covenant Health hospitals.

FROM FRONTLINES TO THE FOREFRONT OF MODERN MEDICINE

Today, Covenant Health is East Tennessee's pre-eminent health care provider, offering state-of-the-art hospitals and facilities, outstanding medical staffs and world-class technology. Covenant Health has brought many "firsts" and breakthrough procedures to the region, including Gamma Knife, robotic surgery, Tomotherapy, TAVR, and photodynamic therapy, to name a few.

Sevierville native and renowned entertainer Dolly Parton at the 2010 opening of Covenant Health's LeConte Medical Center.

Covenant Health includes eight hospitals: Fort Sanders Regional Medical Center, Parkwest Medical Center, Methodist Medical Center, Morristown-Hamblen Healthcare System, LeConte Medical Center, Fort Loudoun Medical Center, Roane Medical Center, and Peninsula Hospital, a behavioral health facility.

The health system also has the Thompson Cancer Survival Center, Patricia Neal Rehabilitation Center, a home health company, specialty outpatient centers and numerous physician practices offering both primary and specialized care.

WORKING TOGETHER FOR EXCELLENCE IN PATIENT CARE

With more than 10,000 employees, volunteers and affiliated physicians, Covenant Health is the largest employer in the greater Knoxville area. Staffs work together sharing expertise, knowledge and an unwavering commitment to excellence, as evidenced by the many awards Covenant Health has received for outstanding clinical quality, innovative technology, and patient satisfaction.

In 2012 Covenant Health was ranked among the top 25 health systems in the U.S. by IMS, a national organization that administers an annual "Top 100 Integrated Healthcare Networks" study. In 2011 Covenant received the "Impact" Pinnacle Award from the Knoxville Chamber of Commerce as the organization most recognized for making a significant difference in the lives of East Tennesseans.

STANDING STRONG FOR THE COMMUNITY'S HEALTH

Covenant Health is a not-for-profit organization and reinvests excess revenues after expenses in new and expanded facilities, advanced technology, and programs and services to improve patient care. No other health system in East Tennessee has come close to matching Covenant Health's long and noteworthy track record of investments in local communities, according to Anthony L. Spezia, Covenant Health President and CEO.

"The mission of Covenant Health is to serve the community by improving the quality of life through better health," Spezia said. "We are focused on community need, not the bottom line. Every dollar is re-invested locally, nearly $1 billion since 2000.

"We are proud to be among the top health systems in the country, but beyond national rankings, we want every patient to experience excellent care in our hospitals. That is the ultimate measure of our success."

For additional information about Covenant Health and its hospitals, physicians, and services, please visit www.covenanthealth.com or call 865.541.4500.

Covenant Health is committed to providing the most advanced technologies, such as (above) multi-slice computed tomography, which provides diagnostic imaging that is faster, clearer and can lead to more accurate treatment of coronary artery and other diseases, and (below) bi-plane angiography, which offers new, minimally invasive options for treating stroke, aneurysms and other vascular diseases in the brain.

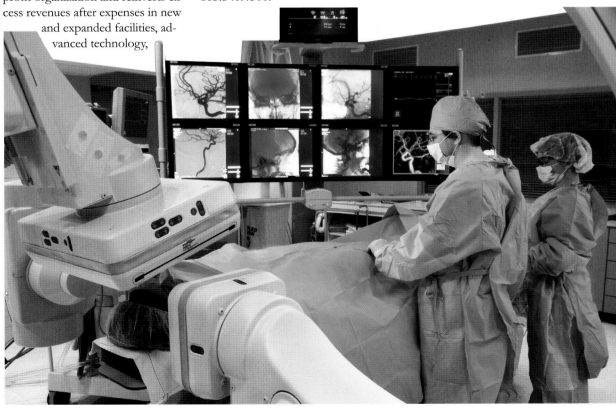

THE TENNESSEE THEATRE

History and Beauty Set the Stage for the Performing Arts in Knoxville

Over the course of its 85-year history, a major element of the Tennessee Theatre experience has been the melodies of the golden-voiced Mighty Wurlitzer organ that continue to enthrall patrons of the venerable performing arts center today. Installed in the Tennessee Theatre when the facility first opened to the public on October 1, 1928, the organ has been witness to a long and impressive list of performers who have graced the theatre's stage over the years. From the opening night film The Fleet's In starring Clara Bow to a live performance by Hollywood legend Helen Hayes in 1935 to a 1940 concert by Glenn Miller and his orchestra, the theatre in its early days built a reputation as one of the finest movie houses and performing arts venues in the country.

The Tennessee Theatre continues to build on the legacy of those early performers. A series of renovations and refurbishments have restored the building to its former grandeur and transformed the facility from a movie palace to a premier entertainment and performing arts facility. The 1,631-seat theatre's most recent facelift, a $25 million project completed in 2005, retained the historic character of the building while providing for state-of-the-art lighting, acoustics, enhanced functionality, and maximum accessibility for the physically challenged. The theatre is now on the National Register of Historic Places and has been designated the Official State Theatre of Tennessee.

"The Tennessee Theatre is the region's leading performing arts center and has led the way towards a complete revitalization of downtown with more than one million guests enjoying more than 1,000 nights of entertainment in our grand auditorium," said Executive Director Tom Cervone. "Knoxville is fortunate to have this community asset when so many other historic theatres have been torn down or have fallen into disrepair."

In addition to showing classic films from the 1930s to the 1970s (On Golden Pond, Godfather II), the Tennessee Theatre today hosts some of today's leading musical groups in a wide range of genres. Recent concerts included performances by Harry Connick, Jr.; Boz Scaggs; Dave Chappelle; Earth Wind and Fire;

The Tennessee Theatre celebrated 85 years on Gay Street in 2013. The theatre marquee and blade sign pictured above when it opened in 1928 and pictured below as it appears today

▼ The grand lobby of the historic Tennessee Theatre stretches for more than half a city block.

▲ Bill Snyder is the house organist and has played the Mighty Wurlitzer organ since 1979.

▲ Since its restoration in 2005, the Tennessee Theatre is the region's leading performing arts center with diverse entertainment from rock shows, like the Grizzly Bear concert pictured above, to orchestra concerts.

and Huey Lewis and the News. Theatre patrons have also enjoyed popular Broadway hits such as Les Miserables and Mary Poppins. Classical music lovers have enjoyed regular concerts by the Knoxville Symphony Orchestra as well as the internationally renowned Moscow Ballet.

The Tennessee Theatre has also become a favorite venue among event planners looking for prime meeting space for corporate functions, seminars, receptions, and private parties. And the Mighty Wurlitzer, with organist Dr. Bill Snyder, former Chancellor and Dean of Engineering at the University of Tennessee, at the keyboard, continues to fill the theatre with the captivating sounds that help to preserve this important chapter of Knoxville's historic past.

"This building is a restored Knoxville landmark and an example of the golden age of movie palaces," noted Tim Burns, the theatre's technical director at the reopening ceremonies in 2005. "This is not a Knoxville thing; this is not a regional thing. It's a national thing and it doesn't happen everywhere."

▼ In 2005, the Tennessee Theatre was restored to its original 1928 majestic splendor with the support of the Knoxville community.

Aqua Chem, Inc.

Comprehensive Water Solutions for a Thirsty World

One of the major logistical problems faced by the American military during World War II was the need to supply fresh water to service personnel locked in the desperate fighting that was taking place in the "island hopping" campaigns in the Pacific Theater of Operations. In 1943, the U.S. government commissioned

Circa 1940, military mobile unit producing 1,000 gallons per hour.

what was then a small company, headquartered in Milwaukee, Wisconsin to supply the critical water needed by troops fighting on the remote, previously unknown outcroppings of coral and palm trees that became household words after the epic battles that took place on them.

Aqua-Chem was founded in 1929 when entrepreneur-engineer John Cleaver joined forces with businessman Raymond Brooks to provide the industry's first "packaged" boiler system. The mobile distillation unit they designed and built for troops in the Pacific converted seawater and brackish well water into 1,000 gallons of purified drinking water per day. An impressive rate of conversion for the time, it was the unit's mobility that made it unique and the solution to the military's problem for

World's largest packaged vapor-compresson distillation unit. Capable of producing 7,200 gallons per hour of USP quality distilled water.

providing potable water in remote locations.

Over the next six decades, the business that Cleaver and Brooks founded has grown to become the premier water purification and micro-utility company in the world. The mobile distillation unit that was producing 1,000 gallons of purified drinking water per day in 1943 has evolved into Aqua-Chem's Portable Reverse Osmosis Water Purification Units capable today of delivering 3,000 gallons of water per hour in field use.

GROWTH OF AN INDUSTRY LEADER

Aqua-Chem is a recognized leader in providing innovative and comprehensive global water solutions through the design, development, and manufacture of state-of-the-art water processing technology. And the company backs its products with after-market parts, supplies, and customer service for a wide range of markets around the globe. Relying on custom engineering, cutting and superior components, Aqua-Chem is proud

to offer complete water solutions to markets including:

► Military
► Offshore Oil and Gas
► Pharmaceutical/Bio Tech/Life Sciences
► Beverage
► Commercial Marine
► Micro-Utilities/Land Based
► Industrial Water Reuse

The company grew to its present position through a series of strategic acquisitions over the years and by pioneering industry-leading technology to continually refine the design and application of its products. In 1951, Aqua-Chem designed and produced a seawater desalinating system for the U.S. Army that combined all the necessary components of water purification systems, including pumps, valves, steam compressors, plate evaporators, and filter components, into a single "package." In the 1960s, company engineers introduced Spray-Film® vapor compression technology capable of producing the water purity levels needed in the most demanding applications. Over the next decade, Aqua-Chem received numerous patents for desalination and its multiple applications. Beginning in the late 1980s and into the 1990s, the company became the product developer and prime production contract supplier to the U.S. government for transportable water purification systems (TWPS) for military and civilian emergency use.

At the dawn of the new millennium, Aqua-Chem purchased the Vaponics brand product lines of still and steam generators to enhance and expand its service to its pharmaceutical and bio-tech customers. The company has also launched more than two dozen new products, including increasingly

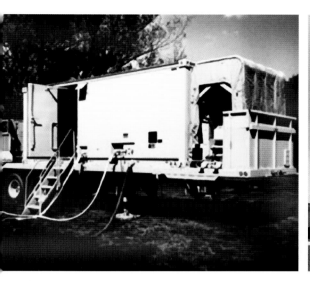

large vapor compression systems, reverse-osmosis water purifiers, pre-treatment and sanitary process distribution systems, waste heat plate type evaporators, vacuum vapor compression units, and titanium and copper/nickel heat exchangers.

At the cornerstone of this phenomenal growth has been a reliance on the expertise and dedication of Aqua-Chem's people.

In-House Engineering: The company's talented engineering staff is fully represented with mechanical, chemical, and electrical disciplines qualified to meet any design need.

In-House Design: With more than 60 years of experience,

the Aqua-Chem design team meets all the demands of GMP and ASME compliant systems design.

In-House Fabrication: Aqua-Chem is vertically integrated, manufacturing all its stainless steel sanitary equipment including all control and power panels at its Knoxville headquarters.

In-House Assembly: Craftsmen with decades of experience in system fabrication bu ild the company's complete product line of water system solutions.

In-House Programming: Aqua-Chem engineers perfor m all the programming required for PLC controls and HMI displays.

In-House Testing and Validation: Product testing takes place in the Knoxville facility under the experienced eye of the Aqua-Chem quality and engineering teams.

AN EYE TO THE FUTURE

Aqua-Chem continues to develop and introduce innovative products and applications to support the needs of its customers and provide solutions to a world increasingly dependent on a dependable supply of fresh water. Aqua-Chem's leading water purification equipment are on six continents, serving in over 100 countries, supported by a world-class global network of sales and service distributors.

Above, left: Military portable reverse osmosis mobile unit producing 3,000 gallons per hour.
Above: Aqua-Chem's world head-quarters and manufacturing facility in Knoxville.

200 associates design, engineer, build and support the leading global water solutions company.

TENNESSEE VALLEY AUTHORITY
Government Partnering with Communities and Business

In the early 1930s, much of the Tennessee Valley region bore a stronger resemblance to some Third World countries than it did to the United States. The land had been eroded and depleted resulting in falling crop yields and downward spiraling farm incomes. Annual family income in places had dropped below $600 and, in extreme cases, was

Historic TVA lineman casting his eyes toward a future brighter than he could have imagined.

less than $100. The best timber had been cut. A full 30 percent of the region's population suffered from malaria.

President Franklin Roosevelt was searching for innovative solutions if his "New Deal" policies were going to lift the nation from the depths of the Great Depression. His vision was of "a corporation clothed with the power of government but possessed of the initiative and flexibility of a private enterprise." That entity became the Tennessee Valley Authority (TVA) and on May 18, 1933, Congress passed the TVA Act and President Roosevelt signed it into law.

TRANSFORMATION OF A REGION

TVA immediately began helping to put America

Along with the rest of the country, Tennesseans faced dire poverty during the "Great Depression"

President Roosevelt signed the TVA into law in 1933, creating what is now the Tennessee Valley Authority.

back to work through the pursuit of its multi-fold mission:

- ▶ Improving navigation on the region's rivers
- ▶ Generating electricity
- ▶ Improving crop yields
- ▶ Sparking economic development

TVA dams were soon harnessing the power of rivers in the area and supplying electricity to homes that had never seen electric lights. Electrification and modern appliances made life easier and farms more productive. It also attracted new industrial operations into the region providing desperately needed employment for thousands.

In addition, improvements to river navigation channels led to a huge surge in commercial barge traffic which previously had been seasonal due to river fluctuations. Educational programs taught farmers how to improve crop yields through the use of newly developed fertilizers. Replanted forests helped control forest fires and improve habitat for wildlife and fish.

Spurred by record economic growth, construction in TVA areas boomed in the years following World War II.

During World War II, TVA was called upon to provide power for critical war industries and embarked upon one of the largest hydropower construction programs ever undertaken in the U.S. By the end of the war, the hydroelectric dams TVA had constructed resulted in TVA becoming the nation's largest electricity supplier.

The following decades saw unprecedented economic growth in the Tennessee Valley, and TVA remained committed to fueling that growth with expanded electrical power. As the utility grew, it became more efficient, cutting operating costs by nearly $800 million annually and developing a plan to meet the energy needs of the Tennessee Valley through 2020.

FROM THE NEW DEAL TO THE NEW CENTURY

Headquartered in Knoxville, the TVA today is the nation's largest public power provider serving more than nine million people in most of Tennessee and parts of Alabama, Georgia, Kentucky, Mississippi, North Carolina, and

Norris Reservoir (now Norris Dam State Park) was the first TVA project begun in 1933.

TVA Headquarters Campus in Knoxville.

Virginia. The utility is now fully self-financed through electricity sales and power system financing to 155 power distributor customers and 56 directly served industries and federal facilities.

TVA's bold vision for the future, to be a leading provider of low-cost, cleaner energy by 2020, embraces three specific goals:

► Lead the nation in improved air quality

► Lead the nation in increased nuclear production

► Lead the Southeast in increased energy efficiency

Pursuant to those goals, TVA focuses on three key areas: Energy, Environment, and Economic Development.

Energy: As the nation's largest government-owned power provider, TVA in 2012 generated $11.2 billion in revenue from reliable, competitively priced energy to homes and businesses that was re-invested into system improvements and economic development initiatives. TVA's average retail price ranked 39th lowest among the nation's 100 largest utilities in fiscal 2012.

Environment: As part of its commitment to limiting the environmental impact of its operations and protecting the natural resources of the region, TVA is improving air quality in the region by reducing emissions at coal-fired plants. Older and less efficient coal units are being replaced with cleaner sources of power. In addition, the utility is integrating renewable energy sources, such as wind and solar, into its generating mix to improve its overall environmental performance. Part of TVA's commitment to good environmental stewardship is its management of 650,000 acres of surface water; 293,000 acres of reservoir land; 11,000 miles of shoreline; and more than 100 public recreation areas.

Economic Development: TVA continues to assist in strengthening the regional economy by building partnerships with communities and the business sector to foster job growth and retention. In 2012, TVA helped attract or retain 48,000 jobs in the region. Businesses receiving TVA financial or technical assistance represented $5.9 billion in new capital investments. An innovative TVA partnership with local communities has successfully marketed major industrial tracts for large-scale manufacturing operations, including Volkswagen's new auto factory in Chattanooga, Tennessee; a new Toyota plant near Tupelo, Mississippi; and a Dow Corning/Hemlock plant in Clarksville, Tennessee. TVA has ranked among North America's top ten utilities for economic development for seven consecutive years by Site Selection, a national industrial development magazine.

TVA headquarters and the Knoxville skyline it powers.

EAST TENNESSEE CHILDREN'S HOSPITAL
East Tennessee's Leading Pediatric Hospital

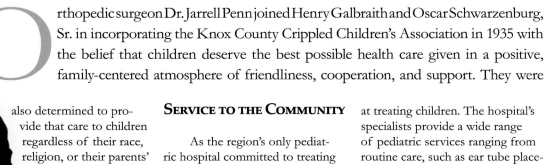

Orthopedic surgeon Dr. Jarrell Penn joined Henry Galbraith and Oscar Schwarzenburg, Sr. in incorporating the Knox County Crippled Children's Association in 1935 with the belief that children deserve the best possible health care given in a positive, family-centered atmosphere of friendliness, cooperation, and support. They were also determined to provide that care to children regardless of their race, religion, or their parents' ability to pay.

The original 28-bed Knox County Crippled Children's Hospital is today the 152-bed East Tennessee Children's Hospital, a group of dedicated professionals operating a series of medical facilities that provide the best pediatric health care to the children and adolescents of the region. Children's Hospital's dedication to the community extends far beyond the medical services it provides. The hospital also returns any revenue back to the organization and uses any budget surpluses to purchase new equipment, expand facilities and enhance services.

Physical therapy helps children develop the strength and range-of-motion they need to move easily and effectively.   Photo by Wade Payne

Children's Hospital's rehabilitation team uses play activities to engage young patients.   Photo by Wade Payne

SERVICE TO THE COMMUNITY

As the region's only pediatric hospital committed to treating children from newborns to age 21, Children's Hospital's primary service area includes the 16 counties in East Tennessee as well as parts of the adjacent states of Kentucky, Virginia, and North Carolina.

Children's Hospital family of services includes a hospital in downtown Knoxville, a surgery center and a rehabilitation center in West Knoxville, and a home health office in Farragut. The 1,900 employees spread over the four facilities have made the hospital the 19th largest employer in East Tennessee. Included in that number are more than 440 physicians and upward of 600 nurses.

Children's Hospital has the largest number of pediatric specialists anywhere in East Tennessee. They are specifically trained in pediatrics—meaning they are experts at treating children. The hospital's specialists provide a wide range of pediatric services ranging from routine care, such as ear tube placement surgeries and tonsillectomies, to highly specialized services, including treatment for cancer, blood disorders, and other diseases that afflict children and adolescents.

The hospital has approximately 160,000 patient visits annually. In addition to operating the busiest Emergency Department in Knox County, the hospital's Neonatal Intensive Care Unit takes care of about 700 premature and critically ill newborns each year.

Family-centered care is an important part of treatment. Having family members close by means they can be involved in their child's treatment, a proven fact in speeding recovery time and shortening the hospital stay.

Child Life Specialists at the hospital provide children with age-appropriate preparation for medical procedures, pain management and coping strategies. They also provide information, support and guidance to parents, siblings and other family members. These services are not often found in adult hospitals.

Children's Hospital has been a pioneer in the treatment of neonatal abstinence syndrome (NAS)—a consequence of the country's prescription drug epidemic. Tennessee actually ranks among the top states dealing with prescription drug abuse. Children's Hospital developed the treatment protocol after seeing the impact this problem was havin g on newborns. In 2012, the hospital treated 283 newborns with NAS—a 110 percent increase from the previous year. In comparison, 600 to 700 infants are treated in the hospital's NICU each year. At this rate, 320 NAS patients are

*Child life specialists make children feel comfortable, so
the hospital is not scary to them.*   Photo by Neil Crosby

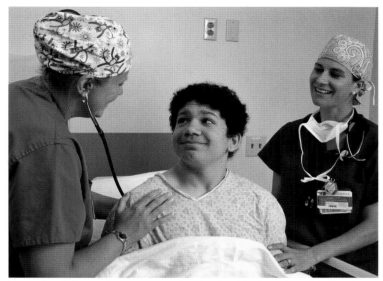

*The staff at Children's Hospital is trained to give the right dose of medicine to all
children—from the smallest baby to a high school student.*   Photo by Neil Crosby

projected for 2013. Opioids, like oxycodone, are the main drugs in these babies' systems. Because NAS is a relatively new problem in the medical community, there is no national protocol for treating it. As a result, several U.S. hospitals have reached out to Children's Hospital for guidance and a toolkit is currently being developed to help other hospitals treat NAS patients.

The hospital has also been a leader in statewide efforts to reduce central line associated blood stream infections.

SERVICE BEYOND THE HOSPITAL

Children's Hospital works closely with numerous groups to enhance the health of the region's children. The hospital sponsors the Knoxville Area Coalition on Childhood Obesity, which seeks to decrease the number of overweight and obese children in East Tennessee, and hospital staff members work diligently to prevent unintentional injuries in children.

In addition to serving as a sponsoring organization for Project ADAM Tennessee, a program designed to work with school systems throughout East Tennessee to address emergent cardiac needs of children and adults in schools, Children's Hospital partners with Fort Sanders

Regional Medical Center's Perinatal Program to provide educational and clinical services throughout the region. The hospital is also a charter member of the Children's Miracle Network Hospitals to raise funds for medical care, research and education benefiting the children of East Tennessee.

"We treat children with everything from life-threatening

*Children's Hospital's nurses use child-friendly terms so patients
understand what is happening.*   Photo by Neil Crosby

conditions to everyday injuries, regardless of their parents' ability to pay," states Keith Goodwin, President and CEO of Children's Hospital. "As the largest pediatric clinical care provider in East Tennessee, hundreds of families trust us to care for their sons and daughters each year."

*Children's Hospital's nurses are
specially trained in pediatrics.*
Photo by Neil Crosby

McGhee Tyson Airport

The Runway to Success

Approximately 1.6 million people travel through McGhee Tyson Airport annually.

W hen it comes to aviation, Knoxville has always been a pioneer. The city's first airport opened only 25 years after the Wright Brothers took their first flight, and from then on, the community has always shown enthusiasm and support for aviation.

In 1929, Knoxville's airport was on Sutherland Avenue and offered a dirt runway, fuel, and hangar space. As years passed, the original site proved unable to handle the evolving needs of aviation in the community and a search began in 1935 for a new airport site. Several locations were considered and the site where McGhee Tyson Airport stands today was chosen in 1936.

McGhee Tyson Airport, named in memory of Knoxville native and fighter pilot Lieutenant Charles McGhee Tyson, was officially dedicated on October 15, 1937, with an air show and community celebration. Fast forward 75 years and McGhee Tyson Airport sees nearly 1.6 million travelers each year and offers travelers and guests an unique and personalized aviation experience.

From the Operations Center

Since 1978, McGhee Tyson Airport has been owned and operated by the Metropolitan Knoxville Airport Authority (MKAA), an independent non-profit agency. MKAA's nine-member, voluntary Board of Commissioners is responsible for setting the course for the future of air travel in East Tennessee through capital improvements, fiscal planning and community development. Appointed by the Mayor of Knoxville and confirmed by the City Council, Commissioners are selected for their significant contributions to the people of East Tennessee and their inspirational leadership in several industries. The Board sets the policies for more than 170 employees in six departments.

"McGhee Tyson Airport's contribution to the economic vitality and development of Knoxville and the surrounding communities

is immense," said Howard H. Vogel, Chairman of the MKAA Board of Commissioners. "Our board must stay in front of travel trends, learn about the needs of the airport's users and work with staff to ensure that passengers in ten, 50, and 100 years will have a safe, affordable, and convenient access to air travel."

Along with McGhee Tyson Airport, the MKAA also manages the Downtown Island Airport, which successfully serves the general aviation community. Together, the two airports provide Knoxville with an efficient, user-friendly air hub that has made the city and region a top contender for business meetings, conferences, trade shows, and vacations.

The Facility Behind the Flights

McGhee Tyson Airport accommodates commercial airline traffic, air cargo, military aviation, and general aviation air traffic with

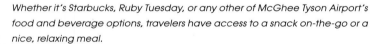

Whether it's Starbucks, Ruby Tuesday, or any other of McGhee Tyson Airport's food and beverage options, travelers have access to a snack on-the-go or a nice, relaxing meal.

Located adjacent to Downtown Knoxville and the University of Tennessee, Downtown Island Airport (DKX) handles more than 83,000 operations a year and has nearly 140 aircraft based on the island.

McGhee Tyson Airport provides East Tennesseans with an efficient, user-friendly air hub that makes the region a top contender for business meetings, trade shows, and vacations.

two 9,000-foot runways on more than 2,000 acres of land. Although the airport still sits on the same site it occupied in 1939, the terminal has received several expansions and renovations.

In 1991, an Air Cargo Complex was added to McGhee Tyson that provides a 21-acre facility for FedEx and UPS, which account for almost 90 percent of the air freight market at Knoxville's airport. In the airport terminal's most recent renovation, which was completed in the fall of 2000, the new airport design was based upon the needs of the traveling public, while embracing the beauty of the region. An Aircraft Rescue and Firefighting Facility was also recently completed to support the airport's emergency response efforts.

"When someone arrives v ia airplane to our city, we want them to immediately feel the culture of our area and see the beauty it holds both artistically and environmentally," said Vogel. "From the art exhibit to the materials used to construct the actual building, visitors are greeted by the warmth of our people and land."

Travelers passing through the McGhee Tyson Airport are the beneficiaries of the improvements

that are constantly underway as the needs of the traveling public changes. With the luxury of numerous food and beverage options, free wireless Internet, electric plug-in stations, and many more accommodations that ensure a memorable travel experience, customers can see their comments and suggestions put into action.

In addition to the aesthetics of the building itself, MKAA and its Board strive to provide flexibility and options in air service to Knoxville. As of June 2013, air carriers at the airport include Allegiant Air, American Eagle, Delta Air Lines, Frontier Airlines, United Express, and U.S. Airways Express. These airlines offer more than 4,000 seats on 120 daily flights to 19 non-stop destinations available.

MASTER PLANNING FOR FUTURE GROWTH

McGhee Tyson Airport will continue to stay at the forefront of aviation in both facilities and customer amenities. With the current trend of smart phone assistance, the airport offers passengers a mobile boarding pass option and an airport mobile app, which makes travel easily manageable using mobile devices. Additionally in 2013, the airport opened a state-of-the-art

airport maintenance facility to help support the needs of growing operations.

"We've come a long way from a dirt runway and 56 acres to more than 2,000 acres and two million annual travelers," said Vogel. "Knoxville's airport has always been at the forefront of aviation, and we plan to continue that legacy for the generations to come."

Installed during the terminal renovation in 2001, McGhee Tyson Airport's fountain emits a welcoming, East Tennessee ambiance for travelers and guests.

CH2M HILL

Providing Sustainable Solutions through Technology, Creativity, and Ingenuity

Dating back to 1946, CH2M HILL was built on honesty, ethics, and morals by a group of dedicated employees who wanted to do the right thing for their clients, the environment, and the communities where they lived and worked. Identifying their venture as CH2M (from Cornell, Howland, Hayes, and Merryfield),

CH2M HILL is a major delivery partner for Masdar City, the first clean-technology cluster to be located in a carbon-neutral, zero-waste city. Masdar City's aim is to show the extent to which cities can be sustainable, while offering world-class living and working environments—thereby changing the global landscape by showing what's possible. Renderings courtesy of Abu Dhabi Future Energy Company.

the four founders set out to fill the post-war void of qualified, experienced engineers. In 1971, the firm merged with Clair A. Hill and Associates and became CH2M HILL.

Today, they are a global project delivery company, helping our clients build a better and more sustainable world. CH2M HILL is recognized as a global leader in consulting, design, design-build, operations, and program management. The original dream of the founders has evolved into a Denver, Colorado-based company with annual revenue in excess of

$7 billion that specializes in performing project and program delivery as well as operations and maintenance services in more than 70 countries around the globe. CH2M HILL professionals have provided sustainable solutions ranging from nuclear cleanup and environmental remediation projects across the country, including Tennessee, to massive construction and support operations and water and wastewater treatment facilities in New Zealand. Whether working in the frigid temperatures of the Arctic or the sizzling heat of the Sahara, CH2M HILL engineers have been the people that clients have turned to with confidence for more than half a century.

The 180 employees based in Knoxville are part of nearly 30,000 workers employed today by CH2M HILL. An employee-owned company, CH2M HILL offers the best of both worlds: the entrepreneurial spirit, local understanding, and personal attention of a small company combined with the long-term stability, expertise, and technologies of a large corporation. The firm's ownership program and entrepreneurial spirit continue to attract high caliber people who have a personal stake in their work. As a result, CH2M HILL is consistently recognized as one of the best companies to work for.

ENVIRONMENTAL STEWARDSHIP

CH2M HILL is a leader in providing comprehensive, integrated sustainable solutions around the world. They bring together strategists, planners, scientists, architects, engineers, economists and others to evaluate opportunities and work collaboratively to deliver lasting solutions that benefit the clients, their communities, and the environment.

CH2M HILL's diverse offering of sustainability services includes facilities and land development, transportation planning, sustainable cities, carbon and energy management, natural resources planning and management, and site remediation. They also have a powerful platform of tools, technologies, and best practices to help clients make well informed decisions and to evaluate the overall sustainability of various options.

The company has been ranked "Number One in Environmental Service and Pure Design" by Engineering News-Record, which sets CH2M HILL apart as the only engineer-procure-construct company that offers a wide spectrum of expertise, knowledge, and services across varied industries and government agencies. This scope and scale sets the firm apart in its capability to partner with clients through the entire lifecycle of a project to achieve strategic and operational goals.

The commitment to sustainable business practices includes protecting and preserving the planet's natural resources and inspiring and educating a diverse and inclusive future workforce that will help solve the environmental and engineering challenges of tomorrow. For that reason, CH2M HILL supports its employees as concerned community citizens with a passion and a spirit of service to make a meaningful and lasting impact on people and communities around the world.

PROGRAM MANAGEMENT

Engineering News-Record consistently ranks CH2M HILL as the leading program management firm because of their proven track record of rapidly implementing large programs. Most of the large, complex sustainability projects involve partnering with other firms, universities, institutes, nongovernmental organizations, and equipment suppliers. This allows them to create and lead the best team of partners to provide innovative, customized sustainable solutions for clients. CH2M HILL's diverse technical skills and niche expertise focused in a programmatic approach helps them create the most robust solutions. They have used this approach in the major programs they have led, including work with the London 2012 Olympic and Paralympic Games and the Panama Canal expansion.

CH2M HILL has been part of the east Tennessee business community since the early 1980s serving both federal and local governments, municipalities, industries and organizations. The firm originally provided comprehensive infrastructure and public works-related services for the Community Reuse Organization of East Tennessee (CROET). CH2M

HILL managed water and wastewater treatment systems; steam, air, and natural gas distribution; boiler operations, and fire-protection systems. CH2M HILL is most notably part of a new team charged by the U.S. Department of Energy (DOE) with the environmental remediation and cleanup of Oak Ridge's East Tennessee Technology Park (ETTP). Today, CH2M HILL continues to provide a wide range of services to clients within Knoxville and the surrounding communities.

In partnership with the local communities, CH2M HILL has a vested interest in helping clients develop sustainable solutions to their toughest challenges. CH2M HILL's Area Manager, Robert Cook, shared, "It's exciting to be part of the CH2M HILL team as we strive to solve the complex issues that our clients face in today's world. Our team looks forward to continuing to build a sustainable future for the Knoxville community and surrounding region."

CH2M HILL is managing the decommissioning and demolition of the K-25 building, a former gaseous diffusion facility, located at the Oak Ridge East Tennessee Technology Park.

As a Delivery Partner, CH2M HILL fulfilled the Olympic Delivery Authority's (ODA's) vision of a sustainable legacy that provides national benefits in culture, sport, volunteering, business, and tourism for the 2012 London Olympic and Paralympic Games.

ORAU

Impacting the U.S. Scientific Mission

For more than 65 years ORAU has provided innovative scientific and technical solutions for some of our country's most pressing issues. From advancing scientific research and education to protecting health and the environment and strengthening national security, ORAU integrates specialized teams of experts, unique laboratory

University of Tennessee engineering students Maxwell Robinson (left) and James Earle (right) stand by "the terminator"—a figure composed of durable-plastic parts made using 3-D printers. The two spent their summer at Oak Ridge National Laboratory in the Volkswagen Distinguished Scholars Program, managed by ORAU, gaining hands-on experience in 3-D printing, robotics, and other elements of engineering.

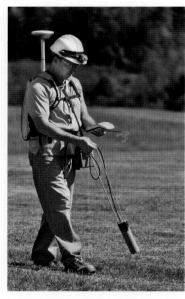

In FY12, ORAU's independent verification expertise was sought to provide support for several ongoing DOE cleanup initiatives such as Hanford Nuclear Reservation, West Valley Reprocessing Plant and on the Oak Ridge Reservation.

capabilities and access to its consortium of more than 100 major Ph.D.–granting institutions to support government and private sector customers in advancing national priorities and serving the public interest.

A 501(c)3 nonprofit organization and federal contractor, ORAU employs more than 1,200 people in 19 locations across the country, nearly 1,000 of whom are in Oak Ridge, Tennessee.

Long-time managing contractor of the Oak Ridge Institute for Science and Education (ORISE) for the U.S. Department of Energy (DOE), ORAU is impacting the U.S. scientific mission through expertise in science, education, scientific peer review, worker and public health, environmental assessments, national security and emergency management, and radiation emergency medicine. In 2012 alone, ORAU's impact included:

- ▶ 8,300+ students, faculty and postdocs from 1,000 universities participated in ORAU and ORISE science education programs.

- ▶ Scientific peer review support was provided for government allocation of hundreds of millions in research funding.

- ▶ 5,000+ workers were tested for beryllium sensitivity and chronic beryllium disease at the ORISE Beryllium Laboratory, one of only four in the U.S. capable of performing the lymphocyte proliferation test for the diagnosis of these conditions.

- ▶ Hundreds of square miles and thousands of square feet of property and facilities were deemed safe for reuse through

independent environmental surveys.

- ▶ 4,100+ soil, water, and air samples were analyzed at ORISE's Radiochemistry Laboratory to support environmental initiatives.

- ▶ 2,100+ professionals received radiation emergency training through the Radiation Emergency Assistance Center/Training Site, a one-of-a-kind DOE facility and 24/7 internationally deployable asset for the medical management of radiation emergencies.

- ▶ Facilitated national security exercises involving 11 federal agencies, nearly 2,000 personnel, and the ORISE Cytogenetic Biodosimetry Laboratory, one of only two labs in the U.S. using radiation dose analysis for radiation injuries.

POSITIVELY IMPACTING EAST TENNESSEE

With the majority of its workforce in East Tennessee, ORAU diligently supports important needs in its own backyard. "Our goal is to be a strong community partner that enhances lives and improves education, the environment and the health of our fellow residents," states Andy Page, ORAU president and CEO.

Through Race to the Top funding, ORAU hosts Tennessee's STEM Leadership Academy promoting teaching skills in science, technology, engineering, and mathematics. Additionally, ORAU's annual Extreme Classroom Makeover provides $25,000 in technology upgrades to a deserving East Tennessee middle or high school teacher. ORAU Education Grants also annually provide

$35,000+ for tools and technology for multiple teachers in Oak Ridge, Clinton, and Anderson County school systems. And each summer, ORAU provides free workshops to area teachers through its Center for Science Education.

To inspire students in math and science, ORAU manages the Tennessee Science Bowl for DOE and supports the Tennessee Middle School Math Competition with Pellissippi State Community College. ORAU works closely with the University of Tennessee and other universities to provide research experiences with national labs for faculty and students, and is working with Oak Ridge National Laboratory (ORNL) and Roane State Community College to enhance workforce development for ORNL's Carbon Fiber Technology Facility through a specialized training program.

With important work in science and energy also comes environmental and health risks. With 40+ years of independent environmental assessment expertise, ORAU supports various DOE cleanup initiatives such as the footprint reduction effort of 22,000+ acres on the Oak Ridge Reservation. ORAU's ecological assessments helped determine which land parcels were safe for public use. With more than 40 years of independent health assessment expertise, ORAU was also tapped by the Tennessee Valley Authority to provide free health screenings for area residents after a coal ash spill at its Kingston Fossil Plant.

EXPANDING ITS IMPACT BEYOND THE REGION

From working with the National Oceanic and Atmospheric Administration to research greenhouse gases in the Arctic to helping Kazakhstan universities

ORAU health experts at the ORISE Beryllium Laboratory performed beryllium lymphocyte proliferation tests on 5,200 workers in FY12. These tests help agencies and sites protect the health of employees exposed to beryllium in the workplace.

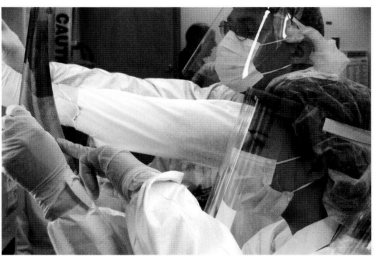

The Radiation Emergency Assistance Center/Training Site (REAC/TS) strengthens the medical management of radiation emergencies by training emergency responders and healthcare professionals to provide care to patients with a radiation injury or illness. In FY12, REAC/TS trained 350 personnel in Kuwait, Singapore, and Thailand, and more than 1,750 personnel in the REAC/TS Oak Ridge, Tenn. facility.

improve faculty research through peer review, ORAU is enabling scientific research and discovery around the globe and continues to expand its capabilities to support challenges in the U.S. and abroad.

For the Japan earthquake, tsunami and nuclear crisis, ORAU provided radiation emergency medicine, emergency management, health communication, and environmental assessment support to the U.S. response effort and assessed the radiological safety of U.S. humanitarian aid ships. Closer to home, ORAU partnered

with a Vanderbilt University professor and a handful of federal agencies to study one million U.S. workers with occupational exposure to low-dose radiation. ORAU has also designed an emergency preparedness tool–Exercise Builder Nuclear–to help make nuclear power plants safer through comprehensive emergency exercises. In support of other public health issues, ORAU is working with the Centers for Disease Control on a nationwide campaign to increase awareness of adolescent vaccines for illnesses such as human papillomavirus.

"These examples represent only a small number of the wide-ranging programs ORAU supports, but they share a common theme: they positively impact science and benefit from a strong commitment to advancing education and research to enhance scientific discovery," says Page. "We are making a difference in our own backyard as well as helping our customers strengthen the overall U.S. scientific mission and global competitiveness, improving the future for our community, our nation, and the world."

ORAU's Extreme Classroom Makeover provides a local teacher with $25,000 to outfit his or her classroom with the latest in technology upgrades to enhance learning, especially in the science, technology, engineering and mathematics subjects. ORAU has been awarding this technology makeover annually since 2009 when it opened a new Center for Science Education in Oak Ridge, Tennessee.

KNOXVILLE ZOOLOGICAL GARDENS

Education. Conservation. Research. Recreation.

One of the most visited educational resources in East Tennessee and Knoxville's largest year-round attraction has a very healthy appetite. The weekly shopping list (which totals about $200,000 annually!) for the more than 750 animals housed and lovingly cared for at Knoxville Zoological Gardens typically includes 5,200 pounds of hay, 120 pounds of bananas, 735 pounds of grain, and untold numbers of fruits and vegetables.

The mission of Knoxville Zoo is to celebrate the wonders of the natural world and, through education, conservation, exhibition, research, and recreation, to tell the stories of the animals, plants, and people who make up the communities across our planet. Since its opening in 1948, the zoo has worked to develop positive attitudes and actions about nature and about conservation as a local and global issue.

Each year approximately 400,000 guests stroll the 53 wooded acres which today make up Knoxville Zoological Gardens. The zoo's visitors are treated to an eyeball-to-eyeball look at some of the world's most fascinating animals in a number of naturalistic habits such as the Boyd Family Red Panda Village, Grasslands Africa!, Stokely African Elephant Preserve, Meerkat Lookout, Penguin Rock, Chimp Ridge, The Valley of the Kings, River Otters, Gorilla Valley, The Clayton Family Kids Cove, Black Bear Falls, and the Williams Family Giraffe Encounter. The zoo also features indoor exhibits, such as The Night Club, The Barn Loft, and Wee Play Zoo. Another guest favorite, The Clayton Safari Splash water play area, is also the most popular place to cool off in the spring and summer months.

A COMMITMENT TO CONSERVATION

Knoxville Zoo is nationally accredited by the Association of Zoos and Aquariums (AZA) and is committed to the highest standards in animal care and well-being, ethics, conservation, and education. The zoo actively participates in the AZA's Species Survival Programs (SSP) which seeks to specifically manage species in order to ensure healthy, self-sustaining populations that maintain maximum genetic diversity and are demographically stable.

The zoo's Gorilla Valley was selected by the Western Lowland Gorilla Species Survival Plan, which manages the breeding and social placement of gorillas in AZA-accredited zoos, to be the new home for a family group of Western Lowland gorillas as part of their efforts to protect these endangered creatures.

Knoxville Zoo is one of the world's leading zoos for the breeding of red pandas, another threatened species in the wild. Since 1978, more than 100 cubs have been born at Knoxville Zoo and the Boyd Family Red Panda Village gives visitors the opportunity to view these irresistible creatures up close.

The zoo's Herpetology department has achieved an international reputation for its success in breeding rare, threatened, and endangered species of reptiles. With more than 400 specimens representing over 80 species, Knoxville Zoo has the distinction of being the first in the world to breed Papuan pythons. It is also one of the few zoos in the country to successfully breed the little-known Philippine pit viper and to have consistent success in breeding tiger rattlesnakes.

Knoxville Zoo has focused its breeding effort on critically endangered tortoise species from Madagascar. It was the second zoo

in the world, and the first in North America, to successfully hatch Madagascar flat-tailed tortoises and have notable success with radiated tortoises and common spider tortoises, Northern spider tortoises, and Southern spider tortoises. Knoxville Zoo received the honor of being chosen as one of only three zoos in the country to house four ploughshare tortoises, the rarest species of tortoise on earth, that were confiscated from the illegal pet trade, and plans are in place to begin a breeding program for this species when they are mature.

Knoxville Zoo has also taken a leading role in local conservation efforts that focused on the threatened bog turtle native to the wetlands of East Tennessee. Researchers combined the study of the species in the wild with a successful captive breeding program that has given the turtles a head start and resulted in more than 180 of these young turtles being released back into the wild.

A COMMITMENT TO EDUCATION

Knoxville Zoo offers programs for college undergraduates that provide practical experience for students interested in working in a zoological facility. The zoo's Department of Conservation Science offers an off-campus study program to provide students the chance to gain hands-on experience working in a zoological facility. Internships are offered in every department of the zoo.

In addition, the zoo's Education Department offers a wide range of programming, including field trips, zoo camps, and overnight stays in the zoo.

These educational initiatives are designed to give visitors of all ages a better understanding of the need to preserve our wild heritage.

"When Knoxville Zoo got its start in 1948, I doubt that anyone would have imagined that eclectic menagerie would evolve into what it is today," states Lisa New, the zoo's Executive Director. "We're now a leading zoo doing important conservation work with a multitude of species, including many that are critically endangered. While conservation is a key part of our mission, we have also established ourselves as an important educational resource for not only East Tennessee but also the surrounding states, welcoming thousands of schoolchildren each year. Perhaps most surprising of all is the economic impact Knoxville Zoo brings to Knox County.

We are Knoxville's largest year-round attraction, and the impact of more than 225,000 tourists visiting the zoo brings in more than $22 million dollars to the local economy each year and supports 423 local jobs. Doing the right thing for the animals entrusted to our care has also been the right thing for Knoxville."

THE UNIVERSITY OF TENNESSEE MEDICAL CENTER

To serve through healing, education and discovery

With a three-fold mission of healing, education and discovery, The University of Tennessee Medical Center holds a unique prominence in the area. As the region's only academic medical center, Magnet® recognized hospital and Level I Trauma Center, The University of Tennessee Medical Center serves

as a major referral center for East Tennessee, Southeast Kentucky and Western North Carolina. UT Medical Center is the home of the Knoxville campus of UT Graduate School of Medicine, UT College of Pharmacy and University Health System, Inc.

Recognized as one of America's best hospitals by US News and World Report, the 581-bed hospital also is home to the region's only

dedicated Heart Hospital, only adult and pediatric transplant center, the region's first certified primary stroke center, houses the region's only private-room neonatal intensive care unit and serves as a regional perinatal center.

HEALING

In an effort to provide comprehensive care to our patients, The University of Tennessee

Medical Center is made up of the five Centers of Excellence including the Brain and Spine Institute, the Cancer Institute, the Center for Women and Children's Health, Emergency and Trauma Services and the Heart Lung Vascular Institute. The dedicated professionals at the medical center thrive in a fast-paced, challenging environment, where expert commitment plays a critical role in the hospital's ongoing success. The

▼ In 1956, UT Medical Center opened its doors to the region, which now serves 21 counties in East Tennessee and into areas of Southeastern Kentucky and Western North Carolina.

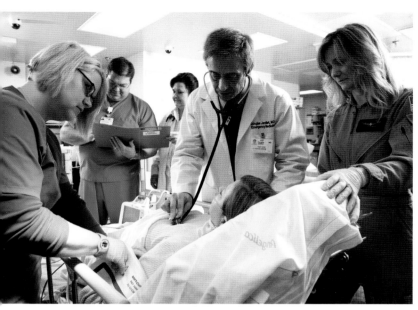

▲ UT Medical Center services as the region's only Level I Trauma Center and is certified by The Joint Commission as a Comprehensive Stroke Center.

▲ UT Medical Center is at the forefront of medical research in working with the UT Graduate School of Medicine.

strength and success of the hospital comes from the work of exceptional team members who dedicate themselves to patient care excellence while upholding the hospital's values of integrity, excellence, compassion, innovation, collaboration and dedication.

EDUCATION

Although the primary purpose is to provide excellent patient care, the medical center also prepares tomorrow's healthcare providers. The UT Graduate School of Medicine has a national reputation in education and is building research programs of national merit. Currently with 12 residency programs and nine fellowship programs in medicine and dentistry, more than 200 faculty members mentor and teach the 190 residents and fellows.

Another component of the Graduate School of Medicine is the Preston Medical Library. The library provides reference, research and instruction for UT Graduate School of Medicine faculty, residents, students, physicians, as well as outreach to the community. Through the Consumer & Patient Health Information Service, library staff assists patients, families, and community members in finding

information on health-related topics and provides the information free of charge.

In addition to the pharmacy students and the medical and dental residents and fellows, there are nursing students from area colleges, School of Radiography students and Clinical Pastoral Education (CPE) students.

In 2006, the UT College of Pharmacy expanded its programs in Knoxville with the construction of a new 15,000 square foot facility. The UT College of Pharmacy provides tremendous learning, research, and clinical experiences for its students and staff, while providing real-life opportunities for clinical and advanced professional training throughout the state.

DISCOVERY

Doctors and researchers at the medical center and Graduate School of Medicine, work together diligently to discover new and better ways to detect and treat disease through various research projects and clinical trials. Research projects at the medical center help advance medical knowledge in areas such as imaging and diagnostic technology. Several of our basic science researchers are funded by the

National Institutes of Health and related agencies to bring the best of medical care to East Tennessee. In addition, our physicians provide clinical trial opportunities unique to our setting making them readily available to those who seek new medications and treatment. Our research teams work closely with researchers throughout the University of Tennessee system as well as others throughout the nation.

▼ As the region's only academic medical center, UT Medical Center and the UT Graduate School of Medicine work together to prepare the doctors of tomorrow.

PILOT CORPORATION

Serving East Tennessee for more than 50 years

Brothers Bill Haslam and James A. "Jimmy" Haslam III are photographed with their father, James A. "Jim" Haslam II, at a Pilot gas station in 1977. Jim Haslam founded Pilot in 1958.

When President Dwight Eisenhower signed the Federal Aid Highway Act of 1956, he authorized the creation of a national highway system in the United States that grew into what has been termed the "largest public works program since the Pyramids." Just two years after the highway act was signed into law,

James A. "Jim" Haslam II opened a single, family-owned gas station in Gate City, Virginia. As the Interstate Highway System has been expanded over the years to include more than 47,000 miles of thoroughfares, so too has Haslam's single gas station evolved.

GROWTH AND EXPANSION

Six short years after Haslam purchased his first gas station, Pilot had grown into a $2 million-a-year business. Within seven years, Pilot had twelve locations in three states.

"In the 1960s, to stand apart from our competitors in customer service, we'd find out customers' names, then put a piece of tape with their name on it inside the gas cap so that when they left, the attendant could say, 'Thank you, Mrs. Smith,'" said Haslam, founder and chairman emeritus of Pilot Corporation. "Today we get their name from the credit card. But that's how you thank people. You use their name."

By 1973 the company was operating more than 50 service stations with annual sales of approximately $30 million. Pilot built its first convenience store in 1973 and began converting its other locations to convenience stores. The following year Pilot bought Lonas Oil Co. in Knoxville and converted the new locations to convenience stores. In 1981, with 100 convenience stores and total annual sales of $175 million, Pilot opened its first travel center in Corbin, Kentucky.

In 1988, Pilot began concentrating on expanding its travel center operations into a nationwide network and opened its first travel center with a fast-food restaurant. By 1996, Pilot operated 96 travel centers and 50 convenience stores. Its total fuel sales had reached 1.2 billion gallons. In 2001 Pilot partnered with Marathon Ashland Petroleum LLC to form Pilot Travel Centers LLC. Two years later, Pilot acquired Williams Travel Centers.

In 2006, Pilot was recognized as the tenth largest restaurant franchisee in the United States. That same year, Pilot became an international company, opening its first travel center in Canada. In 2007, Pilot was recognized by Area Developer magazine as one of the "Top 99 Megafranchisees" and by SAP Retail Inc. as No. 30 in the Top 100 Retailers.

Pilot Corporation sold a substantial interest in Pilot Travel Centers to CVC Capital Partners in 2008, facilitating the sale by Marathon Petroleum Company

(formerly Marathon Ashland Petroleum) of its interest in Pilot Travel Centers LLC. Pilot Corporation retains its majority ownership of Pilot Travel Centers LLC. Pilot's convenience store operations, located in East Tennessee, continue to be fully owned by Pilot Corporation. Pilot Travel Centers merged with Flying J Inc. in 2010 to form Pilot Flying J, the nation's largest operator of travel centers and travel plazas in North America.

"I'm really proud of what Pilot has become," Haslam said. "Our reputation is built on cleanliness and customer service. The most important customer is the one walking in the door right now. I want to make sure we keep this culture going. We have an incredible team of employees, and our customers deserve and appreciate the fast, friendly service they receive at our stores."

Pilot Corporation now operates 40 convenience stores in Tennessee. Headquartered in Knoxville, the company has more than 450 employees.

A COMMITMENT TO COMMUNITY

Pilot takes seriously its commitment to its customers, employees and community. The company's culture is based on several key principles that encourage all members of the organization to show a bias for action, to focus on people, to possess a strong work ethic and a drive for results, and most importantly, to always do the right thing.

Pilot's strong sense of community spirit and philanthropy was established by the company's founder, Jim Haslam, when he began the business more than a half century ago. Through the Pilot Volunteers program, the company provides employees the time and opportunity to give back. Every

In 2008, Pilot Corporation announced a $1 million donation to Knoxville's Legacy Parks Foundation to build a lasting legacy for the people who use parks and to celebrate the company's 50th anniversary.

In 2010, Pilot Travel Centers merged with Flying J Inc. to form Pilot Flying J, the nation's largest operator of travel centers and travel plazas in North America.

employee receives one full day off each year specifically for volunteer service.

"Knoxville has been Pilot's home for more than 50 years and has been an ideal place to build a business – and a family," Haslam said. "The quality of life, talented workforce and support of the community are just a few of the reasons we're fortunate to be headquartered in Knoxville. We're proud to be located in East Tennessee and proud to give back to the communities where our employees, customers, business partners and their families live and work."

Since its inception in 1992, Pilot Corporation's annual "Pilot Celebrity Pumpers" event has raised more than $1 million for the United Way of Greater Knoxville. Pilot also supports a multitude of Knoxville-area organizations through donations, sorships, volunteerism and other means. Pilot was named one of five finalists for the U.S. Chamber of Commerce 2008 Corporate Citizenship Stewardship Award for Large Business for its contributions to business and society.

In 1981, Pilot opened its first travel center in Corbin, Kentucky, like this Pilot Travel Center on Strawberry Plains Pike in Knoxville.

PILOT FLYING J

Making Life Better for America's Drivers

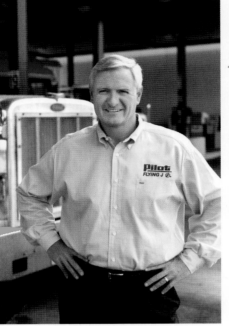

Jimmy Haslam serves as CEO of Pilot Flying J.

Built upon the successful foundation of Pilot Corporation, Pilot Flying J exudes an entrepreneurial spirit and desire to serve professional drivers and travelers. The Knoxville-based company—the largest operator of travel centers and travel plazas in North America—remains true to its roots and is committed to making life better for America's drivers every day.

TRAVELING A SIMILAR ROAD

Pilot Corporation was founded by James A. "Jim" Haslam II in 1958 as a single, family-owned gas station in Gate City, Virginia. He focused on providing convenient, clean facilities and fast, friendly service. Haslam transformed Pilot into a burgeoning convenience store and travel center business, serving the skyrocketing number of professional drivers and travelers across the U.S. that were taking advantage of the newly created network of interstate highways. Pilot Travel Centers LLC, formed in 2001, was named in the "50 Most Influential Franchisees in the World" by Nation's Restaurant News and in 2009 was ranked Number 23 among top 100 retailers in the U.S. and Canada by the National Retail Federation's Stores magazine.

"One of the secrets to success is adding new products and creating new ways to do business," said Jim Haslam, founder of Pilot Corporation and chairman emeritus of Pilot Flying J. "We have to keep changing because our customers are always changing. That's what pushed our company to expand and grow early on, and it's why we continue to be successful today."

While Haslam was building Pilot Travel Centers on the east coast, Flying J founder Jay Call began his business out west. Incorporating his love of flying into the name of his start-up, Call established Flying J as a small, family-owned petroleum marketing company in 1968 with four retail gasoline stations in Utah. The company grew to include a nationwide network of travel plazas.

MAKING AN HISTORIC MERGER

After decades of traveling similar paths as family-owned travel center businesses, on July 1, 2010, Pilot Travel Centers LLC and Flying J Inc. announced the merger of the two companies into Pilot Flying J.

"We are now one great company, two great brands," said James A. "Jimmy" Haslam III, Pilot Flying J CEO. "Our new organization combines two of the best-known brands in the travel center industry, both with strong family histories and shared values. We look forward to a bright future as our customers' preferred stop for highway hospitality."

Two years later, the company acquired Western Petroleum and Maxum Petroleum, which in 2013 became Pilot Logistics Services, one of the largest independent energy logistics companies in North America with sales and distribution of more than 1.3 billion gallons of refined petroleum products to over 15,000 customers. Together, Pilot Flying J and Pilot Logistics Services generate sales of 9 billion gallons of petroleum products annually.

SERVING AMERICA'S DRIVERS

Leading the industry in serving the nation's professional drivers and fuel customers, Pilot Flying J travel centers and travel plazas feature premium coffee selections, a variety of quality dining options, clean restrooms and fast, friendly service.

Pilot Flying J has over 650 retail locations and is the largest operator of travel centers and travel plazas in North America. The company is the top seller of over-the-road diesel fuel in the nation and is one of the 40 largest private carriers in the country. The company employs more than 23,000 team members, and Forbes ranked Pilot Flying J as Number Six on its 2012 list of America's Largest Private Companies.

After decades of traveling similar paths as family-owned travel center businesses, Pilot Travel Centers LLC and Flying J Inc. merged in 2010 to form Pilot Flying J.

Forbes ranked Pilot Flying J as No. 6 on its 2012 list of America's Largest Private Companies.

"Professional drivers keep this country moving, and we're proud to serve them," said Jimmy Haslam. "We're also honored to contribute to local communities where our stores are located – from serving interstate travelers and motorists to providing local jobs and tax revenue."

Haslam went on to say that Pilot Flying J's tremendous growth could not have happened without an incredible team of employees across North America, including those headquartered in Knoxville. "We are committed to Knoxville. It's a great place to live and do business, and we have an extremely talented group working at our main office. As we grow, we are very fortunate to have our roots firmly planted in East Tennessee," said Jimmy Haslam.

IMPROVING QUALITY OF LIFE

Through financial contributions and volunteer leadership, Pilot Flying J is committed to creating a vibrant, healthy community and an enviable quality of life. Pilot Flying J invests in local and regional non-profit and charitable organizations whose missions and work align with the company's values and priorities including those that focus on education, healthcare and recreation, social services, economic development, and arts and culture.

"Just as we strive to serve our customers in our stores, we want to serve the communities where our employees and customers live and work," said Jimmy Haslam. "We're committed to making life better for America's drivers. That reaches beyond the travel centers to what we can do to enhance the quality of life for our customers, their families and loved ones – from our headquarters in Knoxville and across the nation."

Pilot Flying J is committed to making life better for America's drivers. In 2013 the company launched PJ Fresh Marketplace, a new fast, casual dining concept.

McCarty Holsaple McCarty

Fifty Years of Design Excellence

McCarty Holsaple McCarty is on the eve of celebrating a half-century of providing the highest quality architectural and design services to a wide range of clients. The firm, founded by Bruce McCarty in Knoxville in 1965 as Bruce McCarty & Associates, in its earliest days began designing a series of important

*McGhee Tyson Airport
Terminal Building with HNTB*

Photo by Robert Batey

*The Knoxville Convention Center
with Thompson Ventulett Stainback
& Associates*

Photo by Robert Batey

structures for the University of Tennessee, including the Andy Holt Tower Administration Building, the Communications Complex, the Humanities Complex, and the Clarence Brown Theatre. Rapid growth and expansion in the 1960s and 1970s led to MHM being selected to design the Art and Architecture Building on the UT campus which has become one of the firm's single most iconic projects and has influenced generations of UT's architecture students.

In 1982, Bruce McCarty was selected as the Master Architect for the World's Fair and the World's Fair Park by the Knoxville International Energy Exposition. Continued growth and expansion

led to rebranding of the firm as McCarty Holsaple McCarty with McCarty's son, Doug, joining the business and becoming Director of Design. MHM is led today by Doug McCarty (President/CEO), Jeff Johnson (Executive Vice-President), and David Collins (Vice-President).

A FAMILIAR NAME ON THE KNOXVILLE LANDSCAPE

McCarty Holsaple McCarty's design portfolio includes some of Knoxville's signature landmarks:

- ▶ Knoxville Convention Center
- ▶ McGhee Tyson Airport Terminal
- ▶ Tennessee Theatre
- ▶ Neyland Stadium Renovations
- ▶ City-County Building
- ▶ UT Taylor Law School

- ▶ Volunteer Landing Waterfront
- ▶ Ijams Nature Center
- ▶ Bank of America Building
- ▶ UT Hodges Library
- ▶ UT Baker Center

From its offices on Main Street in the heart of downtown Knoxville, MHM has served clients from Maine to California, but concentrates its practice in the Southeastern states. The firm currently employs 30 people and is consistently ranked among the top three firms in East Tennessee in terms of number of registered architects.

These architecture, design, and planning professionals combine planning and design expertise with skills in project management and construction administration. This range of experience enables MHM to handle all phases of the design process, from the initial master planning and facility

programming through construction administration. MHM is large enough to handle almost any design project, yet small enough to provide personal, responsive service.

Keenly aware that successful design is a collaborative process, MHM regards their clients and other professionals involved as partners in that process. To develop facilities that meet each client's individual needs, the MHM design process emphasizes communication and regular client feedback, as well as research and design expertise.

MHM's emphasis on project management and careful cost controls, along with a dedication to client service and design excellence, has won the firm many repeat clients. MHM has established a reputation for designing functional and appealing master plans, buildings and interiors, and is known for completing projects on time and on budget.

DESIGNING FOR THE FUTURE

MHM recognizes that the design profession has a responsibility to protect the environment and natural resources. A sustainable design is one that meets the needs of the users while responsibly using new materials and reusing existing materials to save resources, minimizing the energy required to operate the facility, allowing for efficient movement of personnel and equipment, and recognizing the site characteristics in development of the design.

To meet those criteria, each of the firm's design professionals strives to provide their clients with designs that meet programmatic and economic needs, while respecting the environment, occupant health, and material resources. MHM has several LEED Accredited Professionals who are a valuable resource for the firm's project design teams. Their goal is to implement each program within the smallest footprint possible

to reduce development cost and allow for future programming flexibility. MHM has also successfully managed the LEED Certification process for several clients achieving Gold, Silver and numerous Existing Building certifications.

Recent projects include the new Student Union at UT (with Barber McMurry Architects), AAA's downtown headquarters, numerous additions to the Green Mountain Coffee Roaster's Knoxville facility, the Clayton Center for the Arts, downtown's Tailor Lofts and the new corporate headquarters for K-VA-T Food Stores Inc. (Food City) in Abingdon, Virginia. MHM also has on-going projects for the State of Tennessee, UT, ORNL and TVA, among other large public agencies.

"Our firm has been involved in achieving successful results in the most significant projects in East Tennessee," states Doug McCarty. "We emphasize customer service and meeting each client's schedule and budget restraints. And we take

great pride in supporting our community through the United Way, the East Tennessee Community Design Center, Knox Heritage, and the University of Tennessee."

AAA of East Tennessee, downtown Knoxville
Photo by Robert Batey

The University of Tennessee, Neyland Stadium Terrace Club with Ross Bryan Associates Photo by Robert Batey

The Historic Tennessee Theatre in association with Westlake Reed Leskosky
Photo by Nels Ackerland

AMEC ENVIRONMENT & INFRASTRUCTURE, INC.

Delivering Excellence On Every Project

The 96 engineers, scientists, and corporate management and support staff in AMEC's Knoxville office are part of the 29,000 AMEC family of professionals who today comprise one of the world's leading engineering, project management, and consultancy companies. Their goal is to deliver profitable, safe, and sustainable projects and services for their clients in the oil and gas, mining, clean energy, environmental, and infrastructure markets, including sectors that play a vital role in the global and national economies and in people's everyday lives.

The company's imprint in the Knoxville area began shortly after World War II when the unusual partnership of four U.S. military veterans and a former German prisoner of war was formed in Tennessee to establish a geotechnical and drilling company. The new company was instrumental in assisting the U.S. Army Corps of Engineers in its efforts to construct a series of dams along the Cumberland River. They quickly expanded their scope of services to include civil and environmental engineering, landfill development, groundwater studies, construction engineering, and air permitting. Further growth and evolution over the years led to an eventual acquisition by AMEC, enabling the Knoxville staff to offer its clients the expertise and vast resources available through AMEC's 220 offices around the U.S. and Canada as well as 40 other countries around the globe.

AMEC professionals in Knoxville have placed the company's distinctive signature on engineering, environmental, and construction related projects throughout east Tennessee and around the world. In North America, Knoxville-based staff have performed construction oversight at the Kearl Oil Sands in Alberta, Canada to beach re-nourishment oversight on the Florida coast. Customers in both the private and public sectors with particularly challenging projects from as far away as Korea or as near as Knox County can rely on AMEC's Project Managers to build a close working relationship with them to find innovative solutions. Those Project Managers rely not only on the expertise of their local staff, but can also bring in specialists from the company's other offices to offer their individual skills on projects in diverse and challenging environments. From sub-zero temperatures in the Arctic to the sweltering heat of the Persian Gulf.

AN INTERNATIONAL COMPANY WITH A LOCAL IMPRINT

In the 1970s and 1980s, it became obvious that Knoxville was an optimal location for providing geotechnical and related services to regional clients, including mining companies, regional railroads, the Tennessee Valley Authority (TVA), Humana Healthcare, and the Department of Energy facilities in Oak Ridge.

AMEC's local imprint is evident now in several of the most recognizable projects in the region:

► AMEC engineers provided floodplain management and flood analysis work in Knox County that led to the development of local storm water management regulations. They continue to work with municipalities and counties locally and across the region on storm water management issues.

► Knoxville staff assisted their Nashville-based colleagues in recovery and flood impact mapping efforts for the 2010 Nashville flood.

► Knoxville office engineers, scientists, and technicians provided the foundation studies for all the infrastructure of the Knoxville World's Fair Site, including the famous Sunsphere. They also assisted with the restoration of the Second Creek for the World's Fair.

▼ AMEC provides construction engineering inspection and other services to TDOT for the rehabilitation of the Henley Street Bridge.

Photo by Miles Watkins

Further afield, Knoxville office staff participated in the site recovery and cleanup efforts at the World Trade Center and in the cleanup and rebuilding efforts at the Pentagon after 9-11. They also designed, led, and managed the demolition of Atlas and Titan rocket launch towers and other former space program facilities located in Cape Canaveral, Florida. AMEC's Air Force client environmental support needs have taken them to Korea, Guam, Europe, and the United Kingdom.

Those efforts and others have been recognized with numerous awards. One of AMEC's chief goals has been to build a strong safety culture and the company is particularly proud of the National Safety Achievement Award they have received consecutively from the National Safety Council over the past few years. AMEC also regularly receives project and client-specific safety awards.

Across North America, AMEC regularly receives project awards for engineering and environmental excellence from regional and national chapters of various professional organizations. Agencies of the U.S. government have also recognized AMEC's efforts in supporting small and disadvantaged businesses. The company was recently awarded the Nunn-Perry Award for its business Mentor-Protégé program and an Outstanding Small Business Subcontracting Award.

Proud as they are of the peer recognition the company has

achieved for its excellence, AMEC professionals are equally proud of the company's record of service to the community. Knoxville staff regularly donate their time, food, or materials to local charities or events, including Angel Tree, Coats for the Cold, and an annual stream cleanup effort sponsored by the Water Quality Forum.

"AMEC is proud to be a part of and a contributor to the Knoxville business community," states Angie Jones, the President of AMEC Academy. "AMEC employs about 100 people in East

Tennessee who have access to 29,000 employees worldwide. Since its formation, AMEC has been active with the local business associations and communities to provide a forum for sharing business opportunities and best practices. We have supported local schools through participation in career day events and have supported our community by assisting many local charities and helping with the cleanup of local streets and streams. These efforts have served to improve the local work environment and community and to provide engineering excellence to local clients."

Photo upper left: AMEC provided flooding and water quality services for Beaver Creek in Knox County TN
Photo courtesy of Knox County Stormwater Management Division

Photo above: AMEC's Knoxville office near I-40 and the Pellissippi Parkway

▼ AMEC managed the demolition of aging rocket launch towers in Cape Canaveral FL
Photo by Teresa Fiorillo, 45th Space Wing, Cape Canaveral Air Force Station

ARTS & CULTURE ALLIANCE OF GREATER KNOXVILLE

Representing the Arts and Culture of East Tennessee

The Arts & Culture Alliance of Greater Knoxville represents an extraordinary industry that attracts and entertains more than 1.3 million people annually from countries as distant and diverse as Japan, New Zealand, the Russian Federation, Liberia, the Netherlands, and across South America. Alliance membership numbers more than 100 arts and heritage organizations and 350 individual artists.

Alliance members present more than 100,000 hours of free education to local school children each year and arts and culture activities have catalyzed a remarkable revitalization of downtown. As a result, the non-profit arts and culture industry's positive impact on education, tourism, quality of life, and economic development is key to Knoxville's health and success. For more information call 865-523-7543 or visit the Alliance website at www.knoxalliance.com.

BRINGING THE ARTS TO KNOXVILLE

Founded in 1974 with Sir Anthony Quayle as Artistic Director, the **CLARENCE BROWN THEATRE** (CBT) at the University of Tennessee is a pillar of the Knoxville arts scene. The CBT boasts three theatres, presenting eight full productions each season, many of which sell out. A League of Resident Theatres D Equity theatre, the CBT has a distinguished history of hosting artists of national stature who perform alongside exceptional University of Tennessee students working toward their Bachelor of Arts and Masters of Fine Arts degrees.

Since 1961, **DOGWOOD ARTS** has celebrated the natural and cultural beauty of East Tennessee each April by producing a Festival featuring blooming gardens and trails, visual arts, music, crafts, theatre, culinary arts, dance, and literary arts. Furthering their mission of promoting and celebrating the arts, culture, and natural beauty in the region, Dogwood Arts produces other events throughout the year: House & Garden Show, Art in Public Places Knoxville, Knoxville Film Festival, and Bazillion Blooms.

The **EAST TENNESSEE HISTORICAL SOCIETY** was established in 1834, only 38 years after statehood. The East Tennessee History Center on Gay Street in downtown Knoxville includes a stunning regional history museum, gift shop, a premier genealogy research library, and archives. Through important pieces, such as Davy Crockett's first gun, the museum brings visitors face to face with history, covering the Cherokee, pioneer settlement, slavery, Civil War, Reconstruction, Hillbilly image, early country music, TVA, and the Manhattan Project.

The history of Knoxville is a wild and often surprising tale marvelously told by the city's seven **HISTORIC HOMES OF KNOXVILLE!** From log cabins to frame houses to stately stone mansions, each house museum is a chapter of history unto itself. Together, they exemplify the pioneering spirit that created Knoxville, the state of Tennessee, and our great nation. Visitors can enjoy each site individually or all of them with a value-packed combo pass.

The **HISTORIC TENNESSEE THEATRE** first opened its doors in 1928 and was hailed as "the South's most beautiful theatre." Listed on the National Register of Historic Places and honored as the Official State Theatre of Tennessee, today's Tennessee Theatre has something for everyone. Its sign reading "Tennessee" can be seen from anywhere on Gay Street. A $28 million renovation and expansion retained the theatre's historic integrity and Spanish-Moorish design, while transforming it into a modern performing arts center.

The **KNOXVILLE JAZZ ORCHESTRA** presents six annual concerts with performances at the Tennessee Theatre, the Bijou Theatre and the Square Room. Concerts, which often sell out in advance, feature world-renowned guest artists backed by a 17-piece professional big band. The organization also presents a variety of small ensemble performances. "Jazz Lunch" occurs the first Wednesday of each month. "Jazz on the Square" is a series of free outdoor concerts every Tuesday night, May through August.

The **KNOXVILLE MUSEUM OF ART** celebrates the art and artists of East Tennessee past and present, introduces new art and new ideas, and educates and serves a diverse community. Significant holdings documenting the development of the region's rich visual traditions, and current art from East Tennessee and around the globe are always on view, complemented by a lively schedule of education programs and special exhibitions. In 2014 the museum unveils a permanent glass and steel installation by internationally acclaimed artist Richard Jolley.

▲ Dale Dickey and Jeff Austin in *Sweeney Todd, 2012, a collaboration with the Clarence Brown Theatre and the Knoxville Symphony Orchestra*

▼ *East Tennessee Historical Society*

▲ Knoxville Jazz Orchestra

▲ This 1913 painting by Knoxville Impressionist Catherine Wiley, a highlight of the KMA collection, is a beautiful expression of East Tennessee's rich visual culture

The **McClung Museum of Natural History and Culture**, a Smithsonian Affiliate, houses anthropology, archaeology, decorative arts, local history, and natural history collections. Exquisite exhibits document ways of life, cultural trends, and technologies from prehistoric times to the present day, and showcase the geologic, historical, and artistic past of Tennessee, as well as cultures from around the globe. In doing so, the museum seeks to promote a better understanding and respect for the world's cultural heritage.

The **Tennessee Valley Fair** is a non-profit organization that exists to celebrate and promote agricultural heritage, family values, and individual life skills in our community with an emphasis on youth development activities through exhibits, tours, and the funding of scholarships. The Tennessee Valley Fair showcases traditions of the past, emphasizes ingenuity in Tennessee through the products of the present, and supports the vision of the future in the areas of agriculture, trade, and industry.

WDVX 89.9 FM is a listener-supported community radio station that creates content to promote the cultural heritage of East Tennessee and the Southern Appalachian region. The station plays a diverse mix of American roots music. WDVX showcases local and touring artists through in-studio performances and live shows such as the free Blue Plate Special, Tennessee Shines Radio Show, and Kidstuff. The station is located in the Knoxville Visitor Center in downtown Knoxville.

▼ Inside the Tennessee Theatre

Photo by Eric Smith

▼ McClung Museum of Natural History and Culture

▲ Tennessee Valley Fair

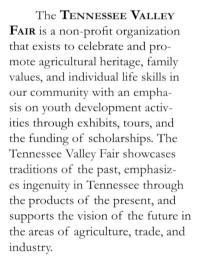

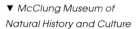

PELLISSIPPI STATE COMMUNITY COLLEGE

Personal Development Through Life-long Learning Opportunities

Pellissippi State and its graduates add nearly $250 million each year into the local economy.

Science classes at Pellissippi State use hands-on techniques to boost students' learning and employment opportunities.

Pellissippi State is a leader in providing manufacturing education, training and workforce development in East Tennessee.

When the State Technical Institute at Knoxville first opened its doors in 1974, the mission of the school was to prepare technical graduates for careers in the engineering field. The explosive growth of the school during its first decade of serving the people of primarily Knox and Blount Counties led the Tennessee Board of Regents in 1988 to approve a major expansion of the school's physical size, its curricula, and it educational offerings. In addition, the name of the institution was changed to Pellissippi State Community College to better reflect its evolving role of serving local communities in the state's third largest metropolitan area by preparing students for challenging careers in a wide range of professional fields.

The College has a present enrollment of more than 11,000 students and 1,000 faculty and staff spread over five campuses in Knox and Blount Counties, including the newest at Strawberry Plains. Indeed, the Pellissippi State Community College of today would be unrecognizable to the 45 students who made up the original student body almost four decades ago. The fundamental reason for which the College was founded, however, remains unchanged: to provide support for teaching and learning, training and workforce development, and opportunities for life, civic and cultural enrichment. And the dedicated faculty strive daily to fulfill the College's mission of providing college-level and non-credit courses and learning support instruction using a variety of delivery methods, including distance learning.

ENHANCED LEARNING OPPORTUNITIES

Pellissippi State Community College focuses on supporting and developing career/technical associate's degrees and institutional certificates, university parallel associate's degree programs, and continuing education opportunities for the citizens of Knox, Blount, and surrounding counties. The College is accredited by the Commission on Colleges of the Southern Association of Colleges and Schools to award the associate's degree in some of today's most in-demand fields:

- ► Engineering and Media Technologies
- ► Business and Computer Technology
- ► Teacher Education
- ► Nursing
- ► Mathematics
- ► English
- ► Liberal Arts

Pellissippi State's faculty does an exceptional job of combining classroom education with hands-on experience to prepare students to compete and excel in a wide variety of fields. And the College enjoys an excellent reputation in the Knoxville area for the exceptionally high long-term job placement rate of its graduates. Approximately two-thirds of the College's students each year will transfer college credits and degrees to other area and regional colleges and universities.

The College continues to expand the teaching of technology, the use of technology in instruction, and the transfer of technology to local business and industry in support of regional economic development. In partnership with the community, Pellissippi State sustains the effort toward an ever-improving quality of life for residents of East Tennessee.

SPURRING ECONOMIC DEVELOPMENT

Pellissippi State's impact on the economy of eastern Tennessee has been impressive. The 24th annual analysis of the economic impact of Pellissippi State on the Knox and Blount County area revealed that the value of business volume, jobs and individual income in the five years from 2006 to 2011 amounted to nearly $1.1 billion, or an average of $215.6 million annually. That roughly translates into a return on investment of about $3.70 in local business volume for each $1 of local revenue coming into Pellissippi State.

On the personal level, the same study estimated that those students graduating with a two-year associate's degree could expect to earn about $350,000 more during their work lifetime than students with only a high school diploma. For the most recent class of Pellissippi State graduates, the difference could mean an additional $264 million in lifetime earnings.

"The results of this study clearly demonstrate that Pellissippi State continues to be a major contributor to the economic base of Knox and Blount counties," stated Fred H. Martin, the educational consultant who completed the study.

NATIONALLY RECOGNIZED

In September, 2012, Pellissippi State became one of only six higher education institutions nationwide to be chosen to receive a grant from the American Council

A Cherokee Millwright apprentice practices welding at Pellissippi State's Claude F. Moon Welding Center at the Blount County Campus.

The Media Technologies program at Pellissippi State offers concentrations in Photography, Communications Graphics Technology, Video Production Technology and Web Technology.

on Education for the College's initiatives to help more working adults in the U.S. earn college degrees. The grant will help expand the process of awarding course-specific credits to adult learners who are in Department of Labor apprenticeship programs or the military. "We're honored to partner with the American Council

on Education on this initiative," said L. Anthony Wise, Jr., Ph.D., the president of Pellissippi State. "This grant helps us reach a growing population on our campuses and contributes toward a more skilled, educated workforce in our region. It will also support our goals under Complete College Tennessee. Pellissippi State has an

important role to play in addressing the educational needs of this community. Our faculty and staff are dedicated to helping each student realize their potential and to making East Tennessee a better place to live, work, and grow."

Pellissippi State students enjoy many cultural opportunities. The college is the top two-year school in the U.S. in terms of the number of students studying abroad.

Visit Knoxville

The Memories Stay with You

What do you feel when you say, "Vacation"?

That word stirs something in every person. It brings the sense of relaxation, time off from reality, and maybe even spending time with those closest to us. There are three phases to every vacation: the planning, the experience, and the memories. We take time to plan the "perfect" getaway, talking about and imagining what a great time we will have while we are away. Then the actual vacation arrives and we are able to relax and unwind and experience new things. Finally, after we return and unpack, we begin to relive and remember all the memories from our vacation, and it seems that those memories are what stay with us for days, weeks, and even years to come.

It is for that reason that Visit Knoxville believes when you Visit Knoxville.....the memories will stay with you.

Knoxville has a tremendous number of events to experience and places to explore. With those assets to work with, Visit Knoxville focuses on developing Knoxville as a travel destination. The organization is committed to driving tourism for the Knoxville community with the goal of keeping our hotels full and generating economic growth for our community.

What Is Visit Knoxville?

Visit Knoxville (Knoxville Convention and Visitors Bureau) is the official destination marketing organization (DMO) for the City of Knoxville and Knox County, Tenn. An accredited member of Destination Marketing Association International, Visit Knoxville is contracted by the city of Knoxville and Knox County to accelerate sustainable economic growth and development by increasing visitor and convention business to our community.

Visit Knoxville is charged with the task of developing an image that will position Knoxville and Knox County as a viable destination for meetings and visitors, bringing in turn an influx of tourism dollars that benefits the local economy.

Visit Knoxville is governed by a board of directors made up of outstanding community leaders who willingly commit their time to further our mission as an economic development driver for Knoxville and Knox County.

Valuable Community Resource

Visit Knoxville continues to communicate the story of Knoxville and promote all the community has to offer to group and leisure travelers. Visit Knoxville has years of experience in evaluating and promoting the strengths of the city and county as it relates to marketing within the conventions, sports and tourism (including group tour) segments.

The professionals at Visit Knoxville bring into play their own expertise and creativity in telling the world about Knoxville and Knox County. They attend trade shows to personally tout the area's amenities to meeting and seminar planners and tourism associations. Advertisements are placed in carefully selected magazines and other print media. The organization's website VisitKnoxville.com offers complete information and assistance to anyone interested in visiting the Knoxville area.

In pursuit of its mission, the Visit Knoxville Team works together to sale and market Knoxville as a leisure and meeting destination. Department responsibilities include:

MARKETING & COMMUNICATIONS
DEPARTMENTAL OVERVIEW

The Marketing and Communications Team promotes Knoxville as a premier travel destination through implementation of consistent, targeted, proactive, cost-effective marketing, and media campaigns. The primary goal of the department is to create compelling online and traditional advertising, promotions, and partner programs that will lead to increased.

SALES & SERVICES
DEPARTMENTAL OVERVIEW

The Visit Knoxville Sales Team markets and sells Knoxville as a destination of choice for meetings and conventions. The Sales/Services Team implements sales and service strategies that secure citywide business that benefits multiple hotels and the Knoxville Convention Center, as well as in-house meetings that provide key incremental revenues to hotels within Knoxville and Knox County.

Visit Knoxville provides meeting planners with extensive and reliable assistance to help them put together the perfect meeting from start to finish. Based on the meeting planners' criteria, the Sales Team will direct RFPs to hotels that can accommodate the specific needs of a particular meeting.

The Sales/Services Team also assists with site visits by planning itineraries, providing transportation to facilities and arranging for complimentary accommodations, if needed. Visit Knoxville is a full-service convention and visitors bureau, and there is no charge to the planner for our services.

VISITOR SERVICES
DEPARTMENTAL OVERVIEW

The Visitor Services Team provides services for leisure and convention travelers, creating collateral materials such as visitor guides, brochures and maps, and stocking gift shop merchandise.

The Visitor Services Team oversees the Knoxville Visitor Center. Regarded as a model for excellence by other communities, the Knoxville Visitor Center not only provides information, it is also home to WDVX Radio and the Uniquely Knoxville Gift Shop. This makes our Visitor Center itself a noted destination among local attractions.

GET INVOLVED
SIGN UP FOR GOTTA KNOW KNOXVILLE

Gotta Know Knoxville is a program that teaches you what Knoxville has to offer so that you can share your knowledge with every visitor you come in contact with! The program, which occurs normally on the third Wednesday of each month, runs between 4 hours and 4.5 hours (beginning at noon). Attendees enjoy lunch, a Powerpoint presentation, as well as a walking and driving tour that includes stop-ins at some favorite local attractions; and...it's FREE!

SIGN UP FOR TEAM KNOXVILLE

Team Knoxville is a volunteer program consisting of more than 3,000 people. Our team members are very diverse in age and background. Volunteers fill a valuable role in the community. The time and talent of our volunteers help make Knoxville a top destination for visitors. Our volunteers continuously provide qualified and caring volunteer services for the great city of Knoxville and Knox County. Come be a part of Team Knoxville and we will watch our community grow together, as a team.

SIGN UP FOR THE WEEKLY E-NEWSLETTER

Receive a Weekly E-Newsletter about events and activities happening in Knoxville.

To learn more about these activities and get involved, email: marketing@knoxville.org

BUDDY GREGG RVS AND MOTOR HOMES

Where Family Memories Begin

Buddy Gregg was an insurance salesman in 1972 when he borrowed a motorhome from a friend for his family vacation. That escape more than four decades ago was an epiphanl moment for Gregg and his wife, Carole, that led them to a career of helping others discover the same wonder and excitement they themselves found in

the gateway to the plethora of recreational activities nestled in the Smoky Mountains, Knoxville is the junction of major interstate highways that shuttle travelers to some of the most breathtaking scenic and historical sights on the eastern seaboard. Gregg opened his "Knoxville Super Center" in 1986 with the same commitment to his new customers that had identified his business in Arkansas.

"I put the same values in our Knoxville location that I have always put in my sales career," Gregg explained in an interview in 2009. "I believe that when I sell a person something, I have to sell it form the heart. That became even more important to me when it was my name on the sign over the door. I realize that I am selling my name and my reputation. My home phone number was even on my business card to show my customers how much I value their business and strive to create a family-type relationship with the people who put their trust in us."

exploring the open road in a luxury motor coach.

After twelve years as a salesman successfully matching customers with just the perfect recreational vehicle to suit their individual tastes, Gregg opened his own sales center for high-end new and pre-owned motorhomes

in Little Rock, Arkansas. There he quickly built a reputation for quality and integrity and, as his reputation spread, Gregg outgrew his original location. Searching for a new cornerstone for his burgeoning business, Gregg was drawn to East Tennessee and found exactly what he was looking for in Knoxville. In addition to being

A REVOLUTIONARY SHOPPING EXPERIENCE

The sales professionals at Buddy Gregg RVs and Motor Homes are extremely proud of the

Below, Right: A huge variety of towables grace the 20+ Acre Supercenter.

Known for hosting many local events, Buddy Gregg welcomes Bruce and Steve Pearl on location for a LIVE broadcast.

way they have revolutionized the experience of shopping for an RV or a motor home. The customer's experience begins immediately upon arrival at the 20-acre Buddy Gregg site. "It's almost like the customer has arrived at a five-star hotel," states Travis Hollifield, the company's general sales manager. "We emphasize customer comfort for the ultimate in a shopping experience. We personalize that experience based on the individual camping or travel needs of each customer. In addition, we are considered a true 'boutique' store carrying the finest names in the industry, including Newmar, Forest River, Heartland, Gulf Stream, Thor, Winnebago/Itasca, and others. It is a privilege for us to represent the best, high-line motor homes and RVs on the market today."

The luxury vehicles and travel trailers on the "Knoxville Super Center" lot offer everything from the ultimate in comfort to economical functionality. Top of the line models feature options ranging from full kitchens with heated flooring to multiple retractable entertainment systems and washer and dryer units. Realizing that the market also includes many shoppers who are more interested in family-centered recreation activities, the Buddy Gregg site includes a wide variety of travel trailers and fifth wheels.

The more than 50 professionals at Buddy Gregg RVs and Motor Homes include experienced sales personnel and factory trained service technicians capable of servicing all brands, makes, and models of motor homes. The Super Center lot includes a complete parts and accessories store, 21 service bays, a full service body shop, and club house for all service guests along with free overnight camping spaces.

CREATING SPECIAL MEMORIES

Bob Wiegand, the company's general manager realizes, however, that being the largest dealer of new and pre-owned motor homes in Tennessee does not in itself satisfy his own personal goals for the business. Nor do the many industry awards the company has received over the years, such as the Winnebago Circle of Excellence (2011 and 2012), Newmar's Medal of Service Excellence and Platinum Dealer (2011 and 2012), and an award from the Knoxville Better Business Bureau for a complaint-free year in 2012. Equally important is the company's involvement with the Knoxville Chamber of Commerce, the Better Business Bureau, and the numerous philanthropic activities undertaken in conjunction with the American Cancer Society, the Muscular Dystrophy Association, and other local charities Wiegand and his staff are justifiably proud of the fact that they

are recognized as the dealership that offers the vehicles that bring people together and create special memories. "Family memories are priceless," Wiegand states. "Motor homes and travel trailers have become an American symbol of personal freedom and a connection between family and friends that combines the excitement of travel and adventure. People who travel in motor homes and recreational vehicles want to be more in touch with themselves and the world around them. They realize that spending time with loved ones is what matters most. That is why they teach their children and grandchildren how to fish, skip rocks, or throw a ball.

"It is this legacy, these memories that we are passing down. That is what we are sharing and what makes us the best in what we do. We are dedicated to providing the finest products and services to help people realize their dreams and create those special memories."

An On-Site parts and accessories store completes the supercenter, making Buddy Gregg RV's and Motorhomes a 'One-Stop-Shop.'

Below, left: The 2013 KING AIRE houses luxurious features within a comfortable living space.

Below: Buddy Gregg RV's & Motorhomes is actively involved with local events. Employees ranging from service to administration make up their team in the News Sentinal Golf Scramble.

KIMBERLY-CLARK CORPORATION

Evolving Products. Timeless Values

Early in 1872, a schoolgirl passed by a paper mill recently established on the banks of the Fox River in Neenah, Wisconsin and was given a small stack of papers by J.A. Kimberly, one of the mill's founders. The grateful child, wanting to use the paper for wrapping a package, later returned to the mill with 15 cents to repay

Kimberly-Clark Loudon Mill

Mr. Kimberly for his kindness. That 15-cent transaction marked the first in a 141-year history of the company's sales that in 2012 reached more than $21 billion.

Charles Clark, Havilah Babcock, and Frank Shattuck had joined Kimberly in founding the mill, then known as Kimberly, Clark, and Company, as a facility for producing newsprint from linen and rags. Over the next almost century-and-a-half, Kimberly-Clark Corporation evolved into a global entity that today supplies household products

Kimberly-Clark is justifiably proud of the fact that it has created five of the eight major consumer product categories in which the company competes: facial tissue, paper towels, toilet paper on a roll, feminine pads, and disposable training pants. Kimberly-Clark has built its reputation and success on inventing new products and then improving them, creating a strong legacy of innovation.

LEADING THE WORLD IN ESSENTIALS FOR A BETTER LIFE

Kimberly-Clark Corporation today produces a long list of well-known global brands that are an indispensable part of life for peo-

the values shared by its employees remain timeless.

The trust that billions of people around the globe daily place in Kimberly-Clark products is a huge responsibility and the company's employees take that responsibility very seriously. The founders' values of honesty, integrity, and courageously doing the right thing are as fundamental today as they were when the first mill opened in 1872. Growth strategies include new ideas that add value and foster respect for each employee and care for the communities in which they live and work.

Kimberly-Clark Corporation is also leading the way in sustainably produced products. In 2009, the company announced stronger fiber sourcing standards to increase conservation of forests globally along with other methods to ensure the resources we enjoy today will be here for generations to come.

Its efforts have led to Kimberly-Clark Corporation being named to numerous prestigious lists, among them:

▶ Best Employer for Healthy Lifestyles

▶ Best Employer in South Africa

▶ Top 20 Great Places to Work in France in 2010

▶ Best Multi-national Workplace in Latin America

A WORLD LEADER COMES TO KNOXVILLE

Almost two and a half decades ago, Kimberly-Clark selected Knoxville as the site for a shared-service center. "There were several reasons for Knoxville winning out over other Southeastern cities that were researched," states

for nearly one-fourth of the people on our planet. During that time, the company has relied on its leadership team, its customers, and users to develop new technologies that have created innovative products and design solutions across its broad range of products.

ple in more than 175 countries. Household names such as Kleenex, Scott, Huggies, Pull-Ups, Kotex and Depend enhance the health, hygiene, and well-being of almost everyone from babies to senior citizens. Approximately 60,000 people in manufacturing facilities in 25 U.S. hometowns and 37 countries daily underscore the fact that while Kimberly-Clark's products have evolved over the past 141 years,

Teresa Hamilton, the company's Information Technology Senior Communicator. "The quality of life in Knoxville, the business climate, and the talent pool, which included the close proximity to the University of Tennessee, weighed heavily in the decision to locate here. Knoxville also had an emerging shared-service/call center industry that was encouraged and valued by government and business leaders."

The administrative center in Knoxville began in 1990 with just a handful of employees. Today, a staff of 365 provides the corporation with domestic and international transportation services, payroll, and employee benefits as well as many accounting and finance functions. "Knoxville continues to be a great place for Kimberly-Clark Corporation to recruit and retain great people who enjoy living here," says Steve Harmon,

the company's Vice-President of Transportation and Kimberly-Clark Knoxville's Site Leader.

At about the same time, the company broke ground on a 230-acre site in nearby Loudon, Tennessee. The $300 million mill, which underwent significant expansion in 2001 and again ten years later, today employs 330 people and focuses on manufacturing paper towel and bath tissue products primarily from recycled waste paper. These products supply commercial and industrial customers such as offices, manufacturing operations, healthcare, and lodging facilities. "Our KC Professional Mill is proudly managed and lead by 330 East Tennessee Partners, who safely produce high quality products, at the lowest cost for our critical customers," says John McCloskey, Mill Manager of the Kimberly-Clark Loudon Mill.

Kimberly-Clark employees in Knoxville and Loudon and their colleagues across the U.S. contributed $2.7 million in gifts and pledges to various charitable causes in 2011, an amount that was matched by the company itself. In addition, Kimberly-Clark Knoxville is an active supporter of numerous other worthy organizations, including the Boys and Girls Clubs, MedShare International, United Way, and the Bright Futures Scholarship Program. Imbued with the same spirit of philanthropy, the company's employees in Loudon have become the largest contributor to United Way of Loudon County.

Kimberly-Clark Knoxville Offices

Martin & Company, Inc.

Planning for the Future

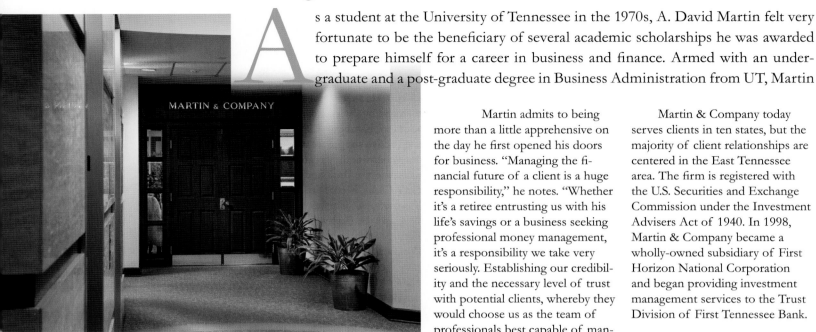

As a student at the University of Tennessee in the 1970s, A. David Martin felt very fortunate to be the beneficiary of several academic scholarships he was awarded to prepare himself for a career in business and finance. Armed with an undergraduate and a post-graduate degree in Business Administration from UT, Martin

began working for his alma mater and went on to become the Treasurer and Chief Investment Officer of the University of Tennessee System.

Passionate about his work in investment management, Martin decided that he wanted to offer personalized investment management services to individuals, financial institutions, corporations, and other entities. "I realized there was a need locally that was not being met," Martin explains. "To do this type of work meant relocating somewhere else and working for an established investment counseling firm or opening my own business. A lifelong resident of Knoxville, I loved this city and wanted to remain. I opted to launch my own business right here."

In 1989, Martin opened the doors to Martin & Company, a professional consulting firm providing investment management services on a fee basis for their clients. Unlike brokers or commodity traders, Martin's staff of nine investment counselors do not receive a commission for buying and selling financial products. They are able to maintain impartiality in the investment arena as they are not driven by commission sales.

Martin admits to being more than a little apprehensive on the day he first opened his doors for business. "Managing the financial future of a client is a huge responsibility," he notes. "Whether it's a retiree entrusting us with his life's savings or a business seeking professional money management, it's a responsibility we take very seriously. Establishing our credibility and the necessary level of trust with potential clients, whereby they would choose us as the team of professionals best capable of managing their financial security, was the single most daunting challenge we faced."

Martin met that challenge and launched his venture in 1989 with three clients and $6 million under management. Almost a quarter century later, as Martin & Company prepares in 2014 to celebrate its silver anniversary of being in business, the company is managing approximately $2 billion in assets for more than 100 clients. Based on assets under management, Martin & Company has been the largest investment advisory firm in Knoxville for the past 20 years and is listed as the largest such firm in the Knoxville Business Journal's "Book of Lists." The firm is the fourth largest fee-only registered investment advisor in the Southeast and one of the top fifty in the U.S.

FINANCIAL STEWARDSHIP

Martin & Company's sole business is managing money on behalf of its clients. The only source of revenue is fees paid by clients based on a percentage of the market value of assets under management. The firm's select group of clients includes pension plans, profit sharing plans, endowments, insurance companies, public funds, financial institutions, trusts, corporations, and individuals.

Martin & Company today serves clients in ten states, but the majority of client relationships are centered in the East Tennessee area. The firm is registered with the U.S. Securities and Exchange Commission under the Investment Advisers Act of 1940. In 1998, Martin & Company became a wholly-owned subsidiary of First Horizon National Corporation and began providing investment management services to the Trust Division of First Tennessee Bank.

Over the quarter-century that Martin & Company has been providing investment counseling services to its clients, the firm has maintained a steadfast focus on the city in which it put down its roots. The same rock-solid trust and confidence that became the hallmarks of Martin & Company's professional services extend to the firm's long-familiar physical location at Two Centre Square in the heart of downtown Knoxville. When Martin & Company marks its silver anniversary in 2014, the celebration will take place in the same building in which the business was launched in 1989.

A. David Martin, the founder and chairman of the company, made a priority of giving something back to the community that he feels gave him so much. "I was a beneficiary of several academic scholarships at UT that were funded by endowments" he adds, "and was intrigued by the endowment concept. I saw how a single gift could create an endowment that would support worthy causes in perpetuity. For that reason, my wife and I have created scholarship endowments at four different colleges and I have committed much of my professional career to endowment building."

The company's philanthropy extends to other areas as well.

Martin & Company portfolio mangers Charles Stewart (left) and Darren Williams.

Martin & Company President and CEO, Bill Woodson (seated, left) and A. David Martin, Chairman & Founder. Standing from left are: Michael Holt, Executive Vice President, David Jagels, Chief Financial Officer, and Ted Flickinger, Executive Vice President.

Committed to community service, Martin & Company employees have served a number of community, civic, and nonprofit organizations, including East Tennessee Foundation, Habitat for Humanity, Helen Ross McNabb Center, Leadership Knoxville, Legacy Parks Foundation, Ronald McDonald House, United Way, and the YMCA.

"Occasionally, I have to step back and take in the huge impact that our work has on the well-being of so many in our community and region," says Bill Woodson, president and CEO. Whether it is the financial security of seniors whose retirement resources we manage or the students whose education is dependent on scholarship endowments or the hospitals whose ability to care for the health needs of our population depends on financial strength, we are making a major difference in the lives of many. As stewards of $2 billion of other people's money, we have established an influential presence locally."

By dedicating itself to its clients and community, Martin & Company will continue to be the "manager of choice" in the region for many years to come.

The highly experienced staff of Martin & Company gathered outside its offices at Two Centre Square in the heart of downtown Knoxville.

SCRIPPS NETWORKS INTERACTIVE

Embracing a Sustainable Work Life Balance

The LEED Gold Certification for the new 150,000 square foot addition completed in 2010.

At the busy intersection of Interstate 40/75 and Pellissippi Parkway exists an oasis of natural tranquility with a tree-lined lake, quietly splashing fountains, waterside benches and walking trails—not to mention an aqua-tinted glass edifice that houses some of the brightest and most creative minds in the media and entertainment industries.

This impressive campus serves as the corporate headquarters for Scripps Networks Interactive, the Knoxville-based company at the forefront of providing lifestyle media content to consumers around the world With a portfolio of top brands including HGTV, DIY Network, Food Network, Cooking Channel, Travel Channel, and GAC as well as incredibly successful digital platforms, print publications, and branded merchandise, Scripps is a beacon of creativity and innovation for East Tennessee.

The company prides itself on being an innovator, not only through its trendsetting brands and original content but by living its core values both internally and within the greater community.

The Scripps entrepreneurial spirit and dedication to its core values is apparent not only in its trendsetting brands and original content, but in its day-to-day corporate operations and its involvement in the greater Knoxville community. The company's commitment to the principles of diversity, clarity in communication, integrity, compassion & support, shared responsibility, work/life balance, openness, and humor is apparent through employee relations and all its business platforms.

In 2010, it became apparent that with the company's continued success and growth a physical expansion of the Knoxville headquarters was in order as well. Scripps designed a collaborative, modern workspace, aligning its dedication to both its employees and the environment. The result was a new 150,000 square foot LEED Gold-certified building that provides a model for environmental stewardship in East Tennessee. The guiding principles for the project were to create a sustainable, efficient facility that allowed more occupant control of individual workspaces while supporting collaborative workflows. Decisions made based on these principles resulted in our ability to obtain LEED Gold certification.

Scripps has a three-pronged approach to green business: recycling and waste reduction, energy efficiency, and community outreach. Recycling is not only practiced extensively in day-to-day operations but nearly 1,000 tons of demolition and building waste were recycled and diverted from landfills during the construction of the new building. The energy footprint of the facility is kept to a minimum thanks to numerous design elements. An exterior made almost entirely of windows eliminates the need for extensive interior lighting while a state-of-the-art under-floor air system allows for individual workplace airflow control.

The Green Team, an employee committee, seeks to spread awareness internally while also supporting sustainability in the community. Due to the team's initiatives and energy, Scripps was honored as GoGreenET's 2012 Community Outreach winner for its employee education initiatives, which included multiple blog posts and a Change the

The stunning Scripps Networks Interactive headquarters located on Sherrill Boulevard in West Knoxville as seen from Packard Park, the private onsite green space and walking trail.

Opened at the Knoxville headquarters in October 2012, the Food Network Kitchen serves employees creative dishes with a focus on the use of fresh, local ingredients.

Scott Atchley, manager of Network Operations, monitors all of the SNI channels in real time to ensure quality control.

World Fair hosted for employees on the Knoxville campus. Scripps also won the 2012 Smart Trips Commuter Challenge competition, which acknowledged the employees' efforts to utilize alternate transportation and/or carpooling for their commutes.

In October 2012, the Food Network Kitchen opened on the Knoxville campus, offering healthy options for employees and demonstrating an enthusiasm for using fresh, local products. With over 400 meals sold in the kitchen each week, employees have enjoyed the healthy eating choices as well as their favorite guilty pleasures.

In accord with Scripps' values as a whole, the Knoxville headquarters, as well as its employees, embraces green building practices and supports a sustainable lifestyle.

Employees from across the company participate in the annual Volunteer Day as part of SNI's Change the World initiative. This group of employees donated their time and efforts to the Second Harvest Food Bank in Maryville.

Pairs of employees, including Rachel Dooley (L) and Chelsey Hallett (R), competed in paddle boat races on the campus lake while the spectators enjoyed the sunshine and ice cream in an event designed to raise funds and awareness for SNI's partnership with the United Way.

THE EPISCOPAL SCHOOL OF KNOXVILLE

Impacting the World, One Student at a Time

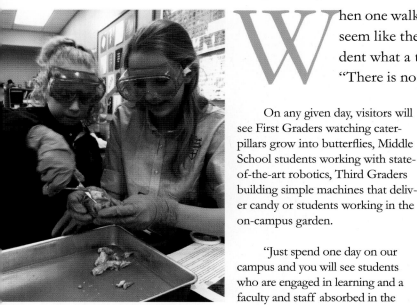

In an effort to connect the Lower and Middle Schools, each fall eighth graders have the opportunity to assist second graders with the dissection of a cow's eye. Here Alexis Farmer is aided by Riley Denton in her dissection which is part of the second grade's annual study of the human eye

In January 2013, ESK launched a FLEx 1:1 Technology Program allowing students to bring their own devices into the classroom to aid in the education process. Below, eight graders Madison Howell and EllieLai use an iPad to record an algebra review. ESK participates competitively with local independent and private schools in seven sports programs. Below right, Seventh grader Sarah Jane Kline drives the ball down the court during a Varsity Girls basketball game.

When one walks through the halls of The Episcopal School of Knoxville, it may seem like the typical elementary or middle school. But ask any teacher or student what a typical day is like at ESK and they will all give the same answer, "There is no typical day." ESK is a school that defines itself on being unique.

On any given day, visitors will see First Graders watching caterpillars grow into butterflies, Middle School students working with state-of-the-art robotics, Third Graders building simple machines that deliver candy or students working in the on-campus garden.

"Just spend one day on our campus and you will see students who are engaged in learning and a faculty and staff absorbed in the education of each child," ESK Headmaster Jay Secor said. "Here at ESK, one is able to make an investment in the lives of our children and that is what makes us unique."

When ESK founders first gathered, they dreamed of a school, which would challenge students to excel, both academically and socially, in an educational environment that taught kindness, compassion, and consideration of others.

In August 1998, the dream became a reality when the school first opened its doors to 28 students in Kindergarten through fourth grade. A middle school was later added and in May 2003 ten eighth grade students were honored as the first graduating class of The Episcopal School of Knoxville. Over the years, fund raising efforts from

donations and from the tireless work of the Parents' Association have led to dramatic expansion of the school's original facilities.

AN INCLUSIVE ATMOSPHERE

The 353 students enrolled in the 2013 school year at The Episcopal School of Knoxville represent a more than tenfold jump from the initial 28 that walked through its doors when the school first opened 15 years ago. ESK is recognized for its academic excellence and character training for students from Kindergarten through eighth grade. The school's interdisciplinary curriculum includes interscholastic activities such as National History Day and Model United Nations; performing and fine arts; world languages; and a full, inclusive athletic program. ESK offers a faith-based environment, including daily chapel for all students, but does not require any student to subscribe to any particular faith. ESK actively seeks children of diverse beliefs and backgrounds.

ESK's mission remains true to the vision of its founders: to prepare students for higher education and a lifetime of learning within the context of a loving, family-centered environment. The learning

experience at ESK enriches its students' intellectual, physical, cultural, and spiritual growth so that they may realize their potential as children of God and involved citizens of local, state, and international communities.

The campus now occupies a picturesque setting of 96 acres of rolling land in West Knox County. The 70 faculty and staff members are justifiably proud of the school's state-of-the-art administrative offices, gymnasium, science labs, dining hall, library, art room, chapel and technology labs. In November 2012, a peer review team from the Southern Association of Colleges and Schools visited The Episcopal School of Knoxville for the SACS evaluation process. In addition to receiving numerous commendations for its facilities and its work, ESK received full recommendation for re-accreditation through SACS as well as from the Southern Association of Independent Schools (SAIS).

Courses of study at ESK's Lower and Middle Schools run the gamut of subjects considered essential to prepare students for high school and college. Everything from Mathematics, Science, and Language Arts to Art, Music, and

An organic garden supplies fresh produce, as seen on the steam table, to the dining hall. Like Bo Fiser, McKenzie Burkhalter, and Sydney Aikens pictured here, students help plant. The school's farm-to-table dining concept incorporates ESK's dedication to teaching students to become environmentally friendly consumers as well as how to live green and care for the earth each day.

► Experiential learning to prepare for real life experiences.

► Cooperation, collaboration and problem solving. Service based learning.

► Cutting-edge technology and sustainability.

► Farm-to-table dining program with student-tended organic garden.

► Nearly-organic lunch each day with homemade bread, local fruits, meat and cheeses.

► Campus security and safety.

► Confidential, need-based financial assistance.

The Episcopal School of Knoxville is situated on a 78-acre, wooded campus overlooking the Smoky Mountains. This is one of three barns that students and families pass on the way up the car pool line.

Digital Literacy is offered. Other programs include involvement with STEMSpark and a recently launched FLEx 1:1 Technology Program that allows students to bring their own devices into the classroom to aid in education. In addition, ESK's Tribes Agreements instill and nurture a strong sense of integrity in each of its students that they carry with them on their educational journey.

Another important aspect of the learning experience at ESK is community service. All students participate in a variety of initiatives that benefit the local community ranging from preparing and serving meals at the Volunteer Ministry Center to environmental work at the Turkey Creek Wetlands and Smoky Mountain Institute at Tremont.

An impressive 92 percent of students at ESK opt to participate in the wide variety of interscholastic athletics the school offers, including flag football, tennis, co-ed track and field, co-ed soccer, basketball, trap shooting and softball. In recent years, ESK teams have won championships in girls' volleyball, girls' basketball, flag football and cross country.

All these factors come together at The Episcopal School of Knoxville to offer an unparalleled experience that instills a love of learning at an early age and establishes a strong academic foundation for the future success of our students.

Below left, George Hall, a 22,000 square-foot Middle School Building, houses the Siler Great Room, library, dining hall, media center, a fully-equipped computer lab and administrative offices.
As part of the K-5 Educational Technology Program, first and second graders use iPads daily and have weekly technology classes. Below, Kindergartners Bella Avery, Greta Whitt and Aidan Brown take their iPad work seriously.

NAVUS

Transforming Dreams Into Reality

David Lawless and his wife, Robin, had considered a number of possible names for the company they were about to launch in 1998, but none seemed to be as appropriate as the one suggested by their pastor. "He offered the Latin word 'nawus' meaning 'industrious'," David explains, "and we felt that was perfect.

We opted to substitute the 'v' for the 'w' in the word as that is how it is pronounced in Latin and settled on NAVUS."

This has been the perfect description for the innovative design company that the couple founded in Knoxville. David and Robin Lawless created NAVUS as a custom machine builder focusing on quality, reliability and an "old school" work ethic. The company's mechanical, weld and electrical designers bring a broad background of expertise in robotic automation integration to the business that has provided custom turnkey solutions for an impressive number of Fortune 500 companies operating in the medical, automotive, and consumer industries as well as the military. "We make the machines that make the products,"

David notes. "If you can dream it, NAVUS can design a machine to build it."

High Tech Company With Old School Values

From concept to finished product, NAVUS specializes in turning the existing manufacturing processes of their clients into highly effective automated solutions, thus increasing safety, quality, and productivity. A vertically integrated operation, NAVUS designs and builds their machines in the company's 23,000 square foot facility in Knoxville. Ranging in size from those that can fit into the palm of one's hand to a weld cell that produces a 30 ton part for industry-leader General Dynamics, NAVUS-produced equipment can be found in businesses and

industries across the country and as part of the U.S. military operating around the world.

The staff of approximately 24 highly talented and trained designers and fabricators has developed a reputation as being among the nation's finest automation integrators. They utilize the latest in three dimensional technology and animation to provide smart solutions for even the most difficult challenges. The NAVUS team of professionals has the knowledge, experience, and skills that enable them to serve as the "one-stop shop" for their clients, partnering with them to offer a wide range of start-to-finish services, including:

Engineering

► Concept Development

► Project Management

► Manufacturing Process Development

► Machine Design

► Reverse Engineering

► Programming and electrical design

► Debugging and Troubleshooting

Fabrication

► 25 ton dual trolley gantry crane

► Certified welding per military specifications.

► Research and development of state of the art weld procedures.

► Assembly and calibration of developed manufacturing processes and machines.

► CNC Machining to customer specification

In its 15 year existence, NAVUS has distinguished itself in the design, fabrication, installation, and servicing of custom-made

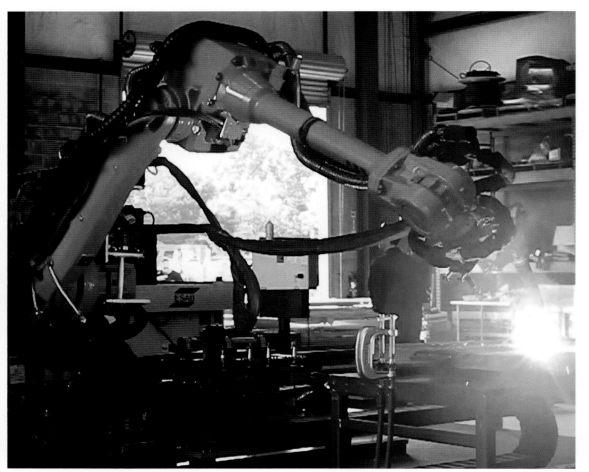

ABB six-axis welding robot in an automated cell built for General Dynamics

machinery. Services also include precision machining as well as the prototyping, fabrication, and assembly of metal and composite materials for aerospace, automotive, medical device, nuclear, and pharmaceutical applications. The NAVUS commitment to quality is the result of having qualified personnel dedicated to meeting the company's unwavering goal of meeting and exceeding the expectations of its clients.

The numerous benefits of NAVUS solutions quickly become evident to the company's clients. Robotic automation today is at the heart of lean manufacturing. NAVUS-designed and produced equipment can reduce operating costs, perfecting both quality and productivity. Companies become more environmentally friendly by reducing scrap, exhaust, and energy. In addition, robotics can remove employees from dangerous and repetitive tasks, allowing valuable human resources to be used in more productive ways.

The economic pressures on businesses and consumers today are forcing both to consider their purchases. Low-cost, high-quality products are the sign of the times. The most successful companies in this economy are realizing that automation, especially the flexibility offered by robotic automation, is the perfect way to achieve both. Those companies with the best, leanest automated manufacturing processes are the ones who are better positioned to respond to the rapidly changing demands of customers. An automated, flexible manufacturing process is able to change product mix and product make-up "on the fly."

"I have lived by the philosophy to treat others like I want to be treated. Truth be known, I have worked my whole life since I was 9 years old. I expect only the best from myself and my employees and I expect the same from my customers."

A COMPANY MAKING A DIFFERENCE

David Lawless points to his own life when asked why the company he and his wife founded has been so active in service to the people of Knox County. "I am a product of the system," he recalls. "I was fortunate enough to have received scholarships from the federal government that allowed me to graduate college with degrees in psychology and religion. I'm pleased to be in a position where NAVUS can play a role in giving back to the people in this area today some of what was given to me."

In addition to the jobs and livelihood that NAVUS has provided over the past 15 years, the company has been active in supporting the area's children and youth through programs that David says, "have helped me develop and move beyond my humble beginnings in West Lonsdale."

"Since I have been with Navus, I have seen the most sincere dedication to customer satisfaction and owners that really care about their business and their employees. I believe the team's diversity, versatility and personality are what keep things moving forward here at Navus. I hope we can continue to move forward for the benefit of the companies that rely on our work and for our local community that we rely on for support." –Buck Barber, Navus Automation

23,000-square foot facility located on three acres in West Knoxville

Automated weld cell for Bath Iron Works' military vessels

VISIONARY SOLUTIONS, LLC

Leading the Way with Creative Solutions for an Ever-Changing World

Visionary Solutions, founded in 2000, provides technical solutions on large-scale, material management and waste disposition projects for the federal government and its contractors. The company is a leading service provider for both the government and commercial nuclear industry addressing the complex issues that span transportation and its related services. We are also expanding our presence in both the national and international commercial waste and material disposition markets.

Our company has developed and improved its resources with a focus on effective project management, customized training and consulting, regulatory analysis, and waste profiling, transportation, and brokerage services to meet the demands of the waste and material management industry. With 85 employees company-wide, about 45 of whom are in the Knoxville area, the company is considered a small business, but provides services on a scale sufficient to effectively meet the needs of large projects.

Visionary Solutions established its positive reputation with the federal government early on, when it successfully managed the transportation and disposition of nearly 6,000 cylinders of depleted uranium hexafluoride from Oak Ridge to Portsmouth for the Department of Energy. Our training team also led emergency preparedness training for the Department of Energy across several regions of the nation and continues to provide on-going support for hazardous and radioactive material awareness to Y-12 and other federal contractors. Simultaneously, Visionary Solutions completed a similar transportation management project for Low Level Radioactive Waste Shipments in Silos 1 and 2 Containers for nearly 4,000 containers from Fluor Fernald, OH to Waste Control Specialists facility in Texas.

Visionary Solutions was also awarded a small business prime

contract with the Department of Energy to provide Transuranic transportation services in 2007, which was recently re-awarded in 2012 based on our performance and reputation for successful project completion and safe operations. These key projects helped Visionary Solutions gain the trust of our federal clients and established our company as a competitive business in the industry. We continue to maintain a positive relationship as a prime contractor to the Department of Energy and other Federal customers while extending our reach into the commercial waste and materials disposition market. Visionary Solutions is strengthening its capabilities with new technology, the best equipment, and successful project management.

Today, the company has locations in Knoxville, TN; Carlsbad, NM; and Corona, CA. Visionary Solutions is proud of its reputation as a total solution provider for material disposition projects. As a federally approved motor carrier and logistics company, Visionary Solutions strives daily to provide safe, compliant, and comprehensive solutions to complex waste management and material disposition needs. Visionary Solutions also features 24/7 tracking and

communications to provide an accurate status of shipments and to enhance the safety and security of government materials.

Visionary Solutions is currently expanding its line of services to include new technologies that will not only create jobs, but also solve many real world environmental problems that our communities face. For example, the company intends to implement a two-part recycling process in the Knoxville area, designed to achieve the goal of "Zero Landfill." Rather than just a hypothetical "go green" alternative, this will be a real system working daily to eliminate waste in its entirety by converting it into a renewable energy source. Additional offerings include medical and pharmaceutical waste management, as well as environmental management and asset recovery and recycling.

SERVICE TO COMMUNITY

Visionary Solutions officers lead by example and every employee takes the company's commitment to being a good corporate citizen very seriously. We provide mentoring services through the Knoxville Chamber of Commerce

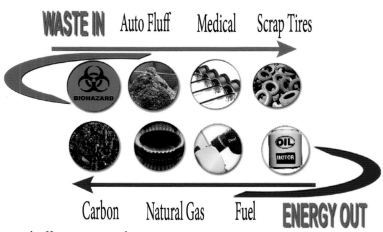

and offer support and resources to other local community associations and small businesses where a need is determined. Assistance in achieving driver certification is also offered to small companies in the Knoxville area. Visionary Solutions is proud to support the efforts of local and national charitable organizations and civic groups. We work diligently to achieve our ultimate goal of managing and mitigating risk in a constantly changing environment while building lasting relationships with clients in the public and private sectors to ensure that all of our projects and services include effective management and resourcefulness, within budget while remaining on schedule.

MANAGEMENT SOLUTIONS, LLC

Comprehensive Project Management Services

Walter Perry, the administrator of the Small Business Administration (SBA) in Tennessee, remarked in 2012 when Management Solutions, LLC was named U.S. SBA National Subcontractor of the Year that the company had "put Tennessee business on the map." The award, which honors small businesses that provide outstanding goods and services to the federal government as subcontractors, was an affirmation of what Management Solutions' many clients have realized since Misty Mayes founded the company in 2002.

Misty Mayes, Founder and President, Management Solutions, LLC
Photo by MSLLC

"This is a wonderful acknowledgment for our entire team," Mayes stated at the award ceremony. "We have worked hard to understand the needs of our clients and to deliver innovative solutions that will help them reduce time and costs on projects. It is simply wonderful to have our small company recognized on the national level."

Mayes' pride in her company and her team was again spotlighted when Management Solutions was awarded the Pinnacle Woman-Owned Business Excellence Award from the Knoxville Chamber in May 2013. The award has become an emblem of business excellence in East Tennessee.

A DECADE OF GROWTH AND SERVICE

Launched just over a decade ago with three employees and a single contract with the U.S. Department of Energy's Oak Ridge National Laboratory, Management Solutions today is a multi-million dollar company that boasts more than 40 employees and dozens of clients and customers throughout the Southeast. The company's client list and high visibility projects include the Department of Energy; the U.S. Army Corps of Engineers; UT-Battelle; Oak Ridge Associated Universities; Alstom Power; Cannon & Cannon; and Pro2Serve among others.

Having successfully established Management Solutions as one of the leading project management companies in the Southeast and with growing demand from the commercial construction industry, Mayes and her husband, Sam, who helped lead Management Solutions through its successful early years, spun off a new business in 2010, Construction Project Solutions, LLC (CPS), to expand services to the construction industry market.

Management Solutions specializes in comprehensive project management services that help its clients deliver their projects on time and on budget every time. Those services include project management/control services, project management training, construction management services, information systems application/integration, application hosting services, process improvement services, and cost estimating services.

To succeed in today's highly competitive funding environment, successful organizations are adopting project management practices on an enterprise-wide basis. Management Solutions has the experience, expertise, and tools to resolve the most complex project management challenges.

Below: U.S. SBA Administrator Karen Mills (3rd from left) presents Misty Mayes (2nd from left) with the 2012 U.S. SBA National Subcontractor of the Year award
Photo courtesy of SBA

Below, left: U.S. Senator Lamar Alexander, Misty Mayes, Sam Mayes, U.S. Senator Bob Corker
Photo courtesy of Senator Alexander's office

The company's staff of civil, environmental, industrial, mechanical, and construction engineers work in close collaboration with clients to provide innovative solutions to even the most challenging projects. Three-quarters of the staff have more than 15 years experience in the industry and senior staff average more than 25 years experience. Half are Certified Project Management Professionals.

These professionals specialize in helping companies establish an integrated planning and portfolio management system that not only formalizes the processes for estimating project-level scope, schedule, and budget needs, but also analyzes groups of projects (portfolios) and their interdependencies, milestones, float, and risk. This seamless process takes a project from formation through the planning and approval phases, through execution and closeout, all within one integrated system.

"We operate as a full-service project management solution provider supplying our customers with 'best value services' through our experienced professionals who have successfully applied project management concepts in a variety of different industries," Mayes explains. "We have impacted financial bottom lines and elevated project management skills for individuals and companies throughout the area. We have helped our customers – local businesses and government agencies – deliver on time and on budget. As a result of our vast federal contact experience, we also help local firms enter the federal market."

A NATIONAL COMPANY MAKING A LOCAL DIFFERENCE

Management Solutions is headquartered in Knoxville and maintains satellite offices in Louisville, Kentucky and Atlanta, Georgia. There are also on-site staff at multiple sites including Oak Ridge and Nashville in Tennessee;

Fort Campbell and Fort Knox in Kentucky; St. Louis, Missouri; Olmsted, Illinois; Indianapolis, Indiana; and Dayton, Ohio.

"We are proud to be headquartered in Knoxville, a place where many of us grew up and in a community that is rich in history, culture, active outdoor living, and offers tremendous support of local business success," states Mayes, who, along with her husband, Sam, vice president of CPS, graduated from the University of Tennessee School of Engineering. "For more than ten years, Management Solutions has provided excellent project management and customer service to clients throughout the region. Creating employment opportunities combined with our business focus and dedication to helping businesses succeed has had a positive regional economic impact. We are proud of our Knoxville heritage and the positive business impact our entire team brings to the region."

Misty and Sam Mayes take great pride in promoting a work environment that stresses a strong sense of community and the belief that they are part of something larger. They believe in being good

stewards in their local community and offer opportunities to their employees to participate in charitable work with organizations they support such as The Restoration House of East Tennessee, Mission of Hope, St. Jude Children's Research Hospital, Knox Area Rescue Ministries, and others.

A strong supporter of the greater Knoxville community throughout the year, Misty Mayes serves on several local boards, including the Christian Academy of Knoxville, Knoxville Chamber, The Restoration House of East Tennessee, and Mission of Hope.

Employees from across the company show their team spirit and compete in the Dragon Boat Races to benefit Knox Area Rescue Ministries

Photo by MSLLC

Management Solutions LLC headquarters, Awarding Winning Way, Knoxville

Photo by MSLLC

STUDIO FOUR DESIGN INC.

Design for people to see, to use, and to feel

Studio Four Design began in 2002 with a simple idea: Help clients go further, faster. By uniting a select group of planners, graphic artists, architects, interior designers and consultants, they focus obsessively on every client's needs. This approach is expanding their ability to work on projects from public to private, local to national.

The team at Studio Four Design proudly helps communities, corporations, and congregations plan for growth; creates brand identities for startups and entrepreneurs alike; and designs office buildings, educational facilities, athletic venues, retail spaces, medical centers, churches, banks, museums, multi-unit housing and single-family residences for a growing list of clients. On projects of all types they are passionate about design for people to see, to use and to feel.

TOGETHER, THEY MAKE DESIGN HAPPEN

To do their work, they meet, research, sketch, model, evaluate and stay involved. But most importantly, they listen. Beyond all else, their projects respond to their client's philosophy. Design, they believe, is an outcome of the process; a collaborative exploration to accomplish a specific purpose. When giving shape to projects, they take cues from clients, ask questions to guide the process, and take the lead with suggestions and direction when appropriate. This process serves as a foundation that supports all of the design work to follow. Around their office, it has been said that, "Every

front porch tells a unique story," and a review of Studio Four Design's portfolio shows their work is not about developing a signature style.

USER DELIGHT, DOWN TO THE LAST DETAIL.

Some ideas flow effortlessly. Others take superhuman effort. But the team perseveres because it is their job to create memorable solutions from complex constraints. From the needs of a single family to the collective voice of 25,000 cheering fans, they uncover the unique qualities inherent within each design problem.

This is evident in how they helped the University of Tennessee build on the success of its basketball program; transforming their aging arena into an NBA-caliber sports and entertainment venue. The elevated fan experience resulted in accolades from Coach Emeritus Pat Summitt who said, "I went in there and just sat in the chairs and looked around. I was like a little kid. I was just in awe."

They've also helped transform a graph paper idea into a national brand. "When Altar'd State began to seek design partners, we were a startup, with the limited finances and infinite visions associated with most new companies," according to Aaron Walters, CEO and co-founder of Altar'd State, a retail apparel brand. "Studio Four Design was a partner with a unique perspective and a shared passion for design that we could grow with, and that could grow with us."

Three Rivers Market turned to Studio Four Design to guide their relocation and expansion after 30 years in their original location. To succeed required taking into account the community, the people and the environment as part of the design process. According to Greg Terry, one of the Studio's principals, "Ultimately, nourishing healthier people is about creating a unique place where they feel welcomed, where they can add their own mark, and where they feel pride as a part of their community."

Altar'd State. A unique storefront engages customers and creates brand identity for the growing retailer.
Photo by Greg Terry

Layton Residence. The family's personality allowed for a unique implementation of traditional forms and modern functions.   Photo by Greg Terry

Three Rivers Market. The focus was about creating a building that doesn't do less than it needs to, but doesn't do more than it can afford to.   Photo by Tyler Thayer

RIO Revolution Church. The church's vision was to be able to make a difference; not just be a 'status quo' church. Something that's alive. Something that's actually breathing.

Green McAdoo Cultural Center. 50 years after Clinton, Tennessee became the first Southern town to desegregate a school, the former 1935 Clinton Colored School reopened as a civil rights museum.   Photo by Greg Terry

These same values were visible in the firm's approach to preservation when the City of Clinton, Tennessee asked Studio Four Design to help mark the 50th anniversary of desegregation in our nation. The Green-McAdoo Cultural Center focuses on the day in August 1956 when 12 black students attended an all-white high school in Clinton, the first Southern town to desegregate a public school. The project extends beyond an historic renovation to include an interactive exhibit, a full-length documentary narrated by James Earl Jones, and life-size bronze statues of the Clinton 12, inspired by a 1956 photo.

Sustainability of the future is also a critical part of the process at Studio Four Design. They create buildings that are fiscally sensitive, environmentally responsible, and healthy spaces to live and work. With their custom design of the Fowler residence in rural East Knoxville – which received LEED Silver certification – the home's sustainable features reflect an understanding that we must meet the needs of the present without compromising the ability of future generations to meet their own needs.

Clearly, their performance and thoughtful impact on the built environment is recognized by the people that count most; their clients. "We're creative simply to make our clients more success-ful" is a core value of the firm,

according to the principals. "They all have compelling stories about what it's like to work with us, but a common theme keeps popping up: we're not a vendor, we're more like a trusted partner."

A PLAN WITH PURPOSE, STRUCTURE AND FOCUS.

At Studio Four Design the creative process is not a 9 to 5 job… it's a way of life. And it's paying off. In addition to being honored with design awards from the American Institute of Architects and other industry or-ganizations, the firm has earned local, state and national business excellence honors for their corpo-rate culture and financial growth.

Studio Four Design has vast capabilities and limitless ideas, but according to the entire team, "our passion makes the difference, and that difference makes it worth it." In a fully collaborative atmo-sphere, shared ideas contribute to the hallmarks of their work: sound planning, strong concepts and ele-gant execution.

Thompson – Boling Arena. Studio Four Design transformed an aging, 25,000 seat facility into an NBA-quality arena for 1/10 the cost of a new building.
                                                                                  Photo by David Massengill

GREEN MOUNTAIN COFFEE ROASTERS, INC.

Quality Coffee From Tree to Cup

Bob Stiller numbered himself among the millions of Americans who begin each day with a cup of coffee when he veered into a small café in Waitsfield, Vermont in 1980. So impressed was he with the quality of the coffee he was served that Stiller bought into the café. The coffee world has never been the same since.

Armed with the mission of making high quality, specialty coffee accessible to all coffee drinkers, Stiller set in motion a chain of events that would have a monumental impact on the coffee industry. He incorporated Green Mountain Coffee Roasters, Inc. (GMCR) in 1981 and moved production to Waterbury, Vermont. The company then began introducing innovative initiatives that not only guaranteed a consistently good cup of coffee, but also improved the methods for brewing the beverage that an estimated 54 percent of Americans over the age of 18 begin their day with.

Green Mountain Coffee Roasters, Inc. sources coffee from many different countries around the world.

In 2006, GMCR acquired Keurig, Incorporated. Since then, the Keurig® single cup brewing system and the company's family of coffee and beverage brands have revolutionized the way North Americans brew and enjoy coffee at home and in the workplace.

GMCR's coffee team, led by VP of Coffee Lindsey Bolger, often conducts calibration cuppings with coffee producers to develop a common language of quality.

GMCR's portfolio of brands is representative of the geographic taste preferences of coffee drinkers across the United States and Canada. The company's growth has been driven by its owned coffee brands such as Green Mountain Coffee®, the leading brand in the Keurig® system, as well as by strategic partnerships and manufacturing and distribution agreements with some of the best known beverage brands, including Dunkin' Donuts®, Starbucks®, Folgers Gourmet Selections®, Millstone®, Newman's Own® Organics, and Swiss Miss®.

Moving beyond great coffee, GMCR has expanded its portion pack offering to introduce hot teas; Brew Over Ice iced coffees and iced teas; and other beverages including hot apple cider and fruit brews. In all, GMCR sources, produces and sells more than 200 varieties of coffee, cocoa, teas and other beverages in K-Cup® and Vue® packs for Keurig® brewers, as well as a wide variety of specialty whole bean and ground coffees in more traditional package formats.

GMCR's commitment to quality extends beyond supplying award-winning coffees and beverages. The company has become known for its environmentally and socially responsible business practices, including:

► Increasing its commitment to sustainably sourced coffee. GMCR was named the world's largest purchaser of Fair Trade Certified™ coffee in 2011 by Fair Trade USA.

Fair Trade helps farmers receive a fair price for their beans, resulting in quality coffee and a higher quality of life in coffee-growing communities.

► Working with International Paper to launch the first hot beverage paper cup and lid made from polylactic acid, a renewable resource.

Working to develop a sustainable solution for its single serve offerings. In 2012, GMCR launched Vue® packs in the U.S., which can be recycled anywhere that polypropylene/#5 plastic is accepted. Currently, approximately half of communities in the U.S. recycle #5 plastic, and that number is increasing. In addition, GMCR's Grounds to Grow On™ program allows workplace Keurig® customers in the U.S. to divert used K-Cup® packs from landfills.

► Working to raise awareness of food security issues in coffee-growing communities. From 2008-2011, GMCR funded 36 food security projects through 17 NGO partners in communities where

Roasting coffee is an art and a science at GMCR's Knoxville facility.

GMCR sources Fair Trade Certified™ coffee.

► Sponsoring "source trips" to bring employees to coffee-growing communities since 1992, to enable employees to get a first hand glimpse of where and how quality coffee is grown and the impact the agricultural crop has on local communities.

A 21ST CENTURY COMPANY

GMCR's business model has served the company well. GMCR sold 8.6 million Keurig® single cup brewers in fiscal 2012 helping boost net sales company-wide to $3.8 billion, a 46 percent increase over 2011 numbers.

That success and the company's focus on sustainability have translated into numerous awards, including past recognition from Corporate Responsibility Magazine, Fortune, Forbes, the Boston Globe, and others. GMCR was also recognized with McDonald's Best of Sustainable Supply in 2012.

In addition, the Harris Poll 2012 EquiTrend© named Keurig® the "Coffee Maker Brand of the Year" and voted Green Mountain Coffee® the coffee "Brand of the Year."

Not content to rest on its laurels, GMCR continues to evolve its corporate citizenship and community outreach efforts. Since 2009, GMCR has donated upwards of $1 million to various civic and charitable organizations in Knox County and rural East Tennessee Appalachian communities, including $830,000 donated in 2012 to 32 regional non-profits. Knoxville employees actively give back to the community as well, with more than 25,000 hours volunteered by employees through GMCR's CAFE (Community Action For Employees) volunteerism program. The efforts in Knoxville support the overall purpose of GMCR: "To create the ultimate coffee and beverage experience in every life we touch from tree to cup, transforming the way the world understands business."

"As we look to the future, we remain committed to bringing fresh ideas to light; pushing forward disruptive technologies; and capturing true innovation in products that delight consumers," stated Brian Kelley, the President and CEO of Green Mountain Coffee Roasters, Inc.

GMCR's Knoxville facility manufactures K-Cup® packs for the Keurig® single cup brewing system.

GMCR was founded in 1981 in a small café in Waitsfield, Vermont.

BPV Capital Management

Thoughtful, Consistent, Disciplined Investing

"My granddad once told me 'making money is easy, keeping it… that's hard,'" quips Mike West, Sr. Partner/CEO of BPV Capital Management. "I have watched successful people secure economic wealth and then lose some, if not all, of their fortune on the next sure thing."

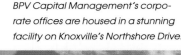

BPV Senior Partner and CEO, Mike West.

BPV devotes its energy to helping investors retain their hard-earned money by adhering to time-tested principles like that of West's grandfather. "As stewards of our investors' money, we take our responsibility very seriously and understand the obligation we have to manage our business and their money ethically and appropriately," West notes.

A Plan for Success

The events of 2008 in the financial markets led many investors to re-evaluate their portfolios and question traditional thinking about investing, asset allocation, and diversification. BPV was founded the following year in Knoxville by four partners who recognized the problems in the financial industry and shared a desire to improve the way people invest. Initially established as an SEC registered investment advisor to enable high net worth clients access to the company's investment strategies, BPV adjusted its approach in 2011 and began offering the same safeguards to everyone by focusing exclusively on the mutual fund industry, making it the only '40 Act mutual fund headquartered in East Tennessee.

BPV Capital Management's corporate offices are housed in a stunning facility on Knoxville's Northshore Drive.

"We initially launched the funds based on the belief that there was a problem in the marketplace and that we could solve that problem," West explains. "We were founded on the principle that thoughtfulness, consistency, and discipline were the hallmarks of good investing. If you are going to be a successful investor, you need the foundation of a belief system. We believed then and now that risk management should be an important component of how you invest."

Today, BPV serves clients across the country in addition to meeting a strong local demand for its services, which it has developed from the time the company was founded. The four original founders have been joined by five partners and numerous professionals personally committed to serving their clients. In addition, BPV has established a nationally recognized advisory board to provide oversight and guidance to the business.

While there are thousands of mutual funds available to investors, there are only a relatively small number of those funds that are considered to be in the liquid alternative category. BPV introduced its mutual funds from strategies that had been originally

constructed to serve the needs of Mike West's family office. The net result is that BPV's funds are more purpose driven and solution driven than merely marketing focused. Simply put, these strategies were designed to solve problems.

BPV financial advisers respond to their clients' needs by helping them understand and access information, including BPV products and services, in order to help them reach their financial goals. "Whether it's an ocean view or mountains in the landscape, a state of mind or some other financial objective, we all have some 'back porch vista' out there," says Jeremy Floyd, Chief Marketing Officer. "BPV exists to take our clients to their vista."

An Impact on the Region

BPV today continues to recruit and attract the best and the brightest employees to the Knoxville area. . The firm's leaders have found that the region's many amenities have made it a highly desirable location to live, work, and raise a family. "While we have coast to coast representation, we like to call Knoxville home for the same reasons so many national brands based in Knoxville do," West says. "It's a great way of life and we can do everything that the guys on Wall Street do, except we see the Great Smoky Mountains out of our windows instead of skyscrapers." BPV is also engaged nationally in discussions about the importance of risk management investing, lending its voice as a leader in liquid alternative investing.

To demonstrate their commitment to supporting the local community, the staff at BPV is actively involved in a variety of civic and charitable organizations:

▶ Alzheimer's Tennessee, Inc.

Corporate branding greets employees and clients as they enter the building.

The globe in CEO Mike West's office is an ongoing reminder of the global investment climate.

- ► Big Brothers Big Sisters of East Tennessee
- ► Boys and Girls Club
- ► Boy Scouts of America
- ► The Hearing and Speech Foundation
- ► The Jason Foundation
- ► Knoxville Chamber of Commerce
- ► Leadership Knoxville
- ► Legacy Parks Foundation
- ► UT Medical Institute Cancer Center – The Man Ride
- ► UT Medical Center Simulation Center Path North
- ► Tennessee Theatre
- ► Tennessee Achieves

- ► United Way of Greater Knoxville
- ► University of Tennessee College of Business Administration— Advisory Board

"BPV remains committed to providing educational information to its clients by discussing and highlighting investment data, trends, definitions, and concepts that are necessary for today's investors," West states. "We want our clients to successfully build their own 'back porch vista' by focusing on the belief that disciplined avoidance of substantial losses drives consistent investment success.

"As BPV continues to grow, it will play an increasingly important role in the community, not only through increased employment and economic impact, but also through community involvement and support. We are poised to be a meaningful part of the region for generations to come."

BPV's familiar Adirondack chair symbolizes the company's "back porch vista"—a desirable place to be or a great state of mind.

www.bpvcapitalmgmt.com

Colleagues gather on the lawn for a company photo.

HR Comp

Solutions for Business Problems

Business owners today realize that charting a course to success requires much more than offering a quality product or service at a competitive price to their customers. Business success (and even survival!) is now dependent on navigating waters often fraught with ship-sinking impediments such as federal and state regulations,

employment law compliance issues, payroll taxes, employee claims, workers compensation renewals, benefits packages, and a host of other potential headaches that can take a disastrous toll on productivity and efficiency.

Savvy business owners in ever growing numbers are turning to professionals trained in providing these services so that their management teams can devote their full attention to their primary goal: successfully operating their business. The outsourcing of these critical business services to a trusted Professional Employer

Organization (PEO) has never been more important.

The leaders in businesses in 13 states across the country have placed their trust in HRComp to handle these critical services. They have come to rely on the skilled professionals at HRComp to help them increase efficiency, productivity, and revenues through the provision of everything from payroll taxes and workers compensation insurance to complete HR packages. Tailor-made co-employment relationships are created between each client company and its workers to ensure that business owners and managers can devote their entire attention to the manufacturing, production, and delivery of their products and services.

An Idea is Born

As a receptionist at a staffing company in Dalton, Georgia,

Andrea Ball quickly climbed the corporate ladder specializing in corporate staffing, accounting, and recruiting. Seeking to own and operate her own business, Andrea decided that the greater Knoxville area would be the perfect location for her new venture. She founded HRComp in 2010 and brought more than a decade of experience in the industry as she began offering clients the professional services crucial to their success.

Andrea realized that business owners are increasingly relying on PEOs to gain access to many professional human resource services, improve risk management practices to reduce liabilities, and improve cost control and efficiency by saving time and reducing paperwork. Employees are benefitting as well with on time and accurate payroll, professional assistance with employment-related problems, efficient and responsive claims

processing, and access to benefits that are often out of the reach of small businesses. Andrea created a business model that would offer those services and create long-term client relationships.

"We are now too big to be little and too little to be big," quips Kelli Jo Wright, HRComp's Director of Marketing. "The business has grown from a start-up to one with 35 employees offering our services to companies from coast to coast. We're not the largest company providing the services we offer and we're happy with that. Our size allows us to be nimble and flexible enough to quickly adapt and custom design individual programs for our clients."

HRComp offers a broad spectrum of services to a wide range of clients.

▶ Payroll Processing Services HRComp's affordable professional payroll processing services, including payroll tax payment and liability, tax form filings, state unemployment, maintaining vacation

and sick leave records, and many more, are perfect for small to medium size businesses.

▶ Workers Compensation Insurance A skilled team offers a workers comp program with features such as better claims management, improved safety training, OSHA compliance assistance, post-accident drug testing, and others that can fit the individual budgets and needs of each client.

▶ Human Resources Today's businesses require innovative solutions to HR issues such as quality employee benefits, employer liability management services, drug free workplace administration, 24 hour injury response, and a host of others. A complete HR department offers solutions to these

issues with the right tools to effectively administer all personnel requirements with minimum time, effort, and expense.

SERVING BUSINESS, SERVING COMMUNITY

Realizing that good corporate citizenship requires service to the community, Andrea Ball leads by example. She launched "Engage", the company's efforts to improving the quality of life for the people in East Tennessee by having employees roll up their sleeves and offer hands-on assistance where needed in the community. They helped raise much-needed funds for Knoxville's revered Love Kitchen in the group's efforts to feed the area's hungry. Other local beneficiaries of HRComp's philanthropy include KARM Ministries, the local

Boys and Girls Club, and local elementary schools where volunteer readers are needed.

"Not giving back is unacceptable," Ball states. "If I look back over my life after years of business and can't see my company's positive influence in the community, I've failed miserably. "

THE OLIVER HOTEL

Knoxville's Boutique Hotel

The term 'boutique hotel' is often overused," notes Ethan Orley, one of the owners of The Oliver Hotel on Market Square in downtown Knoxville, "but we really are boutique. Our plan was to remake an old, classic downtown hotel and re-market a property that for a long time had been a real secret."

Orley, originally from Detroit, and Philip Welker from Nashville, had been partners in the real estate business and had always been interested in developing hotels. Welker had previously known the Kendrick family, the former owners of the hotel, from his time attending the University of Tennessee. It was from their combined vision that the metamorphosis of the city's landmark Kern Building became what numerous magazines and hundreds of satisfied guests have hailed as one of Knoxville's downtown treasures. The excitement that Knoxville experienced during the

remodeling and refurbishing of the historic building was reflected in a statement released by the president of the Market Square District Association at the announcement of the plans for The Oliver. "Having it in the hands of somebody who wants to fix it up and make it even more attractive is a great thing for Knoxville and a great thing for Market Square," noted John Craig.

A PART OF KNOXVILLE HISTORY

Orley and Welker accepted the challenge of enhancing a property that had been made a part of the Knoxville landscape by a German immigrant in the 1870s. Peter Kern had left his native Zwingeberg and lived in New York City and Charleston, South Carolina before settling in Georgia in 1857 on the eve of the American Civil War. When the South seceded and war broke

out in April 1861, Peter followed his neighbors in enlisting in the Confederate army and was wounded in the early fighting and sent home to recuperate. On his way to re-join his unit in Virginia, his train stopped in Knoxville when the Union soldiers moved in and occupied the town. Kern was arrested but released on the promise that he would not leave Knoxville for the duration of the war.

A former cobbler in Germany, Kern saw the promise of Knoxville and learned a new trade to practice in his adopted hometown. He began baking cookies to sell to the Union troops in town and, after the war ended, expanded his operation. He outgrew the original site of his business on State Street and moved into new quarters on the southwestern corner of Market Square. Kern also expanded his offerings to include everything

from candy, fruits, and nuts to soft drinks, fireworks, fresh oysters, and cigars. He became known for his ice cream and Kern's "ice cream saloon" quickly developed a reputation as the most upscale purveyor of the refreshing dessert in Knoxville.

Kern's success led him to construct a new building in July 1875 that the Knoxville Daily Herald termed "a handsome three-story brick building on the southwest corner of Market Square." Constructed during the height of the "Gilded Age," Kern's building housed his bakery, confectionery, soda fountain, toy and fireworks store, and his chandeliered, late night ice cream parlor. Over the years, the building would house a drug store, pool hall, restaurant, speakeasy, and dance hall. In 1981, the Kern Building became the Blakely House Hotel preparing to welcome VIP guests to the

1982 World's Fair held that year in Knoxville. The hotel later changed hands and became known as the Hotel St. Oliver.

A NEW STAR RISES

Orley and Welker took over the property in 2010. Craftsmen immediately began work on the remodeling and refurbishing that would upgrade and modernize the property as The Oliver Hotel.

Redesigning the hotel with stylish guest rooms that offer the most modern conveniences while retaining the charm, sophistication and historic character of the building required careful planning and close attention to detail. The craftsmen tasked with the renovation spent four months doing exactly that. The hotel where rock stars, actors, and actresses (Patricia Neal was a frequent guest!) often stayed would retain its character as an original expression of Knoxville and celebrate its new look and feel with chic, clean Southern designs that pay subtle homage to the location's rich local culture.

The bright, airy lobby is a reflection of the hotel's storied past. A unique handmade metal chandelier highlights original artwork and imported carpet. Guests are greeted by personable and attentive staff members who are consistently rated as among the best to be found in any hotel.

The 28 guest accommodations feature several layouts, each with its own distinctive eclectic style. Interior designer Cortney Bishop focused on maintaining the eccentricity of the old hotel, while adding an "Appalachian-quirky" edge. Each elegantly appointed suite and room features handcrafted furniture, original artwork from Knoxville's own irrepressible Yee-Haw Industries, and luxury branded bath amenities you would expect form a property its caliber. Suites offer the convenience of separate sitting rooms with pullout sofas and the corner suites have 15 foot ceilings. Standard guest rooms offer ultra-comfortable king beds with down pillows, down comforters, bathrooms with walk-in showers and marble vanity sinks.

Guests are invited to experience the cuisine of Tupelo Honey Cafe, the award-winning restaurant occupying the bottom level of the hotel and fronting Market Square with its open terrace seating. The Cafe extends The Oliver Hotel's inventive, imaginative approach to Southern hospitality with both its whimsical interior as well as its innovative take on Southern food and craft cocktails. Tupelo's transformation of just about everything Southern—from fried chicken to sweet potatoes to catfish—allows guests to experience the bold and unique flavors that have made it one of the premier restaurants downtown.

When the day winds down, a tradition has begun for hotel guests and local Knoxville residents to meet with friends at

the Peter Kern Library lounge. A throwback to the days of Prohibition, the outdoor hotel alley entrance is akin to that of a speakeasy of the 1920s.

That feeling quickly evaporates, however, as visitors are greeted by an entirely different atmosphere inside. Bookshelves and a cozy fireplace combine with soft wood tone paneling and plush low back booths to create the warm, casual feel of a library in a whimsical estate home. Like the carefully crafted libations served by the lounge's professional mixologists, the Peter Kern Library is a perfect blend of hospitality and creativity, charm and sophistication. Hidden within the pages of old encyclopedias are the lounge's quirky drink menus. In keeping with the literary motif of the Library, each libation is named after a character from classical literature. It is perhaps fitting that a portrait of Peter Kern, who went on to become a mayor of Knoxville, hangs behind the bar.

The Peter Kern Library was created out of the sitting room of the former St. Oliver Hotel. Having seen a resurgence in the interest in prohibition style drinks and the lack of small downtown lounges, Orley and Welker quickly found a following to their non-advertised speakeasy. Welker adds, "One of the great things about the lounge is the diversity of people who you will find packed into the small room. Very few downtown bars gather from such a wide audience with only 45 seats"

The transformation of the historic Kern Building into one of Knoxville's premier hotel properties has been highlighted in numerous publications, among them *The Tennessean, Southern Living, Garden & Gun, Georgia Magazine,* and *Tennessee Living.*

BGT Recruiting & Consulting, Inc.

Connecting Talent With Opportunity

Christine Bell and Jill Green took the two letters from their respective last names as part of the name of the company they founded in early 2012, but it was the "T" in BGT Recruiting & Consulting that they felt was the true essence of their business.

"We placed the 'T' in BGT to represent 'team'," Bell explains, "as Jill and I were both passionate about our unique team approach to providing outstanding recruiting and consulting services for organizations and professionals in the greater Knoxville area. With 25 years of combined experience in the field of recruiting, we saw a need for professional/corporate-level recruiting in the region.

limitations, its primary focus is on the East Tennessee market from the Tri-Cities area to Chattanooga.

The company's consulting services help organizations with the "people" aspect of their businesses through partnering on search processes and alleviating the administration and communication burden of the hiring process for small to medium sized organizations. Each search is tailored to the specific needs of the individual client. The BGT approach ensures the highest level of confidentiality for all parties.

TRACK RECORD OF SUCCESS

In just over a year and a half, BGT has written a remarkable chapter in the story of Knoxville's rise as a magnet for growth among Southern cities as the corporate headquarters for numerous regional and national companies as well as entrepreneurial startup ventures. From its inception, BGT

established a unique approach to recruiting that has assisted many of the area's companies with their recruiting needs saving them significant time and money while providing them a level of talent they are not often able to effectively reach through traditional hiring methods. The company's team also works closely with local universities to track talent and retain professionals in the Knoxville area rather than lose them to other markets.

"We like to say we're business people in the people business," notes Jill Green. "Our approach is people focused. We strive to create long-term relationships which, in turn, result in a network of trusted professionals we can reach out to when we are assisting a client in finding just the right person for their business. Our low-volume approach is very efficient and effective because we strive for an accurate match between candidates and corporate culture."

BGT Recruiting & Consulting Team, left to right, Christine Bell, Lisa Coulter, Kathryn Bradley, Ashley Franklin, and Jill Green   Photo by Christy Foreman Photography

BGT owners, Jill Green and Christine Bell
Photo by Christy Foreman Photography

We felt that our understanding of the recruiting and staffing industry and the culture of the various organizations we work with would allow us to fill a void in the marketplace. Our own individual business backgrounds as well as the skills and talents of the professionals we assembled would be the path for us to leverage the relationships we'd built over time and provide quality services that focused on people, culture, and integrity."

BGT maintains a sharp focus on contingency-based recruiting services for degreed professionals in corporate roles such as accounting, finance, human resources, marketing, and operations located in the East Tennessee area. While the company has no geographical

BGT Recruiting & Consulting, Inc. Ribbon Cutting—November 1st, 2012

BGT has built an impressive reputation in the industry following that approach. "Whether it be finding highly qualified candidates for job openings or performing behind the scenes work for the local chapter of a prominent business organization we've grown from the ground up, I've seen BGT's commitment to excellence time and time again," stated Frank Southall, the Principal Accounting Officer of Ruby Tuesday.

The greatest testament to the success of BGT may be the fact that the company works mainly on a referral basis—repeat business and satisfied clients telling others about their positive experience with BGT. In addition, the company relies on referrals rather than advertising to find talented candidates. "People don't refer people who are not qualified and great at what they do. Our approach allows us to work with a higher quality talent pool who are likely not going to answer an ad," adds Green.

One of Bell and Green's signature accomplishments has been their role in the establishment of Knoxville's chapter of Financial Executives International (FEI). Bell and Green were instrumental in launching FEI in Knoxville in 2009 and promoting its efforts to advance the success of senior-level financial executives. The Knoxville chapter, which now numbers approximately 100 members, has won an award each year since its founding for either growth in membership or outstanding chapter practices at the annual international FEI Summit Conference.

A KNOXVILLE STORY

While Bell and Green both gravitated to Knoxville from other parts of the country (Bell from California and Green from Ohio), both share a strong passion for their adopted hometown. "Jill and I found our way here and are very committed to the area," Bell states. "Having lived in many places, we are keenly aware of all that

Knoxville has to offer in the way of business opportunities and an exceptional quality of life. We feel we can be true ambassadors of the area, especially as we work with talent from out of town."

That commitment has led each of the women to immerse themselves into the waters of corporate citizenship. Bell in 2012 was named "Woman of the Year" by the Leukemia & Lymphoma Society and has served on the Board for TSCPA for many years. In 2011, she was named to the Greater Knoxville Business Journal's "Top 40 Under 40" and is an active member of Nucleus Knoxville. Green has served as Chamber Ambassador for the Knoxville Chamber since 2003 and became part of the Knoxville Chamber Board in 2013. In addition, she is involved with Knoxville Area Rescue Ministries where she engages as a volunteer and instructor at the Serenity Shelter, and also serves on the Board of the East Tennessee Arthritis Foundation.

BGT's passion for helping people is clearly the driving force behind their success and they are excited about continuing to serve their clients and grow their business in this great community.

2012 Knoxville FEI Chapter Achievement Award Presentation, left to right, George Boyadjis, Kyle Kirchhofer, Jill Green, Christine Bell, Frank Southall, and Marie Hollein

PROVISION HEALTH ALLIANCE

Provision Center for Proton Therapy

Provision Health Alliance is a thriving outpatient healthcare campus located at Dowell Springs in West Knoxville. The idea for a comprehensive medical park started with Terry Douglass, co-founder of CTI Molecular Imaging, Inc., as a result of working with physicians who expressed a desire to have a central location for services. The

Entrance to Provision Health Alliance at Dowell Springs.

— Photo by Bobbie Wyatt

The Provision Center for Proton Therapy, open and treating patients in Spring 2014.

—Photo by Andrew Tessler

co-founder and members of CTI Molecular Imaging, Inc., who developed and commercialized PET and PET/CT technology and delivered the technology globally, have continued on a path of innovation after the sale of CTI to Siemens in 2005. During the last 22 years, the team experienced numerous revelations about the business of healthcare. Since the sale of CTI, the team turned their attention to an array of healthcare related projects, including Provision Health Alliance.

Dr. Douglass envisions a world-class health care center and partnership with physicians and hospitals that will focus on patient care, research and education.

Provision Health Alliance is committed to the development of new, innovative, comprehensive healthcare product and service solutions that will make major improvements in patient care, outcomes and value.

In 2010, the Provision team received approval for the first proton radiation therapy center in Tennessee and currently one of only eleven in the country. The 90,000-square-foot Provision Center for Proton Therapy broke ground in late 2011 on the Dowell Springs campus and is slated to begin treating patients in early 2014 with a noninvasive and painless form of radiation treatment that has minimal to no side effects.

The center will be integrated into the outpatient campus that includes comprehensive diagnostic imaging services, traditional radiation therapy, a health and wellness center, physical therapy center and biomedical research. The alliance also includes on-campus partnerships with Tennessee Cancer Specialist offering medical oncology services and the Knoxville Comprehensive Breast Center.

Through Provision Healthcare Foundation, Provision Health Alliance is a community stakeholder and supports many charitable causes in the local community such as United Way, Salvation Army, American Cancer Society, East Tennessee Children's Hospital and

The radiation therapists at Provision always have smiling faces.

— Photo by Bobbie Wyatt

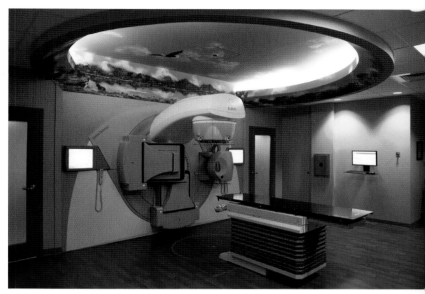

Provision Radiation Therapy's treatment room, with a comforting environment.

— Photo by Bobbie Wyatt

numerous other organizations that provide crucial services for people in the local and regional communities.

A CULTURE OF INNOVATION

Innovation is what has always driven Provision. During the 22 years at CTI they were able to develop every major advancement in PET technology from the first full-body PET scanner to the implementation of industry-leading resolution. The focus was always on improving outcomes for cancer patients and creating value for clinicians. Provision is taking the same innovative approaches and applying them to the local healthcare community.

This desire ultimately evolved into the vision to create a world-class comprehensive center. They

quickly determined that in order to reach that stage, they needed to have the most advanced treatments. That decision led to the implementation of Proton Therapy.

Opening in early 2014, the Provision Center for Proton Therapy is the first of its kind in Tennessee. The center offers one of the most advanced cancer treatments in the world providing a culture of care that will set a new standard of excellence.

Provision Center for Proton Therapy will be able to treat up to 1,500 cancer patients annually when it is fully operational, and will bring in many patients from outside the area. The Provision Center for Proton Therapy will be open to all credentialed physicians and health systems in the region with an advanced cancer treatment

capability that presently is available in only a handful of cities. When completed, it will be one of only 14 in the nation.

Proton therapy is an advanced form of radiotherapy that uses a single high-energy proton beam to treat various forms of cancer. Different from conventional radiation therapy—in which beam energy dissipates as it passes through the body—proton beams can be fine-tuned within millimeters of accuracy to deliver maximum energy within the controlled range of the cancerous tumor.

Because of the nature of proton therapy treatments, clinical benefits to patients include: significant decrease in side effects; improved outcomes; decrease in secondary cancers from unnecessary radiation exposure; and significant

Provision's medical staff.

— Photo by Bobbie Wyatt

Provision Health Alliance's beautiful campus and walking trails.
—Photo by Bobbie Wyatt

Provision Health Alliance's tent during the Provision Center for Proton Therapy's ground breaking event.
—Photo by Patrick Murphy Racey

cost savings by decreasing complications and secondary cancers.

ProNova Solutions: Redefining the Future of Cancer Treatment

The idea for forming ProNova Solutions, LLC was born from the early planning stages of the Provision Center for Proton Therapy. As the team evaluated the existing proton therapy technology available in 2010, they were struck by its size, cost, and complexity, which is a major barrier inhibiting market growth and for patients that need this advanced treatment. Applying their combined expertise in technology development, medical device production, and delivering integrated solutions, the founders conceived an innovative technical approach using proprietary superconducting magnets and

advanced imaging. These innovations dramatically lower system cost while actually increasing functionality. Very similar to the mission of CTI, ProNova's vision is to make proton therapy more accessible for cancer patients and physicians around the world.

ProNova is collaborating with leading proton suppliers and providers to develop the most optimal solutions to address the needs of the market. They have harnessed the power of proton therapy and created a compact system that incorporates the latest technology developments at less than half the cost, one-tenth the weight, and half the size of current systems available today. It differs from other proposed compact systems in that it will feature the full

functionality of full-size systems available today on a highly expandable treatment platform, allowing for growth into the most advanced forms of treatment.

ProNova has assembled a strong technical and commercial team of experienced and knowledgeable entrepreneurs who have demonstrated success in the development and delivery of advanced technology to the medical device market.

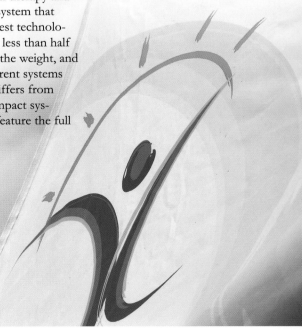

An inside look at Provision Center for Proton Therapy's cyclotron.

—Photo by Talbott Paynter

Provision Center for Proton Therapy's cyclotron room.

—Photo by Bobbie Wyatt

ProNova Solutions' compact SC360 gantry unit in production.

—Photo by Bobbie Wyatt

ProNova Solutions' next generation proton therapy treatment room.

—Rendering by Jon Huber

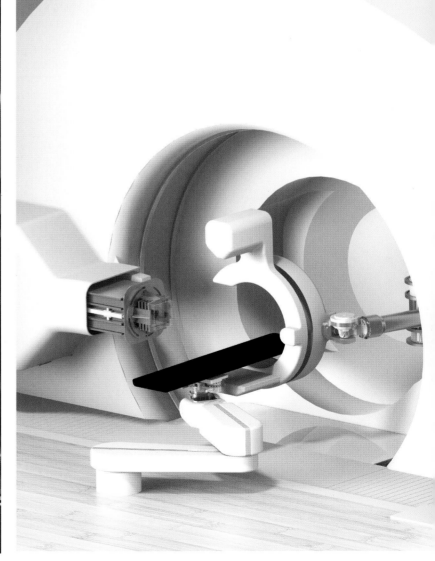

MEET OUR PHOTOGRAPHERS

SCOTT BUSBY

Scott Busby, AIA, is a Knox-ville-based architect and amateur photographer. Some of his work has been selected for local calendars featuring historic architecture. He reports having "about a billion" pictures of his children, none of which are printed.

www.smeebusby.com

sbusby@smeebusby.com

865-521-7550

JACQUES GAUTREAU

Jacques Gautreau is from Angers, a medieval city in western France. After university he moved to Paris and then, for an extended period, lived in Germany. He returned to Paris where he spent most of his adult life. Gautreau is an entirely self-taught photographer, having started his career as a hobby when he was a teenager.

In 2004 he moved to Knoxville, where he works in medical imaging technology for Siemens. He has exhibited his work at the Emporium, the Northshore Brasserie and McGee-Tyson Airport. His work has been featured in Metro Pulse, the Knoxville News Sentinel, and the French art magazine Photo Fan.

Gautreau lives in Knoxville with his wife, Julie, and his son, Sacha.

jgautreau64@hotmail.com

865-755-3393

GARY HEATHERLY

Gary Heatherly has spent 25 years providing fine photography for clients on a regio;nal, national and international scope. Specializing in architectureal, advertising, editortial, stock and photographic arts, his work has appeared on the covers and in feature stories of manu national magagzines.

Gary graduated with honors from the University of Tennessee and although he still resides in Knoxville, he is available for assignments world-wide.

Gary Heatherly Photography
gary@garyheatherly.com
865-971-4870

DAVID LUTTRELL

Career steps ranging from being manager of a contemporary photography gallery to a 5-year stint shooting for TVA's Engineering Design Group and Information Office led David Luttrell to open the doors of his own photography business in 1985.

Luttrell, who attended the University of Tennessee, counts his photographic areas of expertise as being industrial and architectural/engineering as well as the ability to capture images of individuals of all ages in work or leisure settings.

David Luttrell Astral Atelier
www.astralatelier.com

dluttphoto@comcast.net

865-689-5760

STEPHANIE NORWOOD

A Memphis-area native, Stephanie Norwood studied Graphic Design and Fine Art at Parsons The New School for Design in New York City.

She takes a photojournalistic approach to her lifestyle and fine art photography and specializes in portraits, figure, cultural events and architecture. Stephanie developed her passion for photography during a 30-year career as an international model.

Her work has been featured in Cork It and Memphis Downtowner magazines.

Studio Norwood Photography
www. StudioNorwood.com

info@StudioNorwood.com

901-217-2509

SHEENA PATRICK

Currently residing in Austin, Texas, Sheena Patrick is originally from East Tennessee.

She has been shooting professionally since 2005 for a variety of commercial and marketing businesses.

Sheena is a regular contributor to Knoxville's alternative weekly, the Metro Pulse.

Sheena Patrick Photography
www.sheenapatrick.com

GARY POPE

Now at home in Chattanooga, Gary Pope is originally from Oakland, California. He earned his Bachelor of Architecture degree from the University of California Berkeley.

Gary specializes in photographing architecture, landscapes, travel scenes, nature and man-made designs. Some of his works were selected for publication in Chattanooga's Heroic Drive and other for miscellaneous architectural promotional materials.

Pope Photography
hgarypope@gmail.com

423-463-9279

DENISE RETALLACK

A photographer whose "passion is to be able to tell the story of a space and bring the experience to those who can't see it in person," Denise Retallack specializes in architectural and landscape photography.

Her work has been part of multiple American Institute of Architects (AIA) Design Awards, both regionally and at the state level in Tennessee.

Retallack is a native of Higganum, Connecticut, and now resides in Knoxville. She received a B.A. in Fine Art from Towson University and earned her B.A. in Commercial Photography from Brooks Institute of Photography.

Denise Retallack Photographer
www.denisephoto.com

info@denisephoto.com

865-381-0943

Knoxville

Index